Nicholson's
guides to the
WATERWAYS

the Midlands

D0239161

Produced and published by
Robert Nicholson Publications
24 Highbury Crescent
London N5

For

**British
Waterways
Board**

Melbury House, Melbury Terrace,
London NW1 6JX

SBN 90056846 1

© Robert Nicholson Publications Ltd

Maps based upon the Ordnance Survey with the sanction of the Controller of Her Majesty's Stationery Office, Crown Copyright reserved, and John Bartholomew & Son Ltd.

Printed by Butler and Tanner Ltd, Frome and London

Robert Nicholson Publications acknowledge assistance from many expert contributors to this book, especially the staff of the British Waterways Board, Mr E. J. Schatz and the East Midland Area of the Ramblers Association.

Further copies of this publication and others in the series can be obtained from your local bookshop or direct from the British Waterways Board, Willow Grange, Church Road, Watford WD1 3QA.

The publishers do not guarantee the accuracy of the information contained in this guide or undertake any responsibility for errors, omissions or their consequences.

Front cover: The Staffordshire and Worcestershire Canal near Kinver (photo: Derek Pratt)

Introduction

This book is the fifth in the new series of Nicholson's Guides to the Waterways, specially commissioned by the British Waterways Board. The Canals of the Midlands is offered as an introduction to the general reader; if you find yourself hearing more and more talk about canals but haven't yet 'got to grips' with them, if your friends have enthused delightedly about their canal holiday last summer and you haven't yet tried it out, or if you would like to find new places to see and new things to do on a weekend afternoon, then read this book.

The canals of the Midlands are a fascinating network of interweaving waterways dating back to the middle of the 18th century. Several hundreds of miles are woven together in this area, passing through towns, villages and remote countryside, within easy reach of large numbers of people. They provide ample opportunities for boating and rambling, at the same time offering great scope for those who are interested in any aspect of natural history or industrial archaeology—and yet they are still quiet, uncrowded and unspoilt. This book will assist you in your individual exploration of the Midland canals. You don't need a boat for it: a car, a motor-bike or a bus or railway timetable will set you on the right track.

It is wise to equip yourself with maps before getting down to looking round the canals. The 1-inch Ordnance Survey are particularly handy as an all-purpose local map, and nowadays these maps mostly indicate public rights of way in the countryside, including those along the canal towing paths. (Not all canal towpaths are public rights of way.) The 2½-inch to 1 mile Ordnance Survey maps also mark public rights of way, and the greater detail these maps afford makes them invaluable for tracing the route of a long-abandoned waterway, and these too should help you to avoid straying on to private property or private roads.

The 1:50,000 O.S. maps covering the Midland canals are the following sheet numbers: 118, 127, 128, 129, 138, 139, 140, 141, 150, 151 and 152.

Contents

Where to see canals 5

Navigation, touring circuits and distances 17

Boatyards 21

Boat clubs 29

Canal societies 32

Water supply for the Midland canals 37

Abandoned canals 43

Canals in the West Midlands 53

Canals in the East Midlands 63

The navigable canals of the Midlands 70

Natural history 105

Patterns of water life in the Midland canals 113

Canal feeder reservoirs and their bird life 117

Bird life of the Trent & Mersey canal 119

Canal walks 125

Angling on the Midland canals 131

Houses and gardens 137

Places to visit in the countryside 143

Museums and galleries 147

Restaurants 153

Index 157

The Country Code

Guard against fire risks.
Fasten all gates.
Keep dogs under proper control.
Keep to paths across farm land.
Avoid damaging fences, hedges and walls.
Leave no litter.
Safeguard water supplies.
Protect wildlife, wild plants and trees.
Go carefully on country roads.
Respect the life of the countryside.

The maps on pages 70–102 are ¼-inch to 1 mile. The north axis is constant.

Stoke Bruerne

Where to see canals

To many people, canals are little more than a stretch of still water seen from a passing car, and a canal bridge is no more than a traffic obstacle—a tiresome reason for slowing down. But the effort to stop, look and explore would be rewarded not just by a length of artificial waterway but by an intriguing new world ready to be penetrated.

To the initiated, locks and bridges, tunnels and aqueducts, canal villages and canal towns are a familiar sight. But how many others realise that they exist? And how many realise that the short stretch of waterway, glimpsed in a flash, is part of a huge and fascinating canal web woven throughout the country?

If you would like to discover some of the more interesting canal artefacts in the Midlands, read on. We have compiled here an analysis of some good places to see canals, showing how to get there and what to look for. Remember that most canal centres and structures are, for historical reasons, rarely related to the modern road system. So if you use public transport to get there you can expect at least a short walk at the other end; and if you are in a car, you may find yourself ending up driving along a narrow or bumpy lane. Either way, it is wise to be equipped with the new Ordnance Survey maps.

CENTRES OF CANAL ACTIVITY

Many of the places in this category are ideal for a family outing, with the attraction of boats, canal architecture, locks and often a canal pub for good measure—sometimes with garden space for children. There will always be some activity at these places on any summer weekend.

Stoke Bruerne

Northants. Stoke Bruerne is the obvious start to any tour of canal sights. It is one of the best surviving examples of a canal village, built to serve the canal, and once totally dependent upon it. The Grand Union Canal runs through the middle, flanked by a terrace of old cottages, a thatched pub and a handsome stone granary. There is a flight of seven locks, the top one paired with a lock that, disused now, is used to display the 'Northwich' (an ancient 'butty' boat) in an unusual weighing machine. There is also a rare double-arched bridge and, to the north of the vil-

lage, the entrance to the great Blisworth Tunnel, over 1¾ miles long. Moored here are a variety of canal craft, including original trading narrow boats. The stone granary has been converted to house the Waterways Museum—a unique collection of waterway relics, photographs and paraphernalia which will fascinate and delight anyone who visits it. All these features combine to make Stoke Bruerne a first-rate introduction to canals. In summer there are boat trips from the pub to Blisworth Tunnel.

Access Car: Stoke Bruerne is off the A508 3½ miles south of junction No. 15 on the M1. Bus: United Counties 330 and 331 from Northampton to Stoke Bruerne.

Foxton

Leics. Foxton Junction, where the Market Harborough Arm leaves the Leicester line of the Grand Union Canal, features a small canal settlement, with a boatyard, cottages and an interesting variety of bridges. A good selection of boats can generally be seen. Immediately south of the junction is the famous Foxton flight of narrow locks. Here ten locks, in two 'staircases' of five, raise the Grand Union Canal from the level of the Market Harborough Arm. Opened in 1814, and virtually unchanged today, the lock flight gives a good idea of the obstacles faced by canal builders and boatmen alike: even a well-practised crew will take an hour to negotiate the flight. To the east of the locks can be found the remains of the even more famous Foxton Inclined Plane, now listed as an Ancient Monument, which was built to replace the locks around 1900. For although locks have always been the simplest method of effecting changes in level, engineers have sought alternatives since the earliest days of canals. Of these, vertical boat lifts and inclined planes were the most frequently tried, although some engineers produced unlikely schemes that were a mixture of personal eccentricity and adventurousness. The Inclined Plane at Foxton, which lifted boats 75 feet up a 1 in 4 gradient, was the last one to be built in Britain: it came from the same last flourish of Victorian inventiveness that produced the Anderton boat lift and the Barton swing aqueduct.

The Old Union Canal, completed in 1814, was built with flights of narrow locks at each end, seven at Watford and

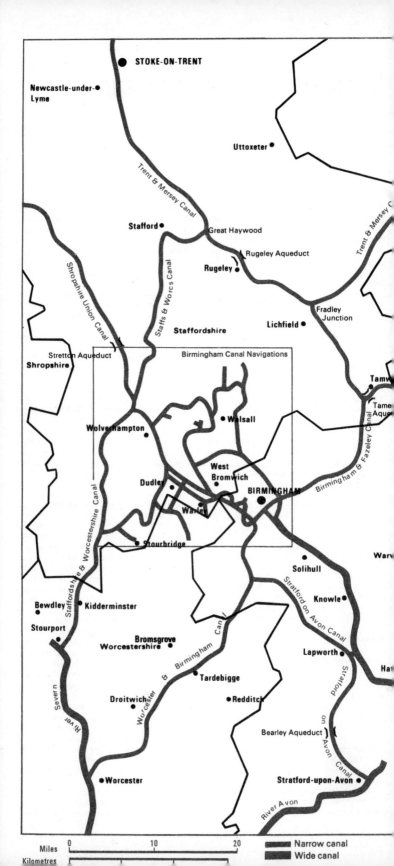

STOKE-ON-TRENT

Newcastle-under-Lyme

Uttoxeter

Trent & Mersey Canal

Stafford

Great Haywood

Rugeley Aqueduct

Rugeley

Trent & Mersey C

Shropshire Union Canal

Staffs & Worcs Canal

Fradley Junction

Lichfield

Staffordshire

Stretton Aqueduct

Shropshire

Birmingham Canal Navigations

Tamw

Wolverhampton

Walsall

Tame Aque

Staffordshire & Worcestershire Canal

West Bromwich

Birmingham & Fazeley Canal

Dudley

BIRMINGHAM

Warley

Stourbridge

Warw

Solihull

Stratford on Avon Canal

Knowle

Bewdley

Kidderminster

Stourport

Bromsgrove

Worcestershire

Lapworth

Ha

Worcester & Birmingham Canal

Tardebigge

Droitwich

Redditch

Stratford

River Severn

Bearley Aqueduct

on Avon Canal

Worcester

Stratford-upon-Avon

River Avon

Miles	0	10	20	▬ Narrow canal
Kilometres				▬ Wide canal

The canal system of the Midlands

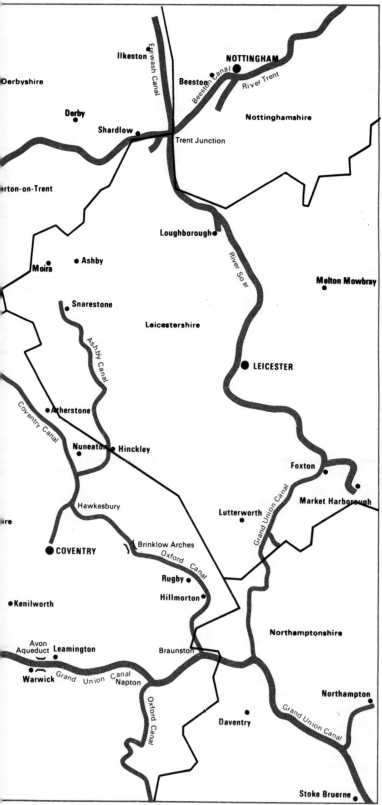

ten at Foxton. These caused long delays, limited the use of through traffic from the Grand Union, and suffered from water supply problems. Various schemes to widen the locks came to nothing, and finally it was decided to build an inclined plane to replace Foxton locks. Work began in 1898, and two years later the plane, designed by G. C. Thomas, was opened to traffic. Two water-filled caissons (tanks), running on four pairs of rails, descended and ascended the concrete slope sideways; each caisson could carry two narrowboats, which floated in the hydraulically sealed caisson. A steam engine powered the plane, although the caissons were designed to counter-balance each other.

Had the plane been powered by electricity it might still be in operation today; but it suffered from continual problems and breakdowns, and the saving in time (12 minutes to negotiate the plane as opposed to up to 1½ hours through the locks) was outweighed by the great maintenance costs, so plans for a second inclined plane to replace Watford locks were abandoned, and in 1909 Foxton locks were re-opened. The plane was closed to traffic in November 1910, but was maintained 'on standby' until 1914. It was then closed permanently, and was dismantled and scrapped in 1928.

The remains of the plane survive to the east of Foxton locks. The overgrown arm that leads to the top of the plane can be traced, a few walls of the boiler house still stand, and the great slope of the plane, recently cleared of trees, runs down to the lower arm which is now used for moorings. Exploration of the slope will reveal the grooves for the pulling ropes and the track bed. There is a good collection of photographs of the Inclined Plane in operation at the Waterways Museum at Stoke Bruerne.

Foxton is a good place for a day out: boat trips operate in summer from the bottom lock, and Leicestershire County Council have built a new car park and picnic site near the top of the locks and the Inclined Plane. In the village there is a pub (the 'Black Horse') near the canal, with a garden.

Access Car: Foxton village is 4 miles north-west of Market Harborough, off the A6. The junction and the locks are half a mile west of the village: the best place to park is in the new car park just off the Foxton–Gumley road. Bus: Midland Red service 656 from Market Harborough and Leicester to Foxton village.

Braunston

Northants. At Braunston the Grand Union Canal joins the Oxford Canal. The area around the junction is well known as a canal centre; there is a large modern boatyard on a short arm that formed part of the original line of the Oxford Canal,

before it was shortened and straightened by Telford between 1829 and 1834. The boatyard also uses some small reservoirs adjoining the canal as a large mooring site. There are several interesting buildings to be seen, including an 18th-century drydock. One mile east of the junction are the six Braunston locks, which take the Grand Union up to its summit level. At the top of the locks are old canal cottages, workshops, a covered dock and a small pumping station. This is very much the 'narrowboat' end of Braunston, contrasting with the smaller fibreglass boats that cluster around the boatyard. Further to the east, just beyond the locks, is the mouth of Braunston Tunnel, which burrows through the Northamptonshire Heights for over a mile. Braunston village, built along a single street parallel to the canal, is also attractive. There are good canal pubs at Braunston–the 'Admiral Nelson' halfway up the locks, and the bigger and more modern 'Rose and Castle' near Braunston Turn. The latter has an unusual canalside restaurant.

Access Car: Braunston village is just off the A45, 3½ miles north-west of Daventry. Visitors should park in the village and then explore the canal on foot, via the towpath. Bus: Midland Red services 511 and 572 (Rugby–Daventry) to Braunston village.

Lapworth

Warwicks. Lapworth is a delightful canal centre. Here the Grand Union and Stratford-upon-Avon Canals run briefly parallel and close to each other, but effectively separated by small reservoirs and the railway embankment. The two canals are on different levels, and so there is a lock in the short arm that links them. The junction occurs in the middle of the long Lapworth flight of 25 locks, which takes the Stratford Canal down towards its junction with the now navigable river Avon. Look for the split iron footbridge on the Stratford Canal, divided to allow the horse towing rope to pass through without being unhitched. Further down is the first of the unusual 'barrel-roofed' lock cottages found on this waterway.

There is a boatyard at the junction, and plenty of boats can generally be seen in the area, including traditional narrowboats. The junction also marks the boundary between the jurisdiction of the BWB and the National Trust, who own the southern section of the Stratford-upon-Avon Canal. (The Trust has a canal office at Lapworth Junction.) The Grand Union Canal is reached via the short arm: it is at this point on an 8-mile level pound between the long lock flights at Knowle and Hatton.

Packwood House, also owned by the National Trust and open to the public, is 2 miles north-west of Lapworth.

Access Car: The B4439 passes through Lapworth, crossing both canals near the junction. Rail: Lapworth Station is conveniently very close. Bus: Not very helpful. Midland Red 150 passes 2 miles west of the junction.

Tardebigge

Worcs. At Tardebigge the Worcester and Birmingham Canal reaches its summit level after the long climb through hilly country from Worcester and the river Severn. On this canal there are 58 locks in 16 miles; 30 of these are in the final Tardebigge flight, which is thus the longest navigable lock flight in Britain. The top lock is also the deepest narrow lock in the country, and an experimental lift was installed here once to save time and water. But it was replaced by the present top lock. Above the lock is Tardebigge Wharf: a BWB maintenance yard is here, and pleasure boats fill the moorings. Nearby is the mouth of Tardebigge Tunnel taking the canal through the first of several hills it meets on its way to Birmingham. (There are three more tunnels on the way to Birmingham.) The many locks and tunnels along this canal reflect the steeply rolling countryside which stretches from Birmingham to Worcester. The railway navvies later faced the same problem; their solution was the notorious Lickey Incline, just west of Tardebigge locks. There is no village to speak of at Tardebigge, but the church with its fine spire stands on a hill overlooking the wharf. **Access** Car: Tardebigge is on the A448, 2½ miles east of Bromsgrove. The road crosses over the tunnel portal. The best way to the lock flight is along the towpath from the wharf. Rail: Bromsgrove Station is about a mile from the middle of Tardebigge locks. Bus: Midland Red services 318 and 319 (Bromsgrove–Redditch) to Tardebigge itself.

Stourport

Worcs. At Stourport the Staffordshire and Worcestershire Canal leaves the river Severn, the start of its long journey to join the Trent and Mersey Canal near Stafford. Stourport is one of the few towns in England to be entirely created by the coming of a canal, for it grew up around the inland port that quickly developed after the canal was opened in 1771. Today the town has little to do with the canal, having a flourishing existence in its own right, but four out of five of the original canal basins are still operational, and the Georgian buildings round about indicate what Stourport was like in its youth. Handsome warehouses overlook the wharves and the locks that lead into the Severn. The four basins are interconnected by locks and short canals, and broad and narrow locks lead down into the Severn. These basins are no longer used for water-borne freight, but they were the very basis of the town's

prosperity and they are still busy today—though now with pleasure boats. The Tontine Hotel—the large pub by the locks—was part of the original canal development at Stourport.

Four miles to the north-west is Bewdley, an elegant 18th-century town and port on the Severn. At one time it was one of the busiest inland ports in England, but its trade was killed by the development of Stourport, and now Bewdley is even inaccessible by river—the Severn has silted up. **Access** Car: Stourport and Bewdley are both very easy, being served by several 'A' and 'B' roads. Rail: Not good. Nearest stations are Kidderminster and Hartlebury, then bus. Bus: Plenty of services to both towns. Midland Red services 312, 313, 314, 133, K13, 293, 294, 192, 291, 292.

Fradley Junction

Staffs. At Fradley the Coventry Canal joins the Trent and Mersey, thus linking the north-west and north-east of England to the Midlands. The importance of the junction to the whole network has inevitably made Fradley into a canal centre, with an attractive canalside pub, cottages and boatyard. In addition the junction occurs in the middle of a short flight of narrow locks on the Trent and Mersey, which add to the interest. The narrow brick lock bridges are particularly appealing. Four miles to the south is another junction at Huddlesford, where the Wyrley and Essington Canal left the Coventry on its journey towards Lichfield and Wolverhampton. This canal is still in water for the first 400 yards or so (and used now as club moorings), but beyond that the canal has been completely abandoned for many years. **Access** Car: Fradley is on a minor road linking the A513 and the A38, 6 miles north-east of Lichfield. It is possible to drive to the junction, which is a mile west of the village. Bus: Not very good. Midland Red services X12, 112, 817 (along A38). Nearest stop 1½ miles away. Huddlesford Junction is accessible only by car along minor roads.

Trent Junction

Derbs. Trent Junction is an important waterway crossroads. The river Trent flows north-east towards Nottingham; the river Soar flows into the Trent from Leicester; while just opposite is a junction with the Erewash Canal, which climbs a flight of locks up to Langley Mill. The situation is complicated by the fact that the Trent itself splits here, the river course flowing over a weir and the navigation channel going down Cranfleet Cut. To the west the Trent and Mersey Canal leaves the Trent on its journey towards Manchester, Wales and the north-west, and to the east the Trent Navigation continues down to Gainsborough and the Humber estuary, joining up with the canals of the north-east. Originally it was possible to travel further north beyond Langley Mill via the Cromford Canal, but this link is now broken and much of the Cromford Canal is filled in. The main focus of Trent Junction is Trent Lock at the mouth of the Erewash Canal. Here there is a boatyard, moored boats, and canal cottages. Two pubs provide a centre of attraction—one of them having a restaurant and a spacious garden beside the river. (There is also a café nearby.) Activity on the Trent hereabouts is generated not only by the constant coming and going of the motor cruisers, but also by the presence of several sailing clubs nearby. This is an extremely busy stretch of water at summer weekends.

Access Car: Trent Junction is 2 miles south of Long Eaton, off the A453; there is a lane to the junction. Rail: Long Eaton Station is just over a mile away. Bus: Midland Red service X99.

Shardlow

Derbs. Four miles to the west of Trent Junction is Shardlow, perhaps the best-preserved canal village in Britain. The Trent and Mersey Canal leaves the river Trent at Derwent Mouth, and Shardlow is the first village encountered; its development was prompted by construction of the canal, which is effectively Shardlow's main street. There is a superb group of original 18th-century and early 19th-century buildings, warehouses, cottages and wharves, which epitomises the natural style and elegance of early industrial architecture. An added attraction is the river Trent, which is still navigable to Shardlow. So Shardlow has two waterways, and one can arrive either by canal or by river.

Access Car: Shardlow is on the A6, a mile west of its junction with the A453. Bus: Trent Motor Traction service to Shardlow.

Worcester Bar Basin, Gas Street, Birmingham

There is an astonishingly extensive network of canals in the Black Country—Birmingham, in particular, is riddled with waterways, mostly still navigable. Few of the Birmingham canals are attractive in the conventional sense, but all of them provide a unique view of the city's industrial development over the last 200 years. Much of the Birmingham canal network is hidden behind walls and factories, and so access is always difficult; but once you get on to the towpath, you enter another world which is peaceful, private and unknown. The only access point in Birmingham that is virtually always open is in Gas Street. A small doorway here in a high brick wall leads to an extraordinary sight: a huge canal basin in the heart of the city, a stone's throw from the Bull

Ring and New Street Station, full of narrowboats, some converted, some in their original state. The basin is also an important canal junction: here the Worcester and Birmingham Canal joins the Birmingham Canal Navigations. At one time there was a physical barrier between the two canals, the famous Worcester Bar, and goods had to be transhipped just for a few yards from one canal to the other. But the two canal companies eventually overcame the rivalry which had created the bar and removed it, replacing it with a stop lock.

Access Gas Street is very close (walking distance) to the centre of Birmingham, but it is completely hidden from all roads, so it is easy to miss. From the city centre, go down Broad Street (which leads off the inner ring road) and turn left into Gas Street. The entrance to the basin is a small opening on the left.

Cambrian Wharf, Birmingham

Not far from Gas Street Basin is Cambrian Wharf, which shows what can be done with a decaying and disused piece of urban canal. The basin (once the beginning of a canal branch into the very heart of the city) has been completely renovated, but great care has been taken to preserve the flavour of the original. There is an old crane, a terrace of canal cottages, and a new canal-orientated pub which has a bar in a converted narrowboat. The basin is also used as a British Waterways mooring site; and a BWB canal shop and information centre is just a few yards away, in a delightful cobbled street (Kingston Row) of 18th-century cottages (also recently restored).

Access Cambrian Wharf is, like Gas Street, close to Birmingham city centre, but although you can walk along the towpath from Gas Street Basin to the top of Farmer's Bridge locks, you cannot gain access from the towpath to Cambrian Wharf itself. The best route through the streets from Gas Street to Cambrian Wharf is as follows: up Gas Street, across Broad Street, into St Martin's Place, along Cambridge Street and into Kingston Row. Cambrian Wharf is down behind the 'Narrow Boat'.

Hawkesbury

Warwicks. At Hawkesbury Junction, in the lee of Coventry Power Station, the Oxford Canal joins the Coventry Canal. During the days of working boats, the junction was a favourite stopping place, especially for the boats that fuelled the power station with coal. Today this commercial traffic is no more, but there is still plenty for the visitor to see at this unglamorous yet rewarding spot. Near the junction there is a stop lock on the Oxford Canal. At one time there were stop locks at most junctions where one canal joined another, built partly to facilitate the collection of tolls, and partly to safeguard the precious water supplies of the canal company that got there first. Today few of these reminders of company rivalry are still in use, but Hawkesbury stop lock is one of the survivors. Beside the Coventry Canal is a large brick pumping house. Now empty, this used to house an historic Newcomen steam pumping engine built as early as 1725. Although it ceased to work in 1913, the engine remained in place until 1963, when it was dismantled and re-erected in Dartmouth, Devon—Newcomen's birthplace—where it can be seen in operation. The junction itself is straddled by a fine old iron bridge cast at Horseley Ironworks in 1836. A variety of traditional boats in working trim can be seen moored around the junction, and there is a boatman's pub, the 'Greyhound'.

Access Car: Hawkesbury is 4 miles north-east of Coventry off the A444, 2 miles south of its junction (No. 3) with the M6. A small lane leads to the junction. Bus: Midland Red services X91, 597, 658 along the A444 (Coventry–Nuneaton road), then a ¾ mile walk.

Great Haywood

Staffs. At Great Haywood the Staffordshire and Worcestershire Canal joins the Trent and Mersey, in an area rich in interest. At the junction there is a mill, a boatyard and a very fine towing-path turnover bridge. A few yards from the junction, an aqueduct carries the Staffordshire and Worcestershire Canal over the river Trent, and beyond it a short walk along the canal leads to Tixall Wide, a delightful and most unusual stretch of broad waterway incorporated into the canal. Just up the hill, outside Tixall village, is the huge square ruin of Tixall Gatehouse, an Elizabethan building that used to serve the now-vanished Tixall Hall. Back at Great Haywood village, there is a shallow lock on the Trent and Mersey Canal, which enjoys a pleasant wooded course beside the Trent. There is a very old packhorse bridge here: it leads to Shugborough Hall, a large 17th and 18th century mansion owned by the National Trust and administered by Staffordshire County Council, who have an excellent 'Museum of Staffordshire Life' in the stable block. Great Haywood village is worth a look (it is an estate village, linked to Shugborough Park, and is now the focus of a local Conservation Area), and to the south is Cannock Chase, 26 square miles of open hills and forest land. Much of this is open to the public and is excellent walking country.

Access Car: Great Haywood is off the A51, 5 miles north-west of Rugeley. A minor road crosses the canal just by the junction. A car park at Great Haywood lock gives easy access to the canal—and to Shugborough Hall via the packhorse

bridge. Bus: Potteries Motor Traction and Greatorex Motor Coaches services to Great Haywood village.

LOCK FLIGHTS

There are few better places to see canals in use than at flights of locks. Here you can study the lock machinery and see how it works, and you can compare the differing skills of the boat crews as they tackle the inescapable obstacle course.

There are many locks flights in the Midlands; the following are a fair cross-section of the whole. If you want to see a big, dense flight, try Hatton locks—they are exhausting just to look at. If it is the urban scene that you are after, have a look at Farmer's Bridge. A complete contrast would be offered by the rural Napton locks, which have a delightfully unruffled, pre-industrial air about them.

Farmer's Bridge and Aston Locks (Birmingham and Fazeley Canal)

These two flights, 24 narrow locks in all, carry the canal down from Farmer's Bridge Junction to Salford Junction. The course is through the centre of Birmingham, but high walls, factories and warehouses shut the canal in, hiding the city completely. Among the familiar old canalside buildings are new structures, towering over the narrow waterway. Some of these have actually been built over the canal, forcing it to take a curious subterranean passage; halfway down the Farmer's Bridge flight the canal passes beneath Brindley House, the new tall circular tower, and the locks are actually in the basement of the building! There is a mysterious passage through the cavern formed by the old Snow Hill Station above. But there are no access points to the towpath, and so the canal and the locks exist in their own private world. Many of the locks are very close together, especially near the top of each flight.

Access The only access point to the towpath in Birmingham that is open at all times is in Gas Street. It is five minutes' walk from Gas Street to Cambrian Wharf and the start of the Farmer's Bridge flight. For precise directions see page 12.

Wolverhampton Locks (BCN)

An extended flight of 21 narrow locks carries the BCN main line down from Wolverhampton to Aldersley Junction, where it joins the Staffordshire and Worcestershire Canal. The surroundings are mainly industrial for most of the flight, but towards the junction the canal comes out into the open country. Busy railway lines accompany or cross the locks; linked to these were several interchange basins, where goods could be transhipped from canal to railway, and vice versa. One of these survives in a good state of preservation. The basins show how the BCN system, alone among canals, benefited from the coming of the railways: this helps to explain why even today there is still a tiny amount of commercial carrying on the BCN.

Access The A449, A460 and A4124 all cross the flight, and there are good towpath access points at these three bridges. The top of the flight is close to Wolverhampton city centre and the railway station. Returning from the bottom of the locks is not quite so easy; the best thing is to turn left when you reach the junction and walk for about a mile along a pleasant stretch of the Staffordshire and Worcestershire Canal to the A41. A bus (Midland Red services X93–96) will take you back to Wolverhampton.

Northampton Locks
(Grand Union Canal)

A long flight of 17 narrow locks takes the Northampton arm of the Grand Union Canal down to join the river Nene; thus the canal system connects with Peterborough, Ely and the navigable waters of the Fens. The flight is attractive, descending through rolling farmland, and the locks are interspersed with old bascule lift bridges, operated by the canal user. A short concrete tunnel takes the canal under the M1 motorway.

Access Car: The A43 runs parallel to the flight, 1 mile to the east. Turn off west along a minor road from Milton Malsor, 3 miles south of Northampton, and join the canal by the road bridge. Rail: Northampton Station. Bus: Midland Red service 512 (Northampton–Towcester) stops at Milton Malsor, ¾ mile east of the top lock. If you walk to the canal and follow the locks downhill, you will arrive back in Northampton.

Hatton Locks

The most impressive lock flight in the Midlands, Hatton consists of 21 locks in 2 miles, many of them only a few yards apart. They are not an encouraging sight for a boatman! The flight lifts the Grand Union Canal by 146 feet, out of the Warwickshire Avon valley towards the uplands of the Black Country. The locks were originally narrow, but the Grand Union Canal modernisation scheme of the 1930's entailed the widening of locks to a 14-foot standard, and so all the locks between Braunston and Birmingham had to be doubled in width—an expensive operation. At Hatton the old narrow lock chambers are still used—as overflow weirs beside the newer locks. The wide locks themselves feature tall, slanting paddle posts. The paddles themselves are big 2-foot-square sluices which ensure that the locks fill and empty very quickly.

The old Warwick and Birmingham Canal Company's workshops at the top of the flight are still in use as a British Waterways Board maintenance yard. There is also a large pub at the top, and a good view down the straight line of locks to Warwick Castle, 3 miles away.

Access The A41 runs right alongside the locks, and the Midland Red buses 547, 557 and 597 follow this route. Rail: The Leamington–Birmingham line follows the canal closely; Hatton Station is on the canal, a mile west of the top lock, and Warwick Station is in the town, 1½ miles east of the bottom lock.

Napton Locks

A delightful and well-known flight of nine narrow locks dropping the Oxford Canal from its 11-mile summit level to the junction with the Grand Union Canal on the north side of Napton Hill. The locks pass through the quiet undulating farmlands of southern Warwickshire. The top lock is at the former canal settlement of Marston Doles, where a canal warehouse still stands; the remaining locks are grouped closer together, towards Napton village itself. The locks are often busy, and interspersed with pleasing arched 'accommodation' bridges, providing an enjoyable stroll up or down the locks. Some of the locks are now fitted with the new hydraulic paddle gear—this is designed to make it easier to open and close the sluices. Between the top and second lock you can see the Engine House Arm. This is a short branch which runs to the site of a former pumping station. The station used to pump water up from the bottom of the locks to the top, but nothing remains of the building now. (The arm was cut so that coal boats could reach the pumping station to fuel its steam-fired boiler.) You can hardly fail to notice that famous landmark, the windmill on Napton Hill, but look twice at the farmhouse set back from the bottom lock. It used to be a canal pub, the 'Bull and Butcher'. (The nearest pub is now in the village.)

Access Car: Napton is just south of the A425, and the locks are south of Napton Hill. Minor roads intersect the canal at several places. Bus: Midland Red services 551 and 596 from Southam.

Atherstone Locks

The original directors of the Coventry Canal Company must have been pleased to have the liability of only 11 locks in their whole 32-mile canal, especially as they were all grouped in one flight at Atherstone. The Atherstone flight enables the canal to continue following the valley of the river Anker. Starting from the top, by the Atherstone–Coleshill road, the locks dodge round the back of the railway, pass under a little road bridge which turns out to be the old A5 (Watling Street), then under major road and rail bridges to finish out in the countryside.

The locks are a little unusual in still having operational side ponds (small reservoirs beside the locks, used for saving lockage water)—which is just as well, for without these the locks would be particularly slow for a boatman to empty and fill. Halfway down the locks, but unattainable from the towpath, is Baddesley Basin. Until comparatively recent years this basin used to be a busy transhipment place, where coal from Baddesley Colliery used to be unloaded from railway wagons into narrowboats for distribution via the canal system. But now, like all the other coal-wharves along this canal, it is silently silting up.

Access Very easy. Plenty of buses to Atherstone from all directions; and the railway station is beside the locks. Motorists would do well to park on the old A5, which crosses the middle of the flight by the station on a deceptively inconspicuous bridge. There is a pub nearby, with a garden leading to the canal.

AQUEDUCTS

Canal aqueducts—i.e. bridges carrying a canal over an obstacle—are the converse of canal tunnels, and often represent a convenient way of negotiating a temporary change in the land level when crossing any form ot valley. In the early days, to build a canal aqueduct was a challenge, mainly because of the sheer weight and bulk of the structure required to withstand the great weight of the water pressing down. In addition the foundations had to be especially strong to prevent movement which could cause cracks and thus leakage. The weight of the structure was in any case augmented by the clay puddle lining.

Many 'aqueducts' are no more than a bridge over a very large culvert, consisting of a single horseshoe-shaped arch carrying the canal over a stream or minor road. Indeed the distinction between a minor canal aqueduct and a culvert has always been blurred. But no such confusion is possible when you consider the bigger aqueducts. James Brindley's first major aqueduct was the Barton Aqueduct on the Bridgewater Canal, opened in 1759. His scornful critics could not believe that bridges could be built for boats just as they could for horses and coaches, but Mr Brindley built his 'castle in the air'—and it worked. Later canal engineers, notably Thomas Telford, modernised the whole technology of aqueduct construction by using a cast-iron trough instead of brick or masonry. This brought the benefits of cheapness, lightness and prefabrication. It also meant that such a trough could be simply placed along the top of a row of brick pillars—which could of course be of great height if so desired. Telford's great Pontcysyllte Aqueduct on the Llangollen Canal in North Wales is the finest example of this technique. More recently, any canal aqueducts that have been built (as re-placements) come in pre-stressed concrete. They are predictably strong and simple.

There are examples of all these types on the canals of the Midlands, ranging from Brindley's heavy-looking aqueducts at Milford on the Staffordshire and Worcestershire Canal, and at Rugeley on the Trent and Mersey, to the delicate cast-iron arch that Telford used on the BCN. There are iron trough aqueducts on the Stratford-upon-Avon Canal, at Bearley and Wootton Wawen, and a late one at Stretton on the Shropshire Union. Another late development is the canal aqueduct over a railway line, where the railway has burrowed through an existing canal embankment; this occurs at Leamington Spa. Then there is the contrast of Ryland Aqueduct, built in 1968 at Dudley Port, where the peaceful canal is sharply contrasted with the rushing road traffic below. And finally there is the large new aqueduct crossing the M5 motorway on the Tame Valley Canal (west of Rushall Junction). But access to this is rather restricted.

There follows a selection of the more interesting canal aqueducts in the Midlands.

Tame Aqueduct
(Coventry Canal)

The opening of this substantial masonry aqueduct in 1790 marked the completion of the Coventry Canal. It carries the canal over the river Tame, which was for a long time a serious obstacle to the canal's builders. Several plans for the crossing were considered, including one locking down to the river and up the other side, but eventually the company—wisely—decided on an aqueduct, and this is the structure that stands today. Half a mile to the west is Fazeley, where the Coventry Canal joins the Birmingham and Fazeley Canal.

Access Car: The A5 and A4091 cross in Fazeley. Join the towpath by the canal junction and walk eastwards to the aqueduct. Rail: Wilnecote Station is a mile east of Fazeley, on the A5. Bus: Plenty of buses between Tamworth and Fazeley.

Avon Aqueduct
(Grand Union Canal)

Opened in 1800, this three-arched aqueduct was built to carry the short Warwick and Napton Canal over the river Avon. Like its neighbour, the Warwick and Birmingham Canal, this small canal company eventually became a part of the Grand Union amalgamation. Just south of the aqueduct is another, later, one which carried the canal over the railway line.

Access The aqueducts are midway between Leamington and Warwick. There are stations in both towns, and plenty of buses between them. A walk along the towpath from the A445 or the A425 leads to the aqueducts.

Brinklow Aqueduct
(Oxford Canal)

Opened in 1778 when the Oxford company completed its line to Banbury, the aqueduct was for long regarded as an engineering marvel. Designed by Brindley, the aqueduct takes the canal across a valley on 12 brick arches, each 22 feet wide, giving it the name of 'Brinklow Arches'. During the shortening of the Oxford Canal in the 1820's, an embankment was added to one side of the aqueduct to widen it, and subsequently many of the arches have been filled in to strengthen them. Today the aqueduct looks much more like a large earth embankment, but it is still possible to distinguish the form of Brindley's original work. One mile to the north-west, the canal crosses a minor road on another aqueduct (once the scene of a disastrous breach in the canal bank) beside a railway embankment.
Access Car: Brinklow village is on the A4114 (A427), which crosses the canal north of the village. A short walk south along the towpath leads to the aqueduct. Bus: Midland Red services 545, 583 and 585 to Brinklow village.

Stretton Aqueduct
(Shropshire Union Canal)

The Birmingham and Liverpool Junction Canal, a direct line linking Birmingham with the Mersey, was opened in 1835. Built well into the railway era, the canal was soon absorbed into the Shropshire Union network to fight railway competition. Many features of the canal typify its late date: its straight line, the deep cuttings; and, not least, Stretton Aqueduct—a wide iron trough carrying the canal over the A5, and looking from the road much like a railway bridge. The aqueduct has recently been renovated.
Access Car: The aqueduct crosses the A5 (Watling Street) 3 miles west of the Gailey roundabout, 5 miles west of its junction (No. 12) with the M6. Bus: Midland Red service X97 along the A5.

Bearley Aqueduct
(Stratford-upon-Avon Canal)

Opened in 1816 when the southern arm of the Stratford Canal was completed, Bearley (or Edstone) Aqueduct carries the canal over a minor road and a railway. Its unusual structure consists of a long iron trough on brick piers carrying the canal with the towpath slung beside and well below the water level. It is more usual with iron aqueducts for the towpath to be carried one or two feet above the water level. A mile and a half to the north, at Wootton Wawen, a similar but smaller aqueduct carries the canal over the A34.
Access Bearley Aqueduct can be approached via the minor road that leaves the A34 at Bearley Cross. Bearley Station is just over ½ mile from the aqueduct. It is a pleasant walk. Wootton Wawen Aqueduct crosses the A34 road about 1¼ miles up the canal from Bearley Aqueduct. There is a station at Wootton Wawen. Midland Red service 149 goes to Bearley, and 150 goes to both Bearley and Wootton Wawen.

Rugeley Aqueduct
(Trent and Mersey Canal)

When it was opened in 1777, the Trent and Mersey Canal included several major engineering features, the most famous being Harecastle Tunnel. The others include Rugeley Aqueduct, which carries the canal over the river Trent on six substantial arches. The aqueduct was built wide, which, in view of the relatively primitive state of the science at that time, makes it an ambitious piece of engineering.
Access Car: The A51 passes just south of the aqueduct, which is 1½ miles northwest of Rugeley. Rail: Rugeley Station is under a mile east of the aqueduct. The quickest way from the station is northwest along the B5013 for ½ mile, then turn left to cross the railway over a small bridge. Bus: Midland Red services 823, 824, 825 and 827 along the A51. There is a short lane down to the canal from the road.

Ryland Aqueduct (BCN)

When Telford engineered the New Main Line of the BCN, he maintained the level of the canal through Dudley Port by building the Ryland Aqueduct, which carried the canal over a main road, now the A461. This aqueduct became too narrow for the demands of modern traffic, and so during a road-widening scheme in 1968 the aqueduct was demolished and completely rebuilt. As such it is one of the very few new canal aqueducts in Britain. The new concrete structure is handsome, and includes a staircase to the towpath. One of the cast-iron name plates from the original aqueduct is in the Waterways Museum at Stoke Bruerne.
Access Car: The aqueduct crosses the A461 1½ miles north-east of Dudley town centre. Rail: Dudley Port Station is right by the aqueduct. Bus: Plenty of buses in this area.

TUNNELS

Tunnels are a vital part of the canal environment and a dramatic interlude in any canal journey. Canal tunnels vary according to the nature of the terrain. Some are 20 yards long, some 3,000; one, Standedge on the Huddersfield Narrow Canal, is over 5,000 yards long—but this is now closed to navigation. There are many tunnels in the Midlands, and their distribution naturally reflects the main geographical obstacles in the path of the canal builders.

In the south-east corner of the Midlands are the Northamptonshire Heights, which are virtually an extension of the Cotswold Hills from north Oxfordshire to Leicestershire. These account for the long tunnels at Saddington, Husbands Bosworth, Crick, Braunston and Blisworth. The other main group of tunnels—on the Birmingham Canal Navigations, the Dudley Canal and the Worcester and Birmingham Canal—is occasioned by the Worcestershire hills which reach north from the Cotswolds on the east side of the Severn valley.

Tunnels presented problems not only to engineers, but also to boatmen: very few early tunnels were built with a towpath, and so boats had to be 'legged' through by the crew while the horses were led to the far end on the surface. Legging means forcing the boat forward by walking against the roof or walls of the tunnel, a slow, exhausting and dangerous activity. In the 19th century steam or electric tugs were used to pull boats through some tunnels, but until the development of the self-propelled boat, legging remained the usual method, often surviving until quite recently—it was practised through Crick, Husbands Bosworth and Saddington tunnels on the Leicester line of the Grand Union right up to the Second World War.

Dudley Tunnel
(Dudley Canal—part of the BCN)

Now the longest navigable canal tunnel in Britain (3,172 yards), Dudley was restored and re-opened as a through route in 1973, along with the Parkhead Locks just south of it. The tunnel was completed originally in 1792, to link Birmingham and the Midlands with the river Severn and the west of England, via the Dudley, Stourbridge and Staffordshire and Worcestershire Canals. Connected to the tunnel is a remarkable series of underground quarries, mine workings and branch canals (disused now), which make it one of Britain's most interesting canal tunnels. Dudley Tunnel is extremely narrow in places (only about 9 feet wide) and since it was re-opened boats have been forbidden to use engines because of the danger from fumes. So legging or 'shafting' boats through the tunnel is again the order of the day.

Above the tunnel are Dudley Castle and Zoo, and the Black Country Museum is being built on a site adjoining the canal. The Wren's Nest geological nature reserve is also close.
Access There is no towpath through the tunnel, but access to both ends is easy. Car: The A4123 crosses the northern portal, the A461 runs near the southern. Rail: Tipton Station is about a mile from the northern portal. Bus: Midland Red service X93.

Netherton Tunnel (BCN)

The most modern canal tunnel in Britain, Netherton was opened in 1858 complete with gas lighting throughout. 3,027 yards long, it runs parallel to Dudley Tunnel, and was built to overcome the traffic delays caused by the latter's limited dimensions. It is a wide tunnel with a towpath on both sides and so it can be easily explored on foot—but take a torch. The remains of an old steam pumping house stand near the southern portal, while a short distance from the northern one is the Tividale Aqueduct, which carries the Old Main Line of the Birmingham Canal over the Netherton branch.
Access Car: The A457 crosses near the northern portal and aqueduct, the A459 runs near the southern. Rail: Dudley Port Station is $\frac{1}{4}$ mile from the northern portal. Bus: Midland Red service X93.

Blisworth Tunnel
(Grand Union Canal)

Opened in 1805 after structural difficulties had delayed the work for several years, Blisworth is the second longest navigable canal tunnel in Britain. It is well situated, Blisworth village being near the northern portal, while a short cutting leads from the southern end to Stoke Bruerne and the Waterways Museum. When the Grand Union Canal was opened from London to Birmingham, Blisworth Tunnel was still incomplete. The problem of through traffic was tackled by building a rudimentary horse tramway—the first railway in Northamptonshire—right over Blisworth Hill from one end of the tunnel to the other. This was obviously very cumbersome, involving double transhipment of the cargo, but it worked for a full five years until the canal tunnel was opened. Remains of the tramway can still be seen in places. In 1861 an unpleasant accident occurred in the tunnel when the crew of a steam boat were overcome by fumes; their deaths led to the opening of more airshafts to improve ventilation, always a problem in long tunnels.
Access There is no towpath through the tunnel, but its course through Blisworth Hill can easily be traced by the line of brick airshafts projecting out of the top. There is a public road following the line of the tunnel shafts from one end to the other. Car: The A43 passes through Blisworth village, the A508 east of Stoke Bruerne. Bus: Midland Red service 512 or United Counties 343 from Northampton to Blisworth. There are boat trips in summer from Stoke Bruerne to the tunnel mouth.

Braunston Tunnel
(Grand Union Canal)

Opened in 1796, this 2,042-yard tunnel cuts through the Northamptonshire Heights. Surveying mistakes made during its construction have given the tunnel a slight 'S' bend. There is still a brick hut at the eastern end—from here the leggers would join the boats before the latter entered the tunnel, while the towing horses would be detached and led over the hill.

Access There is no towpath through the tunnel. Car: The A45 passes through Braunston village, and the B4036 to Welton passes near the eastern portal. Visitors should park in Braunston village and walk up the locks to the tunnel mouth. Bus: Midland Red service 572 to Braunston, United Counties service 307 to Welton.

Shrewley Tunnel
(Grand Union Canal)

Opened in 1799, Shrewley Tunnel is 433 yards long and has pleasantly overgrown portals. There is no towpath through the tunnel, but it is interesting for the clearly defined footpath over the top; this indicates the route that the towing horse took while its boat was being legged through. Above the northern portal this path goes through its own miniature tunnel for 40 yards; when approached from the north-west the mouths of two tunnels can be seen, one above and to the side of the other.

Access: Car: Shrewley village is on the B4439, which branches off the A41 3 miles west of Warwick. A minor road running through the village crosses the northern portal of the tunnel. Rail: Hatton Station is beside the canal, under $\frac{1}{4}$ mile from the tunnel's eastern entrance. Bus: Midland Red services 546 and 557 from Warwick to Shrewley village.

Newbold Tunnel
(Oxford Canal)

During the 1820's the route of the Oxford Canal was considerably shortened to overcome the excessive meanderings of the original line. A part of this operation involved the cutting of a new tunnel at Newbold, to replace the old 125-yard one which was now at right angles to the new course of the canal. The new tunnel, 250 yards long, was built wide, with a towpath on each side, unusual at that date. The towpaths necessitated a turnover bridge at each end, and these were incorporated into the portals. The southern portal of the old tunnel can still be clearly seen by Newbold Church, and the old course of the canal can just be traced as a shallow depression across the fields.

Access Car: The B4112 passes through Newbold village, which is 2 miles north-west of Rugby. Rail: Rugby Station is 2 miles away. Bus: Midland Red service 585 to Newbold.

Newbold

Navigation, touring circuits and distances

A fully co-ordinated network, the canals of the Midlands are not a radial system focused on a well-defined centre, but form a complicated pattern of interlinking trunk routes and branches, a pattern which at first seems random and formless, but which on close inspection turns out to be an accurate reflection of the growth centres and primary trade routes of the Industrial Revolution.

All this is good news for the canal boater today, for he is offered an enormous variety of cruising circuits of all sizes. Some of these circuits take a couple of hours to complete, others take a couple of weeks. Few are free of locks, most offer a balance of rural and industrial scenery, and all have their special features.

Planning a cruise

It is wise when planning a cruise to establish a means of calculating the time it takes to travel any given length of canal. This ensures that you can reliably arrange to meet friends further along the canal at or about a given time—or you can work out whether you will reach a shop or pub before closing time. And of course for those who have hired their boat for a week, it is vital to return on time to the starting point.

The time taken to navigate any canal depends, of course, on the average cruising speed of your boat and the amount of time it takes to negotiate the locks along the way. Both of these vary according to circumstances: for example the optimum cruising speed of a boat depends not only upon the type and size of the boat and its engine, but also the cross-section of the waterway, the amount of wash caused by the hull, and many other factors (bear in mind that a shallow or narrow waterway restricts the speed of any boat). And you must also remember that there is in any case an overall legal speed limit of 4 mph on all the Midland canals. In practice, 3 mph is a realistic canal cruising speed for most boats in the Midlands.

To the uninitiated, 3 mph may sound an unbearably slow rate of progress through the countryside; but a few hours of gentle cruising on a fine day is usually enough to convert most people to this pace. For only by proceeding at walking pace can you appreciate the peace and beauty of the countryside, watch the bird life, and see the scurry of voles, water rats and others as they suddenly notice the slowly approaching boat.

The length of time taken to work through a lock depends on several things: whether the lock is full or empty, wide or narrow, deep or shallow. It depends on the number and size of the paddles that control the sluices, on the presence or otherwise of other boats near the lock, and of course on the number and competence of the boat crew. Most people take around 10 minutes on average to work through a typical lock—or, to put it another way, they take as long to get through a lock as they would have taken to travel another $\frac{1}{2}$ mile. Herein lies the basis for a simple method of estimating time required to travel along a given length of canal: take the number of miles to be travelled and add half the number of locks to be negotiated on the way. This gives the number of 'lock-miles'. Divide this by your average cruising speed, and the result is the approximate length of time it will take, in hours. Thus if you intend to travel 30 miles, and there are 42 locks along the way, the calculation is as follows: 30 + (42 divided by 2) = 30 + 21 = 51 lock-miles. 51 divided by 3 = 17 hours. So this particular journey will take you around 17 hours, assuming your average cruising speed to be 3 mph and assuming you take about 10 minutes to get through the average lock. (If you're a beginner, it might take a little longer than this to start with.)

The lock-mile system is a crude but effective and extremely useful means of working out times taken on canal cruises. To refine the system, simply tailor it more closely to the actual cruising speed of your boat and the efficiency of your lock-operating technique. To fit the lock-mile system to the Midland waterways is not difficult, and it helps to show what a wide choice these canals offer in terms of one-week or two-week holidays. An excellent fortnight's trip, for example, would be the circuit formed by the river Soar and the Coventry, Oxford, Grand Union (Leicester Section) and Trent and Mersey canals. This is 170 miles and 74 locks long, and takes you through some of the very best parts of Leicestershire. You will see the Foxton locks, Braunston Tunnel and the delightful village of Shardlow. You will on this circuit also enjoy one of the longest level pounds in the country; and if you have time to spare you can explore the

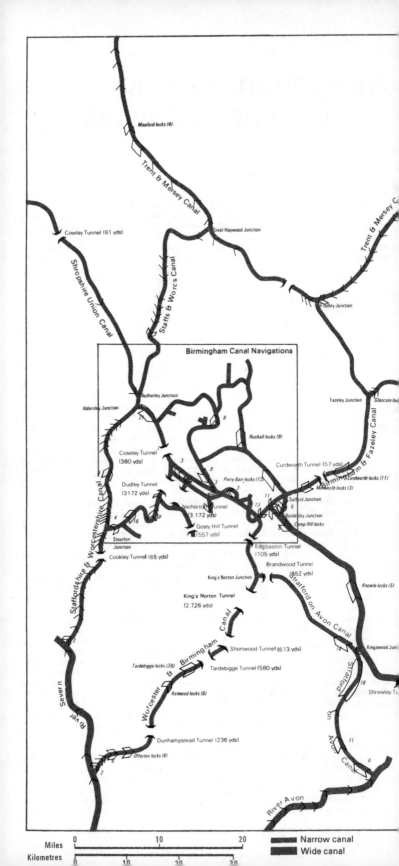

Birmingham Canal Navigations

Meaford locks (4)

Trent & Mersey Canal

Trent & Mersey Canal

Cowley Tunnel (81 yds)

Great Haywood Junction

Shropshire Union Canal

Staffs & Worcs Canal

Fradley Junction

Fazeley Junction

Glascote locks

Autherley Junction

Aldersley Junction

Rushall locks (9)

Coseley Tunnel
(360 yds)

Curdworth Tunnel (57 yds)

Birmingham & Fazeley Canal

Curdworth locks (11)

Perry Barr locks (13)

Minworth locks (3)

Dudley Tunnel
(3.172 yds)

Netherton Tunnel
(3.172 yds)

Salford Junction

Bordesley Junction

Gosty Hill Tunnel
(557 yds)

Camp Hill locks

Staffordshire & Worcestershire Canal

Stourton
Junction

Edgbaston Tunnel
(105 yds)

Cookley Tunnel (65 yds)

Brandwood Tunnel
(352 yds)

Knowle locks (5)

King's Norton Junction

Stratford on Avon Canal

King's Norton Tunnel
(2.726 yds)

Birmingham & Worcester Canal

Kingswood Junction

Shortwood Tunnel (613 yds)

Stratford

Tardebigge locks (36)

Tardebigge Tunnel (580 yds)

Shrewley Tunnel

Astwood locks (6)

Severn

River Severn

Dunhampstead Tunnel (236 yds)

Avon Canal

Offerton locks (6)

River Avon

| Miles | 0 | 10 | 20 | | Narrow canal |
| Kilometres | 0 | 10 | 20 | 20 | Wide canal |

Navigational map of the Midlands canals

lock-free Ashby Canal (22 miles long—2 days there and back) or the meandering course of the unspoilt Market Harborough Arm, 5 miles long.

A good round trip in terms of contrasts would be the Grand Union main line, north Oxford, Coventry and Birmingham & Fazeley canals, which at 106 miles and 88 locks would be a reasonably energetic week's cruising. On this route you could see Braunston and Hillmorton, the long level of the north Oxford canal broken by the 11 locks at Atherstone, and then the industrial outpost of Fazeley. In Birmingham, you could either slip southwards along the Grand Union or have a quick foray into the nether regions of the Birmingham Canal Navigations. Once out in Warwickshire, you encounter the five wide but modern locks at Knowle (built in the 1930's). A few miles further on, the 21 locks of the Hatton Flight will impede your progress considerably; but if you try hard you might get through them in 1½ hours. Then you are in the valley of the Warwickshire Avon, and after passing Warwick and Leamington Spa you start locking up out of the valley again to rejoin the Oxford Canal at Napton.

The most enjoyable week-long cruising route of all is now complete. This is the circle formed by the Stratford-upon-Avon and Worcester and Birmingham canals and the rivers Avon and Severn. It is a 100-mile route of great beauty, taking in the lush fruit-growing area of the Vale of Evesham, the idyllic Stratford-upon-Avon Canal, the handsome but heavily locked Worcester and Birmingham Canal with its great tunnel at King's Norton, and the sweeping reaches of the river Severn. Towns on this circle include such historic places as Tewkesbury, Stratford and Worcester, which are all of enormous interest to the visitor, and the countryside that separates them is green, rich and unspoilt. This circuit of waterways has been broken for over 100 years, because much of the river Avon has been unnavigable for that time, but the Upper Avon Navigation restoration scheme, which has been financed and executed almost entirely by volunteers, is now finished at last.

These three are but a small fraction of the potential number of circular cruising routes in the Midlands. A glance at the map will show the very large number of permutations possible just using these routes as a basis; but the best thing is to make up your own mind. Use the map to work out the number of miles and locks on the various routes, and refer to the individual canal maps to find out where you would like to go and what you would like to see. Relate this information to the amount of time you have available, and you should be able to come up with a few alternative plans. But never make the mistake of undertaking a longer journey than you really want. After all, there is no point in making your holiday a race against time, and even if your party does not want to do much stopping to explore places near the canal, you will still *have* to stop here and there to buy food. So when planning a trip, always leave yourself plenty of time spare. Many a canal holiday has been spoilt by over-ambitious planning.

Watford Locks

Boatyards

The heart of the boating business on the canals is the boatyards. They tend to be the source of most boats, and their present prosperity very much reflects the continued boom in the popularity of canal boating.

The Midlands contain more than their fair share of boatyards, probably because virtually all the canals in the region are good cruising waters. And for hire cruiser operators—which form a very large proportion of the total number of boatyards—a Midlands base is ideal in that it makes available a very wide choice of routes for cruising.

There are very few of the commercial boatyards left nowadays: most of those that have remained have either dropped out of the narrowboat business altogether or turned to making narrowboat conversions to order for the new leisure market. There is a group of three traditional boatyards doing just this on the furthermost reaches of the BCN, at the end of the Cannock Extension Canal. But they are very much in demand and there tends to be a waiting list for the craftsman-built boats from these yards. Other boatyards, such as Harborough Marine at Market Harborough, produce numbers of traditional-type narrowboats—in various lengths.

The majority of canal boatyards have relatively little to do with traditional narrowboats, and most of them have been established less than ten years. Many offer hire cruisers, and if they do this, it is likely to be the main activity of the business. The remainder of the boatyards sell boats, fuels and chandlery; or they have extensive moorings to rent; or they perhaps handle boat or engine repairs.

One of the most important developments in the canals in recent years has been the emergence of canal 'marinas'—which in the normal sense of the word means boatyards covering a large area of water adjacent to the canal. The 'marina' is usually manmade, and provides a very large number of moorings as well, usually, as comprehensive other services. Marinas are sometimes unpopular among canal 'purists', as they tend to take up a lot of space and generate a lot of traffic pressure at one particular spot, but having a number of boats moored in one place is in most respects preferable to having the canal banks lined with boats for several hundred yards. It is also safer for boat owners—and more convenient for those with cars. So marinas are certainly here to stay. (Already there are marinas at Fenny Compton, Braunston, Whilton and Napton.)

The following list shows the addresses of canal boatyards in the Midlands and defines their principal activities. The numbers refer to the map.

Boatyards on the Midland canals

TRENT & MERSEY CANAL

1 Stone Boatbuilding Company,
Newcastle Road,
Stone, Staffordshire.
(Stone 2688.)
Hire cruisers, boat sales, boat building, chandlery, general services.

2 Canal Cruising Company,
Stone, Staffordshire.
(Stone 3982 or 2620.)
Hire cruisers, boat building, repairs.

3 Kingfisher Line,
Hoo Mill Lock,
Great Haywood, Staffordshire.
(Little Haywood 384.)
Hire cruisers, day boats, repairs.

4 Swan Line Cruisers,
Fradley Junction,
Alrewas, Burton-on-Trent.
(Burton-on-Trent 790332.)
Hire cruisers, chandlery, boat building, repairs.

5 Jannel Cruisers,
Shobnal Marina, Shobnal Road,
Burton-on-Trent.
(Burton 42718.)
Hire cruisers, general services.

6 Hopwood Craft,
Horninglow Wharf,
Burton-on-Trent.
(021-445-2595.)
Boat building in steel.

7 Clayton Line,
Stenson Marina,
Stenson, Derby.
(Repton 3113.)
Moorings, fuel, general services.

8 Barrington Narrowboat Company,
Stenson Marina,
Stenson, Derby.
(Derby 515670.)
Hire cruisers.

9 Dobson's Boatyard,
The Wharf, Shardlow,
Derby.
(Derby 792271.)
Chandlery, sales, boat building, repairs.

TRENT NAVIGATION & BEESTON CANAL

10 Sawley Bridge Marina,
Long Eaton, Nottingham.
(Long Eaton 4278.)
Hire cruisers, chandlery, boat sales. Big boating centre.

11 Avondale Marine,
Beeston Marina, Riverside,

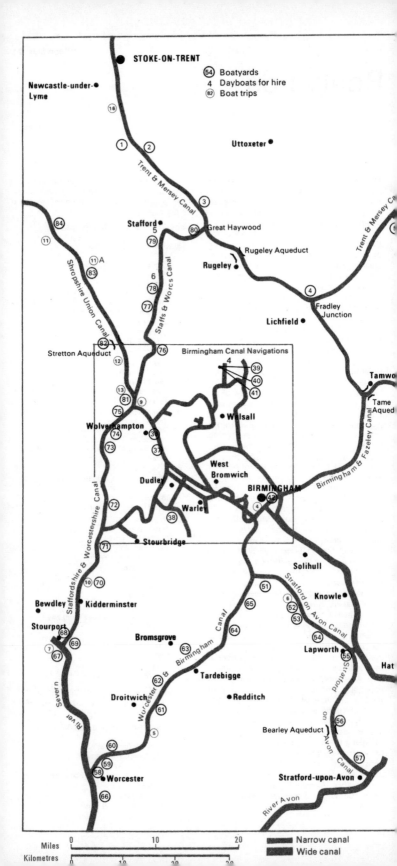

Boatyards, dayboats for hire & boat trips

Beeston, Nottingham.
(Nottingham 254738.)
Hire cruisers, dayboats, chandlery.

12   T. Trevithick,
Gregory Street,
Lenton, Nottingham.
(Nottingham 73467.)
Dayboats (on the Trent at Nottingham),
boat building in wood.

13   Speed Electrics Marine,
Old Pleasure Park,
Trent Lane, Nottingham.
(Nottingham 56550.)
Chandlery, boat and engine sales.

EREWASH CANAL

14   Long Eaton Marina,
Wyvern Avenue,
Long Eaton, Nottingham.
(Long Eaton 66539.)
Moorings, welding facilities.

15   Mills Dockyard,
Trent Lock,
Long Eaton, Nottingham.
(Long Eaton 3657.)
Moorings, drydocking facilities.

16   Davison Bros.
Trent Lock,
Long Eaton, Nottingham,
(Long Eaton 4643.)
Hire cruisers, boat building.

SOAR NAVIGATION

17   Kegworth Marine,
Kingston Lane,
Kegworth, Leicestershire.
(Kegworth 2300 or
Leicester 738938.)
Moorings, general repairs.

18   Inland Pleasure Craft,
Canal Bank, Derby Road,
Loughborough, Leicestershire.
(Loughborough 2019.)
Hire cruisers, boat sales.

19   Soar Valley Boatyard,
Sileby Road,
Mountsorrel, Leicestershire.
(Rothley 2642.)
Boat sales, chandlery.

20   Mountsorrel Marine Centre,
14–18 Loughborough Road,
Mountsorrel, Leicestershire.
(Rothley 2144.)
Boat sales.

21   L. R. Harris & Son,
Old Junction Boatyard,
Meadow Lane, Syston,
near Leicester.
Chandlery, moorings, general services.

22   Jennings & Son
Mill Lane Boatyard,
Thurmaston, Leicestershire.

GRAND UNION CANAL:
LEICESTER SECTION

23   Blaby Marine Centre,
Wharf Way,
Glen Parva, Leicester.
(Wigston 6666.)
Chandlery.

24   Foxton Boat Services,
Bottom Lock, Foxton,
Market Harborough, Leicestershire.
(Kibworth 2285.)
Chandlery, general boat services.

25   Harborough Marine
(Anglo Welsh Narrow Boats),
The Canal Basin, Leicester Road.
Market Harborough, Leicestershire.
(Market Harborough 2594.)
Hire cruisers, steel boat building.

26   Hucker Marine,
The Wharf,
North Kilworth, Leicestershire.
(Husbands Bosworth 484.)
Hire cruisers, chandlery, boat building.

27   Welford Canal Boats,
Canal Wharf, Welford,
Northants.
(Welford 519.)
Hire cruisers, boat repairs, fuel, general
services.

28   Just Boats,
The Wharf, Crick,
Rugby, Warwickshire.
(0788–822371.)
Hire cruisers.

GRAND UNION CANAL:
MAIN LINE

29   Water Gipsy Cruisers,
The Narrow Boat Inn, Stowe Hill,
Weedon, Northamptonshire.
(Weedon 40763.)
Hire cruisers, chandlery.

30   Concoform Marine,
The Boatyard, High Street,
Weedon, Northamptonshire.
(Weedon 40739.)
Hire cruisers, chandlery.

31   Whilton Marine,
Whilton Locks, near Daventry.
Northamptonshire.
(Long Buckby 577.)
Chandlery, hire cruisers, boat sales, boat
building. General facilities, extensive
moorings.

32   Braunston Boats,
Bottom Lock, Braunston,
Rugby, Warwickshire.
(Rugby 890342.)
Narrowboat building and repairing.

33   Ladyline Ltd,
Braunston Marina, Braunston,
near Rugby, Warwickshire.
(Rugby 890325.)
Hire cruisers, boat sales, chandlery, exten-
sive moorings

34   Calcutt Boats,
Calcutt Top Lock,
Tomlow, Stockton,
Rugby.
(Southam 3757.)

35   Boats (Warwick),
Nelson Lane, Warwick.
(Warwick 42968.)
Hire cruisers.

BIRMINGHAM CANAL
NAVIGATIONS

36   James Walton & Son,
Biddings Lane, Deepfields,

Coseley, Staffordshire.
(Bilston 42725.)
Boat building in wood.

37   Alfred Matty,
Biddings Lane, Deepfields,
Coseley, Staffordshire.
(Bilston 42725.)
Commercial carrying and boat repairing.

38   Bumblehole Boating Centre,
St Peter's Road, Netherton,
Dudley, Staffordshire.
(Dudley 55874.)
Chandlery.

39   C. J. Parker,
Norton Canes Dock, Lime Lane,
Pelsall, Staffordshire.
(Brownhills 3179.)
Boat building (steel narrowboats).

40   M. E. Braine,
Norton Canes Dock, Lime Lane,
Pelsall, Staffordshire.
(Brownhills 4888.)
Boat building (steel narrowboats).

41   Canal Transport Services,
Norton Canes Dock, Lime Lane,
Pelsall, Staffordshire.
(Brownhills 4370.)
Boat building (steel narrowboats).

BIRMINGHAM & FAZELEY CANAL

42   Planetfleet Cruisers,
435 Lichfield Road,
Birmingham B6 7SS.
(021-327 0253 daytime.)
(021-783 3105 evenings.)
Hire cruisers.

COVENTRY CANAL

43   Nautocraft Marine,
Boot Wharf,
Nuneaton, Warwickshire.
(Nuneaton 5833.)
Hire cruisers, boat sales, chandlery,
general services.

44   Gilbert Bros,
Charity Dock, Furnace Road,
Bedworth, Warwickshire.
(Bedworth 313122.)
Narrowboat building (in steel and wood)
and repairing.

ASHBY CANAL

45   The Narrow Boat Company,
The Canal Wharf, Stoke Golding,
Nuneaton, Warwickshire.
(Hinckley 212671.)
Hire cruisers, general services.

OXFORD CANAL

46   Maidboats,
Brinklow Marina,
Stretton-under-Fosse, Warwickshire.
(Rugby 832449.)
Hire cruisers, general services.

47   Willow Wren,
Rugby Wharf, Forum Drive,
Rugby, Warwickshire.
(Rugby 4520.)
Hire cruisers (converted narrowboats),
boat building, general services.

48   Rugby Boatbuilders,
Hillmorton Wharf, Crick Road,
near Rugby, Warwickshire.
(Rugby 4438.)
Hire cruisers and general services. Steel
narrowboats built.

49   Gordon's Pleasure Cruisers,
Napton Marina, Stockton,
Rugby, Warwickshire.
(Southam 3644.)
Hire cruisers, chandlery. Steel narrowboats
designed.

50   Fenny Marine,
Station Fields,
Fenny Compton, Warwickshire.
(Fenny Compton 461.)
Chandlery, boat building (steel
narrowboat cruisers) and boat sales
(fibreglass craft).

STRATFORD-UPON-AVON CANAL

51   Earlswood Marine Services,
Lady Lane,
Earlswood, Warwickshire.
(Earlswood 2552.)
General services.

52   Swallow Cruisers,
rear of Wharf Inn, Stratford Road,
Hockley Heath, Warwickshire.
(Lapworth 2418.)
Chandlery, general services.

53   Holwill's Boatyard,
Wharf Lane,
Hockley Heath, Warwickshire.
(Lapworth 3442.)
Dealers in fibreglass boats.

54   E. G. Wheatley,
Old Warwick Road,
Lapworth, Warwickshire.
(Lapworth 2379.)
Hire cruisers and general services.

55   Narrowboat Services,
Lapworth Basin,
Lapworth, Warwickshire.
(Lapworth 2727.)
Boat building and repairing.

56   Anglo Welsh Narrow Boats,
The Canal Wharf,
Wootton Wawen, near Solihull,
Warwickshire.
(Henley-in-Arden 3427.)
Hire cruisers and general services.

57   Western Cruisers,
Western Road,
Stratford-upon-Avon, Warwickshire.
(Stratford 3878.)
Hire cruisers, chandlery.

WORCESTER & BIRMINGHAM CANAL

58   J. H. Everton,
Basin Road, Diglis, Worcester.
(Worcester 20975.)
Boat building and repairs, chandlery.

59   Cathedral Cruisers,
Basin Road,
Diglis, Worcester.
(Worcester 27543.)

60   Tolladine Boat Company,
Blackpole Wharf,
Worcester WR3 8TJ.
(Worcester 54474.)

61 Ladyline Ltd,
Hanbury Marina, Hanbury Road,
Droitwich, Worcestershire.
(Droitwich 3002.)
Boat sales, chandlery.

62 Stoke Prior Boat Services,
Stoke Wharf, near Bromsgrove,
Worcestershire.
(Bromsgrove 31401.)
General services.

63 Tardebigge Boat Company,
The Old Wharf, Tardebigge,
Bromsgrove, Worcestershire.
(Bromsgrove 73898.)
Converted narrowboats for hire, narrow-
boat building.

64 Warwickshire Cruisers,
Scarfield Wharf,
Alvechurch, Worcestershire.
(021-445 2909.)
Boats for sale. General services.

65 Hopwood Craft,
Birmingham Road, Hopwood,
near Alvechurch, Worcestershire.
(021-445 2595.)
General services. Boat building and fitting
out at Burton-on-Trent.

RIVER SEVERN

66 Seaborne Yacht Company,
Court Meadow,
Kempsey, Worcester.
(Kempsey 295.)
Boat building, hire cruisers.

67 Head's Boatyard,
Riverside,
Stourport-on-Severn,
Worcestershire.
(Stourport 2044.)
Boat building, chandlery and general
services.

68 Stirchley Marine,
1240 Pershore Road,
Stirchley, Birmingham.
(021-458 3946.)
Hire cruisers (at Stourport).

STAFFORDSHIRE &
WORCESTERSHIRE CANAL

69 Canal Pleasurecraft,
Stourport-on-Severn,
Worcestershire.
(Stourport 2970.)
Hire cruisers, boat building.

70 Dawncraft,
The Paddock,
Kinver, Staffordshire.
(Kinver 2363.)
Fibreglass boat building. General
services.

71 Dawncraft,
Stewponey Lock, Stourton,
near Stourbridge, Worcestershire.
(Kinver 2481.)
Boat sales, chandlery.

72 Renown Marine Services,
Ashwood Marina, Greensforge,
Kingswinford, Staffordshire.
(Kingswinford 79527.)
General services.

73 Mermaid Hire Cruisers,
Wightwick Wharf,

Castlecroft, Wolverhampton.
(Wolverhampton 763818.)
Hire cruisers and general services.

74 Leisurecraft Marine,
Newbridge Wharf, Tettenhall Road,
Wolverhampton, Staffordshire.
(Wolverhampton 752368.)
Fibreglass boat building.

75 Double Pennant Boatyard,
Hordern Road,
Wolverhampton, Staffordshire.
(Wolverhampton 752771.)

76 Calf Heath Marina,
Kings Road, Calf Heath,
near Wolverhampton, Staffordshire.
(Standeford 420.)
Hire cruisers, general services.

77 Bijou Line,
Penkridge Wharf, Cannock Road,
Penkridge, Staffordshire.
(Penkridge 2732.)
Hire cruisers, chandlery, boat building.

78 Teddesley Boating Centre,
Park Gate Lock, Teddesley Road,
Penkridge, Staffordshire.
(Penkridge 2437.)

79 Radford Marine,
Radford Wharf, Stafford.
(Stafford 3519.)
Day boats, chandlery, boat building.

80 Anglo Welsh Narrow Boats,
The Canal Wharf, Mill Lane,
Great Haywood, Staffordshire.
(Little Haywood 711.)
Hire cruisers, general services.

SHROPSHIRE UNION CANAL

81 Water Travel,
Autherley Marina,
Oxley Moor Road,
Wolverhampton, Staffordshire.
(Wolverhampton 782371.)
Hire cruisers, chandlery, trip boat, general
services.

82 Countrywide Cruisers,
The Wharf,
Brewood, Staffordshire.
(Brewood 850166.)
Hire cruisers, chandlery, general services.

83 Castle Boats,
The Wharf,
Wheaton Aston,
Stafford ST19 9NP.
(Wheaton Aston 840090.)
Hire cruisers.

84 Shropshire Union Cruises,
The Wharf,
Norbury Junction, Stafford.
(Woodseaves 292.)
Hire cruisers, boat building, repairs,
general services.

While every care has been taken in the preparation
of this list, the publishers cannot guarantee the accuracy of the information, which is liable to
change without notice.

Dayboats and boat trips

An easy and gentle introduction to canals
can be enjoyed by taking a cruise in one of
the many trip boats of all kinds that ply up

and down the waterways. This way you can sample for yourself the peaceful charm of Britain's old-fashioned inland waterways at minimum effort. Because of their largely rural nature, the Midland canals have a fairly high density of trip boats, and they range from carefully converted traditional narrowboats running a scheduled public service (these operate principally on summer weekends) for up to 60 people, to restaurant boats serving a meal on the move for a small party of up to about a dozen people. The boats tend, obviously, to be concentrated on the lightly locked stretches of canal—the long level of the Coventry and Oxford canals is a typically suitable area for the operation of regular boat services. The list below gives details of the boat services on the Midland canals—and in case you're the energetic type who prefers self-propulsion to large powered craft, we have included also a list of firms that rent out rowing boats, canoes, etc., by the hour or the day. But if you intend to try one of these, be sure to check the weather forecast beforehand! The numbers refer to the map.

Dayboats for hire

TRENT & MERSEY CANAL

1   Kingfisher Line,
    Hoo Mill Lock,
    Great Haywood, Staffordshire.
    (Little Haywood 384.)
    Runabouts for hire.

RIVER TRENT

2   T. Trevithick,
    Gregory Street,
    Lenton, Nottingham.
    (Nottingham 73467.)
    Rowing boats and canoes for hire on the Trent.

3   Avondale Marine,
    Riverside,
    Beeston, Nottingham.
    (Nottingham 254738.)
    Motor dayboats for hire.

BIRMINGHAM CANAL NAVIGATIONS

4   Canal Transport Services,
    Norton Canes Dock, Lime Lane,
    Pelsall, Staffordshire.
    (Brownhills 4370.)
    Motor boats for hire by the hour.

STAFFORDSHIRE &
WORCESTERSHIRE CANAL

5   Radford Marine,
    Radford Wharf, Stafford.
    (Stafford 3519.)
    Rowing boats, canoes and motor boats available.

6   Teddesley Boating Centre,
    Park Gate Lock, Teddesley Road,
    Penkridge, Staffordshire.
    (Penkridge 2437 or 2477.)
    Rowing boats for hire.

Boat trips

EREWASH CANAL

1   'Erewash Princess'. Operates from Sandiacre: limited public service on summer Sundays, otherwise available for charter. (Max. 54 passengers.)
    Erewash Princess,
    2 Sandown Road, Toton,
    Beeston, Nottinghamshire.
    (Long Eaton 2260.)

GRAND UNION CANAL:
LEICESTER SECTION

2   'Vagabond'. Boat operating from Foxton Bottom Lock: trips in three directions. Available for private charter (max. 51 passengers) and public trips at summer weekends.
    Foxton Boat Services,
    Bottom Lock, Foxton,
    Market Harborough,
    Leicestershire.
    (Kibworth 2285.)

GRAND UNION CANAL:
MAIN LINE

3   'Castle Rose'. Small boat running short trips from Stoke Bruerne to and through Blisworth Tunnel (max. 12 passengers.) Available for private parties only, except at weekends. All profits go to local charities.
    J. Woodward,
    The Boat Inn, Stoke Bruerne,
    near Towcester, Northamptonshire.

WORCESTER & BIRMINGHAM
CANAL

4   'The Brummagem Fly'. 48-passenger narrowboats operating from Farmer's Bridge. Public trips and private charter. Educational cruises a speciality.
    Enquiries to: 021-643 0525.

5   'Cedar'. 40-passenger narrowboat based at Dunhampstead Wharf. Scheduled trips at 16.00 on summer Sundays; otherwise available for private bookings.
    Telephone: Droitwich 3889.

STRATFORD-UPON-AVON CANAL

6   'Franklin', 'Planet' and 'Cepheus'. Narrowboats taking up to 50 passengers each. Private hire only, bar on board. Operate from Lady Lane, Earlswood.
    Earlswood Marine Services,
    Lady Lane, Earlswood,
    Warwickshire.
    (Earlswood 2552.)

RIVER SEVERN

7   'River King', 'Carbolate' and 'Miss Jason'. Steamer boats taking up to 160 passengers: scheduled trips along the Severn every 40 minutes each afternoon from Stourport Bridge. Also available for charter.
    Heads Boatyard,
    Stourport-on-Severn,
    Worcestershire.
    (Stourport 2838.)

8 'Severn Traveller and 'Belle'. Motor boats taking up to 200 passengers. Scheduled hourly river trips every afternoon from wharf at junction of river Severn and Worcester & Birmingham Canal. Also available for charter.
Worcester Steamer Company,
Diglis, Worcester.
(Worcester 27543.)

STAFFORDSHIRE & WORCESTERSHIRE CANAL

9 'Compton Queen'. 40-passenger narrowboat operating from Autherley Junction. For charter only.
Mr Gregory,
83 Aldersley Road,
Tettenhall, Wolverhampton.
(Wolverhampton 753851.)

10 'Bellatrix'. 49-passenger narrowboat operating from Kinver Lock. For charter only.
The Midland Navigation,
Packet Boat Service,
47 Geneva Road, Shrubbery Estate,
Tipton, Staffordshire.
(021-557 7347.)

SHROPSHIRE UNION CANAL

11 'Iona'. 48-passenger, horse-drawn narrowboat. Private hire only. Operates from Norbury Junction.
Shropshire Union Cruises,
The Wharf, Norbury Junction,
Stafford.
(Woodseaves 292.)

'Hyperion'. 42-seat ex-Grand Union narrowboat running trips on summer Sunday afternoons from Wheaton Aston to Stretton Aqueduct. Available for private charter. Bar on board.
Castle Boats,
The Wharf, Wheaton Aston,
Stafford ST19 9NP.
(Wheaton Aston 840090.)

12 'David'. 50-passenger narrowboat for private charter. Operates from Brewood.
Canal Transport Services,
Norton Canes Dock, Lime Lane,
Pelsall, Staffordshire.
(Brownhills 4370.)

13 'Water Tripper'. 42-seat narrowboat based at Autherley Junction. For private charter. Scheduled trip on summer Sundays at 15.00.
Water Travel,
Autherley Marina,
Oxley Moor Road,
Wolverhampton, Staffordshire.
(Wolverhampton 782371.)

OXFORD CANAL

14 'Windlass'. Daily dinners and weekend lunches served aboard this converted narrowboat, which takes diners for trips in the Rugby area. For individuals or private parties: booking essential. Boat operates from Clifton Wharf, Rugby.
Mr & Mrs Pritchard,
n.b. Andromeda, Clifton Wharf,
Vicarage Hill, Rugby.
(Rugby 3570.)

15 'The Lace Plate'. A converted narrowboat designed to carry up to 12 people for mobile meals. Dinner served nightly: boat departs from towpath opposite the 'Rose & Castle'

at Braunston at 20.00 every night. For individuals or parties: booking essential.
Mrs Hargrave,
The Grange, Braunston,
Rugby.
(Rugby 890348.)

TRENT & MERSEY CANAL

16 'Flamingo'. Traditional full-length canal boat available for charter: up to 50 passengers carried.
Trent Valley Cruises,
9 Lindum Avenue,
Trentham, Stoke-on-Trent.
(Stoke 57507.)

Working narrowboats in the Midlands

For various historical and economic reasons, commercial traffic along the canals of the Midlands is now virtually finished, and a loaded working narrowboat is a rare sight. Only two of all the old canal carrying companies have survived into the 1970's, and both of these are based on the BCN, where their work consists mainly of contracts to remove rubbish and liquid waste from canalside factories, and to provide transport for pipe-laying schemes along the towpath.

Several new companies have been recently formed, to try and maintain a minimal flow of commercial traffic along the canals. These are based mostly in traditional canal centres like Birmingham and Braunston. They usually have working boats available to anyone wishing to charter them, and indeed these firms have recently carried goods as varied as oil, gravel and newspapers.

But a cargo which is far more profitable and promising than any bulk material is people. Unconverted narrowboats, with their long canvas-covered holds and primitive facilities, are used as 'camping boats' for groups of hardy open-air types. One may simply charter a working narrowboat (and skipper) for a week or two and then fill it with up to a dozen people who are prepared to 'rough it'. The arrangement works well for everyone: the boat operators find a use for their traditional boats not in commercial use, *without* having to make any concession to modern standards of comfort; youth groups and others can enjoy a very cheap, totally unusual and stimulating holiday, and the organiser finds himself in charge of an easily run constructive expedition. Apart from all this, many like to see the old working boats travelling the canals in their original trim. So camping boats are certainly here to stay.

Information about carriage of anything by canal

National Association of
Inland Waterway Carriers,
c/o British Fuel Company,
Stoneferry Bridge,
Hull HU8 0BD.
(Hull 41325.)

Boat clubs

Many boat owners belong to a boat club based on a canal or river. This has many advantages: it means you will get a good safe mooring for your boat, near other boats, with the use of any boating facilities the club may have—such as a slipway, hard standing, workshops, water point, etc.—as well as all the social benefits of belonging to a club. For the gregarious boatman, belonging to a boat club is an essential aspect of owning a boat.

Some clubs go further than this, becoming more of a dynamic influence on the canal scene by carrying on active campaigns to restore or promote particular canals.

The list below shows the boat clubs on BWB waterways in the Midlands, together with the name and address of the Secretary—to whom all enquiries about club membership, etc., should be addressed.

More general enquiries about canal boat clubs should be addressed to the Association of Waterways Cruising Clubs, whose Honorary Secretary is Mr C. F. Stephens, 38 Sandhurst Drive, Seven Kings, Ilford, Essex.

ASHBY CANAL

Hinckley Boat Club,
Secretary: E. Lockley,
87 Coventry Road, Burbage,
Hinckley, Leicestershire.

BIRMINGHAM CANAL NAVIGATIONS

Longwood Boat Club,
Secretary: Mrs D. Thompson,
89 Edinburgh Drive, Rushall,
Walsall, Staffordshire.

COVENTRY CANAL

Tamworth Cruising Club,
Secretary: Mrs J. Houliston,
15 Orchard Close, Austrey,
near Atherstone, Warwickshire.

Wheatsheaf Boat Club,
Hon. Secretary: J. Stanger,
62 Keresley Road, Radford,
Coventry, Warwickshire
CV6 2JD.

EREWASH CANAL

Long Eaton Boat Club,
Hon. Secretary: Mrs Richardson,
60 Central Avenue,
Stapleford, Nottinghamshire.

GRAND UNION CANAL: MAIN LINE

Barston Boat Club,
Secretary: D. Dugard,
16 Oxford Road,
Moseley, Birmingham.

Black Buoy Cruising Club,
Secretary: S. Hanks,
The White House,
4 Canalside, Hopwood,
near Alvechurch, Worcestershire.

Mid-Warwickshire Yacht Club,
Secretary: Mrs L. M. Reed,
132 Leicester Lane,
Leamington Spa, Warwickshire.
(Leamington Spa 24985.)

Navigation Cruising Club,
Secretary: J. Wood,
35 Moorend Road, Yardley Gobion,
Towcester, Northampton NN12 7UF.

Taverners' Boat Club,
Commodore: J. R. Johnson,
16 Jeansway,
Dunstable, Bedfordshire.

Whilton Marina Cruising Club,
Secretary: A. Warren Allured,
53 Clarence Avenue, Northampton.
(Northampton 39809.)

GRAND UNION CANAL: LEICESTER SECTION AND RIVER SOAR

Soar Boating Club,
Secretary: L. Hales,
The Willows, Mill Lane,
Thurmaston, Leicester.

OXFORD CANAL

Coventry Cruising Club,
Secretary: F. H. Jeanes,
40 Thurlestone Road,
Coventry, Warwickshire CV6 2EB.

RIVER SEVERN

Lenchford Sailing Club,
Secretary:
Rear Commodore K. Rollason,
341 Heath Road South, Northfield,
Birmingham 31.

Sabrina Cruising Club,
Secretary: W. W. Hayle,
19 Park Avenue, Oldbury,
Warley, Worcestershire.

Severn Motor Yacht Club.
Hon. Secretary: N. J. Fisher,
Bowling Green Farm,
Bromsgrove, Worcestershire.

Worcester Rowing Club,
Secretary: C. B. Legge,
145 Northwick Road,
Worcester.

SHROPSHIRE UNION CANAL

Autherley Marina Boat Club,
Autherley Junction, Tettenhall,
Wolverhampton, Staffordshire.

Wolverhampton Boat Club,
Secretary: Mrs A. Clews,
40 Coronation Road,
Pelsall, Staffordshire.

STAFFORDSHIRE &
WORCESTERSHIRE CANAL

Kinver Cruising Club,
Secretary: W. H. Thorp,
127 Charlotte Road,
Wednesbury, Staffordshire.

Stafford Boat Club,
Secretaries: Mr & Mrs Owen,
10 Cherrybrook Drive,
Penkridge, Staffordshire.

Stourport Boat Club,
Secretary: D. C. Siston,
24 Cleriot Close,
Stourport-on-Severn,
Worcestershire.

Stourport Yacht Club,
President: W. K. Woodthorpe,
26 Wolverhampton Road,
(Quinton) Oldbury,
Warley, Worcestershire.

RIVER TRENT

Derby Motor Boat Club,
Secretary: J. W. Calladine,
c/o Robinsons, Market Place,
Heanor, Derbyshire.

Nottingham Sailing Club,
Hon. Secretary: A. B. Inglis,
'Lynton', Haddon Street,
Ilkeston, Derbyshire DE7 8LD.

Nottingham Yacht Club,
Trent Commodore: Dr T. Barry,
3 Cranfleet Lock,
Long Eaton, Nottingham.

Nottinghamshire
County Sailing Club,

Hon. Secretary: N. E. Parr,
51 Fernleigh Avenue,
Mapperley, Nottingham NG3 6FN.

Trent Boating Association,
Secretary: B. F. Holloway,
c/o Robinsons, Market Place,
Ilkeston, Derbyshire.

Trent Power Boat & Ski Club,
Secretary: G. W. H. Walker,
37 Valley Road,
West Bridgford,
Nottingham NG2 6HG.

Trent Sailing Club,
Secretary: J. M. Baron,
28 Tunstall Road,
Woodthorpe, Nottingham.

TRENT & MERSEY CANAL

Ash Tree Boat Club,
General Secretary: G. Seward,
51 Long Bridge Road,
Lichfield, Staffordshire.
(Lichfield 2741.)

Armitage Boat Club,
Secretary: Peter Wild,
The Plum Pudding,
Armitage, Staffordshire.

Fradley Junction Cruising Club,
Hon. Secretary: Mrs M. E. Teager,
5 Beaton Road, Four Oaks,
Sutton Coldfield,
Warwickshire B74 4RU.

Swarkestone Boat Club,
Secretary: R. N. Parkes,
Thorncliffe, Snape Hill,
Dronfield,
near Sheffield S18 6GH.

WORCESTER & BIRMINGHAM
CANAL

King's Norton Motor Cruising Club,
Secretary: R. V. Wright,
52 Fladbury Crescent,
Selly Oak, Birmingham 29.

Shardlow

Canal societies

The development of canal societies is a recent phenomenon. As appreciation of our waterway heritage has grown, so have the number and size of societies who help to support and promote canals. More important, canal restoration projects have moved from the realms of wishful thinking to reality. The societies also reflect the rapidly increasing use of pleasure craft, which on most canals have now replaced the commercial traffic more traditionally associated with waterways. Most societies publish a regular newsletter or magazine, which helps to keep members in touch with canal developments throughout the country.

The spread of boatyards and hire cruiser bases, the production of reports and restoration studies, the use of a volunteer labour force to work on restoration projects, backed by the ability to raise large sums of money privately in the determination to conserve the inland waterways, are all part of a movement that has grown from the initial leadership of the Inland Waterways Association. Here follow details of the canal societies active in the Midlands. The name and address of each Society's current secretary is given in each case, but readers are warned that these change frequently. The BWB keeps an up-to-date list of these addresses.

Ashby Canal Association

Formed after the ending of the coal trade on the Ashby Canal to ensure the continuance of navigation on the canal, and to encourage public support for all waterway activities. The Association owns $\frac{1}{4}$ mile of the abandoned canal at Snarestone which is the base for its activities. In addition a building is being put up here for the use of local youth clubs and other organisations interested in the canal. Boat rallies are held on the canal, and the Association arranges an annual canoe race from Marston Junction to Snarestone Tunnel. The Hinckley Boat Club is affiliated to the Association.

An unusual aspect of the Association is the Trading Section, formed to maintain commercial use of the canal. Their boats operate regularly on the canal, and elsewhere on the canal network, carrying coal, clay and granite. The Association is the only canal society to own and operate commercial boats.
Secretary: T. Henshaw,
5 Chapel Street, Newhall,
Burton-on-Trent,
Staffordshire.

Association of Pleasure Craft Operators

Formed in 1954, this trade association links together in friendly co-operation firms offering inland waterways holidays and facilities. It is recognised by the British Waterways Board as the official negotiating body for the inland waterway holiday industry.
Secretary: H. Arnold,
26 Chaseview Road, Alrewas,
Burton-on-Trent, Staffordshire.
(Burton-on-Trent 790447.)

Birmingham Canal Navigations Society

Formed in 1968 after the Transport Act had reduced much of the BCN to 'Remainder' status. The Society exists to preserve and develop a wide range of interests concerned with the maintenance and improvement of the BCN network. Working parties help with maintenance and restoration projects, youth groups with canal interests are encouraged, and towpath walks are organised. In addition the Society helps local authorities for the future development of urban canals and canalside buildings.

The Society organises regular meetings and lectures, as well as boat trips and rallies. There is also a lecture service for schools and other interested bodies to illustrate the recreational potential of the BCN. The Society magazine is published bi-monthly.
Secretary: B. McGowan,
55 Westwood Road,
Sutton Coldfield, Warwickshire.

Coventry Canal Society

Founded in 1957 to promote and encourage the proper use and maintenance of the Coventry Canal and its connecting waterways. The Society leases the Wyken Old Main Pit Arm and Basin, and has developed this to provide extensive moorings; the Arm, derelict until 1958, was cleared out by volunteers from the Society.

Cruises, walks, excursions, boat rallies and working parties are held, as well as meetings and lectures. A canoe section encourages younger people to enjoy the canal and co-operates closely with the needs of local schools. The Society magazine is published monthly.

A booklet, 'Coventry's Waterway, a City Amenity', was produced recently to encourage local interest in the past, present and future of the canal between Coventry and Hawkesbury.

Secretary: P. J. Williamson,
81 John Rous Avenue,
Canley,
Coventry CV4 8EU.

Dudley Canal Trust

Founded in 1964 to fight for the full re-opening of the longest and most interesting navigable canal tunnel in Britain. The Trust succeeded in preventing the northern portal of the tunnel being replaced by a culvert, and then arranged working parties to maintain the navigation through the tunnel and along the approach canal. These efforts were rewarded by the decision of Dudley Council and the British Waterways Board to restore and landscape Parkhead locks and re-open the tunnel. The re-opening took place at Easter 1973.

The Canal Trust is also closely associated with the plans for a Black Country Museum, which is to be built beside the canal near the south end of the tunnel. The Trust owns several narrowboats, and trips are arranged. Meetings and lectures are held, and a magazine is published.
Secretary: O. W. Pinfold,
14 Pineneedle Croft,
Willenhall,
Staffordshire WV12 4BY.

Erewash Canal Preservation and Development Association

The Association's aims are to encourage the amenity use of the waterway, with the objective of getting the canal promoted to full 'Cruising Waterway' status.

A notable success of the ECPDA has been the recent total restoration of the lock and terminal basin at Langley Mill. Boats navigating the full length of the canal are issued with commemorative certificates at Langley Mill.

The Association publishes a cruising and walking guide to the canal (20p) and a quarterly newsletter 'Erewash Outlook'.
Secretary: E. G. Harrison,
31 Derby Road,
Risley, Derbyshire.

Grand Union Canal Society

Campaigns for the retention, development and restoration of Britain's inland waterways for all uses. The aims and activities of the Society are similar to those of the Inland Waterways Association.
Secretary: R. C. Hampson,
Half-way House, Cassio Bridge,
Watford, Hertfordshire.

Grantham Canal Society

Established in 1970 to stimulate public interest in the Grantham Canal, and to promote the restoration and public use of the canal and towpath, the Society aims to restore the canal to full navigational use. Working parties have started clearing the canal and towpath; gate parts and lock machinery are being collected; and a feasibility study has been produced. In addition the Society has obtained an assurance of the canal being kept in water.

Rallies are organised and regular meetings are held.
Secretary: H. W. O. Walker,
The Old School House,
Kinoulton, Nottingham.

Inland Waterways Association

'The object of the Association is to advocate the use, maintenance and development of the inland waterways of the British Isles and in particular to advocate and promote the restoration to good order of every navigable waterway, and the fullest use of every navigable waterway by both commercial and pleasure traffic.'

This declaration of intent explains the purpose and aims of the Association, which was formed in 1946. It is a voluntary organisation, with over 10,000 members and several regional groups. Apart from general campaigning for canals and navigable rivers, the Association holds rallies, fund-raising events and voluntary working parties to help restoration projects. A monthly 'Bulletin' is published, which keeps members in touch with development all over the country.

General Office

114 Regent's Park Road, London NW1 8UQ. (01-586 2510 and 2556.) There is a 'canal bookshop' here.

Midlands Branch

Secretary: S. G. J. Clover,
Britannic Building, High Street,
Erdington, Birmingham B23 6RH.
(021-373 6251.)

West Midlands Branch

Secretary: R. D. Corser,
73 Gower Road, Halesowen,
Worcestershire.
(021-422 2675.)

North-East Midlands Branch

Secretary: H. Green,
Sa Rumah, Crookes Brook Lane,
Hatfield, Doncaster, Yorkshire.
(Doncaster 841334.)

East Midlands Branch

Secretary: R. J. Godwin,
Lawn House, Main Street,
Etwall, Derby.
(Burton-on-Trent 64290.)

South-East Midlands Branch

Secretary: D. J. Warren,
2 Willow Close, Spratton,
Northampton.
(Creaton 467.)

Lower Avon Navigation Trust

Founded in 1950, the Trust owns and operates the river Avon between Tewkesbury and Evesham, where it becomes the Upper Avon. Between 1950 and 1962, seven of the eight locks on the river were restored and rebuilt, weirs were repaired and other works carried out at a cost of around £80,000—raised entirely from donations and subscriptions. Evesham Lock was restored in 1963.

Administered and operated entirely by unpaid volunteers, the Trust was one of the first organisations of its kind to successfully restore and subsequently operate a derelict navigation.
Secretary: Ivor M. Beard,
Gable End, The Holloway,
Pershore, Worcestershire.

Narrow Boat Trust

Formed in 1971 with the purpose of buying, restoring and operating a small fleet of narrowboats, the Trust aims to keep alive the traditions of commercial carrying on canals. At present the Trust owns two motorised narrowboats—*Alton* and *Nuneaton*—and the butty *Satellite*, which are restored and maintained voluntarily by members. The boats are based at Norton Canes Docks on the Cannock Extension Canal (BCN) and working parties are gradually restoring them to first-class condition. The boats are available for commercial carrying, and when not involved in this, publicity cruises are undertaken to raise funds. In addition meetings are held, and a magazine is published.
Secretary: Miss Claire Johnstone,
Willow Cottage, Timsway,
Staines, Middlesex.

Old Union Canals Society

Formed in 1964, the Society is interested in the preservation and development of the Old Union Line (part of the Grand Union Leicester section) and of canals generally. The Society assisted BWB in the re-opening of the 1½-mile Welford Arm in 1969, and is helping Leicester Civic Society in making the canal and towpath in Leicester into an attractive civic amenity.

Boat trips and sponsored towpath walks are arranged in the summer. Meetings and lectures are held monthly and a magazine is published quarterly.
Secretary: M. Bower,
93 Lubbesthorpe Road,
Braunston, Leicester.

Railway and Canal Historical Society

Founded in 1954 to bring together people interested in the railway and canal history of Great Britain, and to spread historical information among members and the public. Activities include the collection of relevant material from county record offices, museums, libraries and private collections, regular meetings, and organised visits to places of railway and canal interest. There is a monthly bulletin, a quarterly journal, and original papers are produced in the form of Transactions.
Secretary: J. R. Harding,
174 Station Road, Wylde Green,
Sutton Coldfield, Warwickshire.

Shropshire Union Canal Society

The Society grew from the original Shrewsbury and Newport Canal Association, and its aim is to maintain the use and resources of the Shropshire Union network. The Society campaigns for the re-opening of the Montgomery branch. Regular working parties and meetings are held, and a magazine is published.
Secretary: R. Johnstone,
20 Barnfield Crescent,
Telford, Salop.

Staffordshire and Worcestershire Canal Society

Formed in 1959, to safeguard the future of the Staffs and Worcs Canal after the ending of the coal trade, the Society advocates the maintenance and development of the canal as a vital part of the Midlands network. The main achievement of the Society has been the re-opening of the Stourbridge Canal in 1964, a project carried out largely by voluntary labour with the help and co-operation of BWB. The Society still maintains the towpath of the canal, which is a very useful link between the BCN and the Staffs and Worcs Canal. More recently the Society has campaigned for the restoration of the Stourbridge Arm (a short spur from the canal into Stourbridge itself), and has assisted with the Dudley Tunnel re-opening and the Upper Avon project.

An annual rally is held at Whitsun, and a publicity cruise in the autumn. There are monthly meetings from September to June, and a magazine is published monthly.
Secretary: G. Whittaker,
57 Carless Avenue,
Harbourne, Birmingham 17.

Steam Boat Association of Great Britain

Established in 1971, the Association is open to everyone interested in steam boats. The aims are to encourage steam boating, and the building, operating, preservation and restoration of steam boats and steam machinery of all kinds. Regattas and rallies are organised during the summer, and a newsletter is published three times a year.
Secretary: Peter Hollins,
30 Ranvilles Lane,
Fareham, Hampshire.

Stratford-upon-Avon Canal Society

Founded in 1956, the Society aims to encourage interest in and proper maintenance of all inland waterways, with emphasis on the Stratford-upon-Avon Canal and the Upper Avon Navigation. The Society campaigned successfully against abandonment of the southern section of the canal, which was derelict at the time, and against the closure to traffic of the northern section. Helped by the Inland Waterways Association, the National Trust (who adopted the southern section in 1960) and other bodies, the Society completed the restoration of the southern section in 1964. This is now maintained by the National Trust, assisted by the Society. More recently the Society has been assisting the Upper Avon Navigation Trust in re-opening the navigation of the Upper Avon. Fund-raising events, lectures and regular working parties have been arranged to help complete this project.

Monthly meetings are held from September to April, and a monthly magazine is published. The Society also publishes guides to the southern section of the canal, and to the Upper Avon Navigation.
Secretary: Dr A. G. Johnson,
8 Union Road,
Leamington Spa,
Warwickshire.

Transport Trust

Constituted in 1964 to promote the permanent preservation of items of technical or historical interest in all fields of transport. Registered as a charity, the Trust is a fund-raising body to help any suitable transport preservation scheme. Individual organisations can be affiliated to the Trust, which acts as a guardian for the whole preservation movement. A Transport Museum Register is published, and a register of all preserved transport items is under construction. There is a quarterly magazine.
Secretary: J. T. Webb,
18 Ramillies Place,
London W.1.

Upper Avon Navigation Trust

Formed with the awe-inspiring objective of rebuilding a navigation that had been abandoned for a century, the Trust finally triumphed in June 1974 when the Queen Mother officially re-opened the river to boats.

Now navigable from the Severn at Tewkesbury right up to above Stratford, the Avon forms part of a magnificent circle of cruising waterways. The Trust has pushed forward this project despite great difficulty, raising its own finance and relying on voluntary labour, much of which came from prisons and Borstals. Locks, weirs and bridges have been restored or built from scratch, and an extensive dredging programme has been carried out. Through its achievements the Trust has not only made an invaluable addition to the inland waterways network, but it has also proved that the most arduous and unlikely restoration projects can be carried through despite all sorts of physical hindrances; also that a lock can be built in eight weeks and for £10,000 by volunteers, a task that would take contractors six months and cost at least £100,000. Having achieved what it set out to do, the Trust has now turned to the possibility of making the Avon navigable – for the first time ever – from Stratford up to the Grand Union Canal at Warwick, which would forge a wide waterway route from the Midlands to the Severn.
Secretary: J. D. Tomkins,
10 Guild Street,
Stratford-upon-Avon,
Warwickshire.

Waterway Recovery Group

Formed in 1970, the Group co-ordinates voluntary labour on inland waterways maintenance and restoration projects, assists with the financing of work and equipment, and publicises the restoration movement generally.

The knowledge and experience of restoration techniques that the Group has acquired is available as Group sponsored and organised labour or as an advisory service. There are 30 voluntary work groups throughout the country, controlling a labour pool of over 2,000; this ensures an even spread of work at weekends throughout the year. The Group owns a small stock of construction machinery which is moved from site to site; in addition it negotiates the loan or hire of other equipment.

A monthly magazine, 'Navvies', is published, which is essential reading for anyone interested in active restoration work.
Secretary: Graham Palmer,
4 Wentworth Court,
Wentworth Avenue,
Finchley, London N3.

Worcester and Birmingham Canal Society

Formed in 1969, the Society aims to promote the use and preservation of the canal and its associated waterways. Apart from the working parties which help to maintain the towpath and locks, and assist restoration projects, the Society is campaigning for a full restoration of the Droitwich canals. A restoration feasibility study has been produced by Droitwich Town Development with the help of the Society.

Monthly meetings and lectures are held, spring and autumn cruises and outings are arranged, and a magazine is published monthly.
Secretary: Miss Diane Churchill,
Flat 0, College House,
20 Barbourne Road, Worcester.

Hatton Locks

Water supply for the Midland canals

One of the most interesting facets of canal boating is that you cannot help noticing when you are going up or down hills. For example, if you leave London for the north by train or car, you will hardly notice the Chiltern Hills, for powerful locomotives and modern road engineering both make light of the gradients; but the canal boatman finds that there are no less than 56 locks up from the Thames valley to the 3-mile summit level near Tring, and as soon as he arrives at Marsworth he starts locking down again—towards the valley of the river Great Ouse. Similarly, the steep flight of seven locks at Watford Gap in Northamptonshire slows down a boatman's progress considerably, especially if there are other craft about, but a motorist cruising along the M1 past the motorway service area barely notices the change in level.

The hilly nature of the Midlands did not make the task of the early canal builders any easier, for either they had to build locks which were expensive both as a capital cost and as a maintenance liability, or they had to divert the route around the obstacle—which by increasing the length of the route was often just as expensive. Whichever was the particular solution adopted, locks usually had to be built somewhere along a canal's course. An average for the number of locks per mile is rarely found; indeed the Oxford and Coventry canals between Hillmorton and Atherstone form a level 'pound' nearly 33 miles long. If you add the lock-free Ashby Canal, which leaves the Coventry Canal at Marston Junction via a now-disused 'stop lock', you will find a lock-free stretch of canal over 53 miles long—probably the longest in the country.

Such long pounds of water were, when forming a 'summit' level, a great bonus to the canal builders, for they provide a stretch of water that is relatively 'elastic' in the amount of water that it can hold. But a length of canal that takes a long time to empty also takes a long time to fill, and no canal engineer could shirk the most important problem of all—a reliable supply of water to the canal. Without good provision for this, a canal was doomed before it was opened, for an erratic or insufficient level of water in a canal, with the inevitable delays to all traffic, would soon drive away the canal carriers to a rival canal or, later, to the railways. So vast reservoirs were built, streams diverted and coal-fired steam pumps installed to supply the water, and these measures are naturally no less important today than they were nearly 200 years ago—although their physical characteristics have in some cases changed a little.

The key section of any canal, of course, is the summit level, shown on every canal map that marks the locks. For as long as the summit level is adequately supplied with water, the rest of the waterway can, to a certain extent, look after itself—although supplementary reservoirs are sometimes to be found halfway down a flight of locks, mainly in sites which lend themselves very easily to the siting of a reservoir. It is also worth remembering—as of course the original canal engineers did—that broad canals (like the Grand Union, and the Trent and Mersey below Burton-on-Trent) use more water than narrow canals. A typical Grand Union lock draws off up to 100,000 gallons of water every time a boat passes through it. It is no coincidence that the Grand Union Canal in places has a small shed at every lock, in which an electric pump is kept to pump the water back up the lock, nor that the Trent and Mersey Canal crosses the river Trent on the level only a few miles above Burton—a very useful supplementary water supply.

It might be interesting to look at the principal sources of water for the Midland canals a little more closely, for it is a complicated system of reservoirs and feeders that keeps boats afloat in this area. In the Black Country, for example, the great (260-acre) reservoir known as Chasewater supplies most of the Birmingham Canal Navigations. The water flows west along the Wyrley and Essington Canal, then south along the Birmingham Canal main line, thus feeding the Worcester and Birmingham Canal and the Birmingham and Fazeley Canal. The Birmingham Canal main line is also fed by Rotton Park Reservoir at Icknield Port, while the older and higher Wolverhampton level is fed by a pumping station at Bradley. The Titford Branch is maintained by small streams and a small pump at Titford locks.

At the same level as Birmingham is the town of Wolverhampton. A flight of 21 locks here leads down to—and thus feeds—the summit level of the Staffs and Worcs Canal. Near Autherley Junction, another feeder enters the canal in the form of a purified outfall from a sewage works. The Shropshire Union Canal leaves here, drawing partly on the Staffs and Worcs Canal although its main feed comes from Belvide Reservoir, beside the A5. (Another Shropshire Union reservoir, at Knighton, is now de-watered and out of use.)

To the north, the Staffs and Worcs Canal

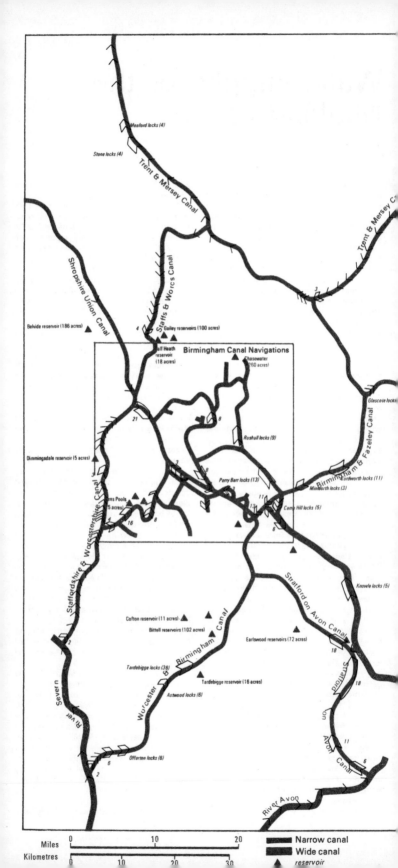

Meaford locks (4)

Stone locks (4)

Trent & Mersey Canal

Trent & Mersey Ca.

Shropshire Union Canal

Staffs & Worcs Canal

Belvide reservoir (186 acres)

Gailey reservoirs (100 acres)

Calf Heath reservoir (18 acres)

Birmingham Canal Navigations

Chasewater (260 acres)

Glascote locks

Rushall locks (9)

Dimmingsdale reservoir (5 acres)

Perry Barr locks (13)

Curdworth locks (11)

Minworth locks (3)

Camp Hill locks (5)

Birmingham & Fazeley Canal

Edgbastons Pools (5 acres)

Staffordshire & Worcestershire Canal

Stratford on Avon Canal

Knowle locks (5)

Cofton reservoir (11 acres)

Bittell reservoirs (102 acres)

Birmingham Canal

Earlswood reservoirs (72 acres)

Worcester

Tardebigge locks (36)

Tardebigge reservoir (16 acres)

Astwood locks (6)

Stratford on Avon Canal

River Severn

Offerton locks (6)

River Avon

Miles	0	10	20
Kilometres	0	10	20	30

▬▬ Narrow canal
▬▬ Wide canal
▲ reservoir

Water supply for the Midland canals

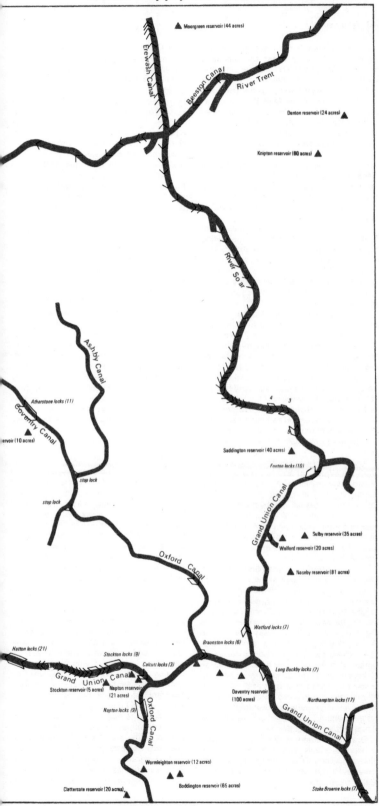

Moorgreen reservoir (44 acres)

Erewash Canal

Beeston Canal

River Trent

Denton reservoir (24 acres)

Knipton reservoir (80 acres)

River Soar

Ashby Canal

Atherstone locks (11)

Coventry Canal

...ervoir (10 acres)

stop lock

stop lock

4   3

Saddington reservoir (40 acres)

Foxton locks (10)

Grand Union Canal

Sulby reservoir (35 acres)

Welford reservoir (20 acres)

Naseby reservoir (81 acres)

Oxford Canal

Hatton locks (21)

Stockton locks (9)

Calcutt locks (3)

Braunston locks (6)

Watford locks (7)

Long Buckby locks (7)

Grand Union Canal

Stockton reservoir (5 acres)

Napton reservoir (21 acres)

Napton locks (9)

Oxford Canal

Daventry reservoir (100 acres)

Northampton locks (17)

Grand Union Canal

Wormleighton reservoir (12 acres)

Clattercote reservoir (20 acres)

Boddington reservoir (65 acres)

Stoke Bruerne locks (7)

locks down towards the Trent and Mersey. Reservoirs at Gailey boost the supplies— these are the reservoirs that decorate the junction of the M6 motorway and the A5. At Fradley the Gailey water joins the Trent and Mersey, whose main feed is way up at Rudyard Lake—a charming reservoir near Leek, between Stoke-on-Trent and Macclesfield at the end of the Caldon branch. (Subsidiary reservoirs are nearby: Knypersley Reservoir and Stanley Pool.) The feed runs down to join the top end of the Caldon Canal and then down to the Trent and Mersey summit level at Etruria, Stoke-on-Trent. From here it makes its way slowly down the canal until it reaches the Trent valley in Nottinghamshire.

The Staffs and Worcs Canal falls south from Compton to Stourport, its flow being boosted only by the influx of the Stourbridge Canal at Stewponey Junction, and by tiny reservoirs at Dimmingsdale, near Compton. At Stourport the wide locks require pumps to maintain the water level in the substantial basins.

The Worcester and Birmingham Canal enjoys a very long summit level from Birmingham to Tardebigge top lock. This level is fed not only by the Birmingham Canal (on the same level) but also by reservoirs. The feeder at Bittell is so wide as to be almost navigable (it was once, for $\frac{1}{2}$ mile), and at Tardebigge the supply is augmented by a reservoir beside the locks. At the lower end of the canal, at Diglis Basin in Worcester, a situation exists parallel to the one at Stourport: wide and busy locks necessitate electric pumps to maintain the level in two big basins.

The Stratford-upon-Avon Canal leads off from the Worcester and Birmingham, with a long summit level before beginning to lock down steeply from Lapworth to Stratford. The summit is fed not only by the Worcester and Birmingham Canal (now that the stop lock is permanently open at King's Norton Junction), but by the big Earlswood Reservoirs that are so beloved of fishermen and naturalists.

Some of Stratford's water finds its way to the Grand Union Canal at Lapworth Junction, joining the water from the summit level between Birmingham and Knowle (fed principally by a reservoir at Olton). From Lapworth the water descends the big Hatton flight of locks and disperses itself in the Avon valley. Up the other side of this shallow valley, the Grand Union receives its water from various directions. At Napton Junction the Oxford Canal arrives, bringing water down from reservoirs at Boddington, Clattercote and Wormleighton on its summit level a few miles to the south. Small supplementary reservoirs are beside the canal at Napton and Braunston.

Braunston summit level also provides a substantial supply both to the northern section of the Oxford Canal, which starts to lock down at Hillmorton, and to the Grand Union Canal on either side of it.

The Braunston summit is kept filled by two main sources. One is the reservoirs at Daventry and Drayton, which enter the canal halfway between Braunston Tunnel and Buckby top lock. The other is the all-important group of three reservoirs above the summit level of the Grand Union's Leicester section. For at Welford high up on the border of Leicestershire and Northamptonshire, Naseby, Welford and Sulby Reservoirs intercept the course of the incipient river Avon and flow down the Welford Arm to feed each way along the summit level of the Leicester section. This water thus not only fills the Braunston summit but also acts as the principal source for the canal northwards as far as Market Harborough and Leicester. It is supplemented by a reservoir at Saddington and feeder streams near Kibworth. At Leicester, of course, the canal joins the river Soar and so water supplies are no problem from here to the Trent—indeed the river frequently floods in winter and navigation traffic is halted until the water level drops again.

The Coventry, Ashby and northern Oxford canals are comparatively uncomplicated in terms of water supplies: they are mostly on the 54-mile lock-free level, although Atherstone top lock naturally has to be carefully guarded against wastage from this level. The Ashby has no locks, so it is supplied only by one or two small streams, the northern Oxford Canal receives adequate supplies from the south, but the Coventry Canal has a very small reservoir at Oldbury, near Atherstone.

Drainage

The other side of the water-supply 'coin' is of course what happens to the canal water after being drawn down from the summit level through the locks to the canal's lowest level and over the weirs that prevent the waterway from flooding. Probably some of the water, getting caught up by the pumps and sent back to the summit level, is circulated several times round the 'system'; but it is all bound to end up eventually in the sea, and it is interesting to consider which of the country's principal river basins the fresh water ends up in.

The canals of the Midlands are in these terms a typical jumble. To the north-east of the region, the Trent valley is the predominant influence. The Trent and Mersey Canal flows parallel to the river Trent most of the way down from Stoke, and the canal joins the river at the junction with the river Derwent, near Shardlow. A little further down the Trent, the valley of the Erewash joins the Trent, so the Erewash Canal finishes here; while opposite this junction is the mouth of the river Soar, which feeds into the Trent not only all of the Soar Navigation from as far upstream as Leicester but all of the water that comes down Foxton locks. The river Trent also catches the water that follows the northern Oxford Canal down Hillmorton locks, and all of the Coventry Canal water that is run down Atherstone and Glascote locks. The Birmingham and Fazeley Canal water finds its way eventually to the Trent, as indeed does much of the water in the canals of Birmingham.

Canal water in the south-west corner of the Midlands tends of course to make for the river Severn. The Worcester and Birmingham and Staffs and Worcs canals both feed straight into the Severn, and the Stourbridge and Dudley canals both end up there, bringing down a proportion of the water from the Birmingham Level with them. The Stratford-upon-Avon Canal locks down southward all the way to Stratford, where it joins the river Avon—which ends up in the Severn at Tewkesbury.

Meanwhile around Leamington and Warwick there is an unfortunate but inevitable constant loss of water from all directions into the river Avon. All the water passing down Knowle and Hatton locks goes down this drain, and any of the Grand Union water from Braunston, or Oxford Canal water from Napton, is doomed to the same fate.

Over in the south-east corner of this region, water descending Watford locks is drawn either west to Braunston and then the north Oxford Canal or the Avon valley, or it continues south down Buckby Locks to Gayton Junction. From here it either proceeds south down Stoke Bruerne locks to Wolverton and the Ouse valley, or it may be drawn east down the Northampton Arm and so join the river Nene in Northampton. Both the Nene and the Ouse lead eventually to the Wash.

The water in the Black Country canals drains off in several different directions. Much of it, as already seen, finds its way to the river Trent, and some of course to the river Severn. But any water drawn down the 21 locks at Wolverhampton and arriving at Aldersley Junction could join any one of three river basins: it is either drawn north along the Staffs and Worcs and down to the Trent and Mersey Canal, which will take it to the Trent and the North Sea; or it might be drawn *south* down the Staffs and Worcs canal to Stourport and eventually the Bristol Channel; or finally it could be run off down the Shropshire Union Canal, which locks down all the way to the Dee and Mersey estuaries.

Stewponey, Staffs and Worcs Canal

Two pubs near Newbold Tunnel

Abandoned canals

Although many canals today are being restored to navigation, this is the reflection of a comparatively new way of thinking. The Midlands canal network is still very extensive, but there are inevitably many canals that have been lost to the navigator. Some of these were branches and arms from surviving main lines, some were main lines in their own right. Some were closed as early as the 1840's, some as late as 1964. Whatever the date of closure, the reasons were generally similar: falling traffic, increasing rail and road competition, and lack of maintenance. But although the pattern of abandonment is clearly defined, the pattern of survival is not. In this respect, chance and the demands of local land users have played a major part. Thus much of the rural Uttoxeter branch of the Caldon Canal can easily be traced although it was abandoned in 1847, while lengths of the Derby Canal, closed only in 1964, are already well on the way to vanishing without trace beneath new roads and housing. It is of course usual to explore navigable canals by boat; but closed canals offer a new dimension to the enthusiast, for they can usually be traced only on foot, with the help of a detailed map and, ideally, aerial photographs. Some canals can easily be followed, as they have remained largely visible, while others are now so hidden or changed that they require a very practised eye. The Oakham Canal, for example, is no more than a faint depression in the ground, and in places only a single stone remains of a lock, with the slightest suggestion of a slope to betray its site.

To help the explorer, the numbers of the relevant new Ordnance Survey sheets are given for each canal: these maps generally give a good indication of the canal's course, but if you need a really detailed map to track down an old canal, then the 2½-inch to 1 mile O.S. sheets are ideal. Explorers should always remember that the one-time existence of a canal gives no right of way whatsoever. Sometimes the towpath survives as a recognised footpath, but more often the land has been sold and put to other uses. The notes below give pointers as to whether the canal is worth exploring, and where, but this does not imply the existence of a footpath or the right of access. (Most new Ordnance Survey maps now show public rights of way.) The simple rule is—if in doubt, ask the landowner's permission.

The Ashby Canal
OS128

Today the Ashby Canal, a cruising water-

way, ends rather abruptly in the middle of a field just north of Snarestone Tunnel. Perhaps few boatmen reaching this point realise that there used to be another 9 miles of canal, and an extensive tramway network linked to it.

When opened in 1804 the Ashby Canal ran from Marston Junction, on the Coventry Canal, to Moira, near Ashby-de-la-Zouch. It was built primarily to serve coal interests, and several tramways were built and operated by the canal company to bring the coal from the pits to the terminus at Moira and so down the canal to the coal consumers in the south. These tramways linked Swadlincote, Ticknall, Dimsdale, Cloud Hill, Coleorton and Ashby to the canal. Trade on the canal took a long time to get going, and it was not until the opening of the famous Moira collieries in the early 19th century that the canal began to make money. These pits ensured both the canal's success and its commercial survival until recent times; as late as 1943 half the production of the Moira pits travelled by narrowboat, and even today occasional boatloads of coal are carried down the canal towards the south. There were schemes to extend the canal to join the Trent and Mersey near Burton-on-Trent, but these came to nothing. The tramway network was soon killed off or absorbed by the railways, but the real enemy of the canal was subsidence: in 1944 the section from Moira to Donisthorpe was closed, in 1957 a further 5 miles to Measham were lost, and then the final closure from Measham to Snarestone took place, prompted by the failure of a small aqueduct near Snarestone.

Subsidence and mining operations have hidden most of the upper section of the Ashby Canal, and so exploration is difficult. However, the trained eye will pick it out as it passes through the centre of Measham, and in a few other places.

The Grantham Canal
OS129

The Grantham Canal is one of the most attractive and the best preserved of the abandoned canals of the Midlands. Except for a short section in Nottingham, the course of the canal is entirely rural.

The wandering 33-mile line, with 18 broad locks, from Nottingham to Grantham was opened in 1797, having been engineered by William Jessop. The canal passes through quiet, flat agricultural land, through the Vales of Belvoir and Trent. It was easy to build and easy to maintain.

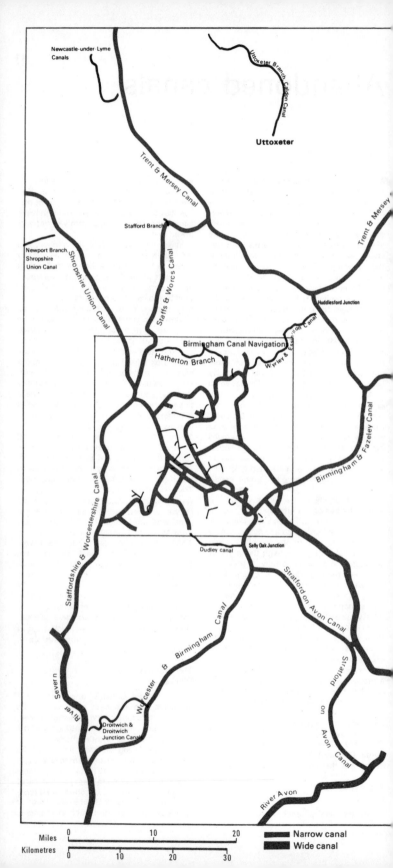

Newcastle-under-Lyme
Canals

Uttoxeter Branch Caldon Canal

Uttoxeter

Trent & Mersey Canal

Stafford Branch

Trent & Mersey

Newport Branch
Shropshire
Union Canal

Shropshire Union Canal

Staffs & Worcs Canal

Huddlesford Junction

Birmingham Canal Navigation

Hatherton Branch

Wyrley & Essington Canal

Birmingham & Fazeley Canal

Staffordshire & Worcestershire Canal

Dudley canal   Selly Oak Junction

Stratford on Avon Canal

River Severn

Worcester & Birmingham Canal

Stratford

Droitwich &
Droitwich
Junction Canal

on

Avon Canal

River Avon

Miles	0	10	20
Kilometres	0	10	20	30

███ Narrow canal

████ Wide canal

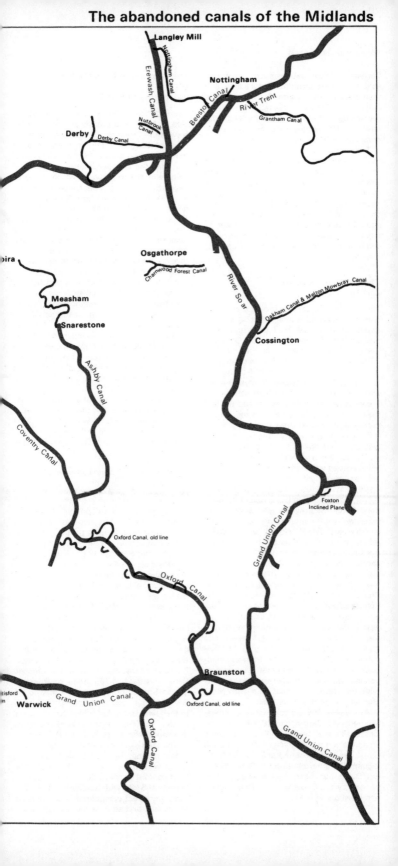

The abandoned canals of the Midlands

Langley Mill

Nottingham Canal

Erewash Canal

Nottingham

River Trent

Beeston Canal

Grantham Canal

Derby

Nutbrook Canal

Derby Canal

Osgathorpe

Charnwood Forest Canal

River Soar

bira

Oakham Canal & Melton Mowbray Canal

Measham

Snarestone

Cossington

Ashby Canal

Coventry Canal

Foxton Inclined Plane

Grand Union Canal

Oxford Canal, old line

Oxford Canal

Braunston

tisford

Warwick

Grand Union Canal

Oxford Canal, old line

Oxford Canal

Grand Union Canal

Carrying agricultural produce, coke and coal, the canal was profitable for a time, and then declined slowly after the advent of the railways. In 1854 it passed into railway ownership, but traffic did not finally die out until the 20th century. (The canal was abandoned in 1936.)

Today the canal is still in a fair state of repair. Weirs have replaced the locks, but most of the canal still holds water. The Grantham Canal Society is engaged in clearing the towpath and old locks, but unfortunately most of the bridges have been dropped. But perhaps one day boats will again be able to lock up out of the Trent, to enjoy the slow, meandering journey to Grantham. In the meantime, the canal is ideal for walking.

The Nottingham Canal
OS129

The Nottingham Canal was built to compete with the Erewash Canal, offering a more direct route for the coal trade into Nottingham from Langley Mill and the Cromford Canal. Jessop surveyed the line, and in 1792 work started. The 15-mile canal from the river Trent in the centre of Nottingham to Langley Mill was opened four years later, with 19 broad locks. The Nottingham and Erewash canals were close rivals: for half their course they run parallel to each other, in places coming so close that only a single row of houses separates them. Yet there was sufficient traffic for them both to be profitable, toll and working arrangements being agreed with each other. Railway competition soon affected the Nottingham Canal, and in 1855 it was sold to the same railway company that had bought the Grantham Canal the previous year. Despite this take-over, trade continued on the canal, and it was not finally closed until 1937 — although the 2½-mile length between Lenton Chain and the Trent is still navigable, and important as part of the through route from the Midlands to the Humber. Little of the Nottingham Canal remains from Lenton Chain northwards to Wollaton (in Nottingham itself), but from here to Langley Mill its course can easily be traced. Parts still hold water, and but for the dumping of rubbish, the canal would be in a reasonable state. As it approaches Langley Mill the canal can easily be explored from its neighbour, the Erewash. Boatmen travelling to Langley Mill can examine this important link with the Cromford Canal, and with Manchester via the High Peak Railway.

At Langley Mill the contrast is complete, for here the Nottingham Canal (and the Cromford Canal) have completely vanished, while the top end of the navigable Erewash Canal has been restored and the old Nottingham Canal terminus in the Great Northern Basin has been dredged out and reopened by the Erewash Canal Preservation and Development Association.

The Charnwood Forest Canal
OS129
(*Not controlled by BWB*)

The Charnwood Forest Canal was authorised in 1791 as a branch off the Leicester Navigation, running to collieries 8 miles west of Loughborough. In order to save money the branch was built on a level contour line, the changes in level at each end being effected by railways, which of course necessitated double transhipment. Opened in 1794, the canal ran from Nanpantan, 2½ miles west of Loughborough, to Thringstone, with a short branch to Barrow Hill. A railway linked it with the main line of the Leicester Navigation in Loughborough, and other railways were built at the western end to serve the various collieries. Although built cheaply, its isolation doomed the canal to a short life. The delays caused by transhipping goods from boat to railway at Nanpantan, and back again at Loughborough, limited the canal to traffic that was largely local. Floods caused the canal to be closed in 1799, and though it was repaired by 1801, the small amount of traffic it had carried before the temporary closure never returned. Problems of ownership of the land on which it lay caused the formal closure to be delayed until 1848.

In view of its short life and early disuse, it is not surprising that this former canal is hardly recognisable nowadays. The best place to see it is the old junction (with a former branch) south of Osgathorpe village, where the tollhouse still stands.

The Newcastle-under-Lyme canals
OS118/127
(*Not controlled by BWB*)

The extensive redevelopment of the Potteries in recent years has buried for ever many important traces of the industrial past of the area. Today it is rare to see the unmistakable shape of the bottle kiln, although hundreds survived until 10 years ago. Likewise canals have suffered in the upheavals, and today it is difficult to trace the three canals that were built in Newcastle-under-Lyme at the end of the 18th century.

Sir Nigel Gresley's Canal, opened in the late 1770's, was built to bring coal from Sir Nigel's mines at Apedale to Newcastle. The canal, 2 miles long, ran to a basin north of Newcastle beside the present Liverpool Road. The Newcastle-under-Lyme Junction Canal, opened in 1799, and also promoted by the Gresley family, added a mile to the Gresley Canal, and brought the coal virtually to the town centre. Both these canals closed in the 1850's, under pressure from the developing North Staffordshire Railway.

The third canal was more substantial, and longer lasting. The Newcastle-under-Lyme Canal was authorised in 1795. A 4-mile-long contour canal, it linked the Trent and Mersey at Stoke with Newcastle. Its Act forbade any direct competition with the Gresley canals, and so it carried limestone and depended on the pottery industry for its revenue. Despite these limitations it survived in operation until 1921, when part was closed. The rest followed it in 1935.

Today there are few remains of these canals. Sections of the Gresley Canal exist near Apedale, and sections of the Newcastle-under-Lyme Canal can still be found south of the town. But the explorer needs a trained eye and a very detailed map to be sure of tracing these relics.

The Birmingham Canal Navigations

Apart from being the heart of the English inland waterway network, the Birmingham Canal Navigations (BCN) are a unique canal phenomenon in their own right—a vast and predominantly urban canal complex with a string of lock flights, tunnels and aqueducts, and a great wealth of industrial archaeology interest.

The BCN as it is today represents the surviving elements of a large system formed originally by the merging of several companies. The old Birmingham Canal and the Dudley Canal were its backbone, dating from the earliest period of canal development; to these were later added the Walsall Canal, the Bentley Canal, the Tame Valley Canal, the long meandering Wyrley and Essington with its many branches; parts of the Birmingham and Fazeley; and a great variety of arms, branches and basins. At its peak there were 159 miles of canal, endless small private arms, and 26 railway interchange basins which made the BCN the only canal network that was able actually to benefit from the coming of the railways. The tentacles of the BCN connected with the Coventry Canal, the Stourbridge Canal, the Grand Union Canal, the Staffs and Worcs Canal, and the Worcester and Birmingham Canal, and via these links boats from companies in the Black Country could trade with almost every part of England. Commercial carrying survived on the BCN until recent times; a million tons per annum was still travelling by boat immediately after the 1939–45 war.

Today it has all changed. Over 50 miles of the network have been lost, and there is very little commercial operation. The future of a considerable mileage is still uncertain, as inevitably an urban canal network takes much longer to adapt to an amenity role. At present it is mainly the dedicated canal enthusiast who will explore the BCN for fun, although there are many welcome signs of a general shift in people's attitudes towards urban canals: the Cambrian Wharf development and the re-opening of Dudley Tunnel are conspicuous examples of progress in this respect.

Much of the BCN that has been closed consisted of branches, or duplicated routes, but there have been some serious losses: the Dudley Canal's line through Lappal Tunnel to its junction with the Worcester and Birmingham (closed as long ago as 1917), the Bentley Canal, the Wyrley and Essington from Ogley to its junction with the Coventry Canal at Huddlesford, and the top section of the Cannock Extension, with its link to the Staffs and Worcs Canal via Churchbridge locks. Some of these closures were quite recent: the Wyrley and Essington was closed in 1954, and the Cannock Extension in the mid-1960's, but this was partly prompted by serious mining subsidence, an ever-present threat throughout the history of the BCN. Because of the demands on land in an urban environment, most of the closed canals of the BCN have already vanished, having been either filled in or buried beneath new roads and buildings. Thus it is very difficult to find any trace of these canals on the ground.

The best way to explore the BCN is probably by boat: pedestrian access to the towpaths of the BCN is very limited, except in the outlying areas, and so explorers on foot must be prepared for a frustrating time. There is only one access place in Birmingham that is always open, and that is Gas Street Basin (see page 12).

Because of these difficulties, there is little point in listing all the surviving remains of every closed canal. Instead, we give here a few details of some of the most important relics.

Many of the abandoned canals in the Black Country are already of interest only to the archaeologist of the future. There is no trace of the closed section of the Dudley Canal with the Lappal Tunnel (3,795 yards long), nor of the Newhall Branch which used to continue through tunnels from Cambrian Wharf into the centre of Birmingham, nor of the other great basins that used to penetrate like tendrils into the city. Elsewhere there is more to be seen. The course of the old Wyrley and Essington to Huddlesford can be traced, although parts have vanished completely; there are even the remains of a boat to be seen abandoned in the canal, and a short section over at Huddlesford Junction is still in water. The remains of the old Black Delph locks, now serving as overflow weirs, still stand beside their later replacements. The Titford Canal and its branches, and the Engine Arm, can be explored on foot beyond their navigable limits, as can parts of the Anson Branch and the Bentley Canal.

But the most rewarding field for study is the Old and New Main Lines of the Birmingham Canal between Gas Street and Tipton. Here much of Brindley's original line still survives, wandering along in contour loops, and contrasting sharply with Telford's straight canal, with its steep cuttings and dramatic bridges. At Smethwick there is the work of three engineers to be seen, side by side: Brindley's original short summit, now disused, Smeaton's longer summit on a lower level, and, far below, Telford's New Main Line. There is more scope for the 'canal archaeologist' concentrated into a small area on the waterways of the BCN than anywhere else in the country.

Droitwich and
Droitwich Junction canals
OS150
(*Not controlled by BWB*)

The two Droitwich canals, one built early and the other very late, had a varied career, plagued for most of their existence by rivalry and an uneasy relationship with the Worcester and Birmingham Canal. However, the Droitwich salt trade sufficed to keep the canals open until comparatively recently.

The Droitwich Canal was authorised in 1768, with Brindley as consultant engineer. The 6¼-mile line from Hawford on the river Severn to Droitwich was opened in 1771, with wide locks to enable Severn barges to reach Droitwich.

The owners of the Worcester and Birmingham Canal took over the responsibility of the Droitwich Canal in 1810, and remained responsible for it for the rest of its existence.

The Droitwich Junction Canal was opened in 1852, a 1¾-mile line linking the Droitwich Canal with the Worcester and Birmingham Canal at Hanbury Wharf. The Droitwich Junction Canal was equipped with narrow locks, in line with the latter. It thus provided an alternative route for narrowboats to the river Severn and Stourport, avoiding Worcester. There were altogether 15 locks along the two canals, rising from the river Severn to Hanbury Wharf.

Trade declined slowly throughout the 19th century, and in 1874 both the Droitwich canals were taken over by the Sharpness New Docks Company, who remained the owners until they formally closed them in 1939.

Much of the two canals still survives in reasonable condition, although sections in Droitwich have been filled in. The locks still exist, although they are rather dilapidated. Recently a campaign has been mounted to re-open the two Droitwich canals, and Droitwich Town Development has been foremost in promoting their possible amenity value to the town. Major working parties have now made a start on the canals, and it seems likely that at least partial restoration will take place.

The Droitwich Junction Canal can be easily followed by road, for it runs right alongside the old Roman road Salt Way (B4090) from Hanbury Wharf to Droitwich. There are several overgrown locks quite close to Hanbury Wharf. The more winding Droitwich Canal follows the valley of the river Salwarpe, and is best approached from the A4133 or the various unclassified roads that cross it. The 1-inch Ordnance Survey map (No. 130) is very useful for locating it.

Hatherton Branch of the
Staffordshire and Worcestershire
Canal
OS128

In the 19th century the Staffs and Worcs Canal Company became increasingly dependent upon the BCN for its revenue, for most of the former's trade came via the old Wyrley and Essington Canal. This close co-operation encouraged suggestions for further physical links between the two companies: a branch was proposed from the Staffs and Worcs eastwards to Churchbridge, to serve the collieries in the Cannock area. Eventually a plan was accepted, and the branch was opened in 1841, locking up from the Staffs and Worcs to Churchbridge, where it connected with several colliery railways. It was named the Hatherton branch, after the chairman of the Staffs and Worcs company.

When the Cannock Extension Canal was planned by the BCN company, it was agreed between the two companies to build a junction between this new canal and the Hatherton branch. Thirteen locks were built at Churchbridge to carry the branch down to the Cannock Extension, and the whole was opened in 1863. Despite its late construction, the system was very profitable; it was well supported by a railway interchange basin at Churchbridge, traces of which still survive. There was regular coal traffic along the branch long after the decline of the Staffs and Worcs and much of the BCN, and final closure did not take place until 1949.

Today little remains of the eastern end of the branch; Churchbridge locks have vanished along with the top of the Cannock Extension. More survives of the original branch, and it is not too difficult to follow its course towards Churchbridge from its junction with the Staffs and Worcs main line.

Stafford Branch of the
Trent and Mersey
OS127

Although the course of the Staffs and Worcs Canal took it within 1½ miles of Stafford, there was originally no connecting link with the city. At the end of the 18th century various schemes to overcome this were suggested, but nothing was done until 1816, when a short cut, with one lock, was made between the canal and the River Sow. The river was navigable into Stafford, and by this means narrowboats could reach the city centre. At first this short branch and its lock were owned privately by Lord Stafford, who imposed various restrictions on its use, but in 1838 the Staffs and Worcs Company bought it (for £50). The branch remained in use until the 1920's.

The average boatman passing along the Staffs and Worcs nowadays has little reason to suspect that there was ever a canal junction near Weeping Cross bridge, 2 miles east of Stafford. And even if he stopped to explore this short canal he would find little trace of it—the Stafford Branch has covered its tracks well. The river Sow is of course unnavigable now, but it is possible to walk along the river into Stafford, where remains of the wharves may still be found.

The Newport Branch of the Shropshire Union
OS127

When the Birmingham and Liverpool Junction Canal (now part of the Shropshire Union network) was opened in 1835, it included the 10-mile Newport Branch. This left the main line at Norbury Junction and ran westwards, descending through 23 narrow locks to join the Shrewsbury Canal at Wappenshall. There was a short arm to Lubstree. Apart from the inevitable coal traffic, the Newport Branch served as an important outlet for the Coalbrookdale Iron Company, which ensured its survival into the 20th century. The Newport Branch, like the Welsh canals, survived until the passing of the 1944 Act, which authorised the closure of 175 miles of the old Shropshire Union system. But a rearguard action by the forerunner of the Shropshire Union Canal Society failed to prevent final closure of the canal.

There is still plenty to see of the Newport Branch, although the locks are now decayed and the water channel is becoming very overgrown. Its junction at Norbury with the navigable Shropshire Union main line is conspicuously marked by a towpath turnover bridge, and the lock flight starts only a few yards beyond it.

The Derby Canal
OS128
(Not controlled by BWB)

Opened in 1796, this canal ran from Swarkestone on the Trent & Mersey to Sandiacre on the Erewash. There was also a branch to Little Eaton, north of Derby. The Derby Canal played an important part in the Midlands canal complex, and its closure has meant that Derby is the biggest Midland town to have lost its waterway link. Coal, cement, corn and local cargoes kept the canal profitable during the 19th century, although it suffered inevitably from railway competition. Curiously, it remained the property of the Derby Canal Company until its final closure in 1964. Thus it never had a chance to develop a second life as an amenity waterway, for the company were more interested in selling off the remains of the canal for building land.

Today much of the canal has already vanished. There is nothing to be seen in Derby itself. Where parts do survive, they exist only as a rubbish dump. The only section to hold water is the first 20 yards or so at the junction at Swarkestone, which is used by a boat club. At Sandiacre, at the junction with the Erewash Canal, the bottom lock is derelict and the toll-keeper's cottage is ruined and in danger of demolition. It is all rather depressing. A happy contrast is provided by the well-kept lock cottage a few yards away on the Erewash Canal. The latter cottage is the base of the Erewash Canal Preservation and Development Association.

The Nutbrook Canal
OS128/129
(Not controlled by BWB)

The Nutbrook grew from the same enthusiasm that prompted construction of the Nottingham and Erewash Canals, and from the same desire to link the Nottingham coalfields to the Trent and thus to the rest of the waterway network. A small undertaking, this 4½-mile canal was opened in 1796. Thirteen broad locks took the canal down from Shipley (not the same Shipley as on the Erewash near Langley Mill) to a junction with the Erewash near Stanton. Reservoirs were built at Shipley to feed the canal. Despite—or perhaps because of—its size, the canal quickly became profitable, and remained so throughout the 19th century. The development of ironworks in the Stanton area ensured its continued success long after grander undertakings had fallen by the wayside. The Stanton ironworks used the canal not only for transport, but as a vital source of water supply, a role that the Nutbrook still carries out today, although it is no longer recognisable as a canal. Traffic to Shipley ceased at the end of the 19th century, but the last boat did not leave the Stanton length until 1949.

Although the canal has never been formally closed, it was bought by the ironworks in 1946, and much has subsequently disappeared. Today there is nothing to be seen in Stanton, and all that remains of the junction with the Erewash is a pipe carrying water from the ironworks: a passer-by would never believe that this had once been a junction of two canals. Traces can be found further north, but in spite of its recent demise most of the Nutbrook Canal is no more than a memory.

The Uttoxeter Branch of the Caldon Canal
OS128
(Not controlled by BWB)

The construction of a branch from the Caldon Canal's terminus at Froghall to Uttoxeter, 13 miles to the south, was authorised in 1797. After several changes of heart the company finally began work in 1807, and the extension was completed in 1811. There were 17 narrow locks, and a short tunnel at Alton; the river Churnet was crossed on the level, and there was an iron trough aqueduct over the river Tean. The canal was used to transport coal and lime, and to serve the copper and brass works at Oakamoor; it played a large role in the development of Uttoxeter, but was never very profitable. In 1847 the canal was closed, and a railway was built along much of its course through the Churnet valley.

Despite its early closure, much of the canal still survives, and parts even hold water. The remains of locks and bridges can be found, but the tunnel has disappeared, and only the abutments of the Tean aqueduct still exist. There is no trace of the terminal basin in Uttoxeter.

Watford Locks, Leicester section, Grand Union Canal

The rural course of the canal along the narrow Churnet valley is very attractive, and makes an excellent walk, well illustrated by gentle reminders of a long vanished industrial post. With the re-opening of the Caldon Canal to Froghall, the long-dead Uttoxeter Branch should take on a new lease of life, as an added interest to a restored canal environment.

The Melton Mowbray Navigation and the Oakham Canal
OS129/130
(*Not controlled by BWB*)

These two waterways were built and operated by separate companies, although the one was wholly dependent upon the other. Neither was a success, and both were among the early casualties in the canal's fight against railway competition.

Authorised in 1791, and opened six years later, the Melton Mowbray Navigation ran eastwards for $14\frac{3}{4}$ miles from Cossington on the Leicester Navigation (now the Grand Union Canal Leicester line). The navigation was based on the river Wreake (it was sometimes known as the Wreake Navigation), and 14 broad locks were built to make it navigable to Melton Mowbray. At first trade was predominantly agricultural, but coal became the mainstay of the navigation in the 19th century. Traffic was never heavy and the closure of the traffic-supplying Oakham Canal in 1846 aggravated the situation, but the navigation struggled on until its formal closure in 1877. Its winding course can still be followed along the river Wreake, but there are few signs today that the river ever carried boats.

The authorisation of the Melton Mowbray Navigation prompted the construction of a canal from Melton Mowbray to Oakham. Work started in 1793, under the direction of the engineer William Jessop, and ten years later the 15-mile canal was opened. 19 broad locks took the canal up to its summit at Oakham. Traffic was always slight, coal and grain being the main cargoes, and the canal was never really profitable. However, it played a large part in the growth and prosperity of Oakham, by linking it to the national waterway network. For most of its life the Oakham Canal had to compete with the Grantham Canal to the north, and various schemes to extend it to Stamford, to the river Nene, and to Boston via the Black Sluice Drain came to nothing. The canal was sold to the Midland Railway in 1845, who closed it the following year and used part of its course for laying down their new line from Melton Mowbray to Oakham.

The course of the Oakham Canal today presents a varied picture to the explorer. Little can be seen of it between Melton and Saxby, since the railway line runs along the canal bed for most of the way; but from Saxby to Oakham the canal's course is independent of the railway, and can therefore be followed. In places the canal holds water, but after over 120 years of disuse much of the canal has simply faded into the fields, its course indicated only by a slight depression in the ground. Keen explorers may be well rewarded: there is at least one original iron canal milepost to be seen, left high and dry with not a puddle of water in sight. In another place, near a railway level crossing, the site of a former lock is indicated only by a gentle rise in the ground and the tell-tale shape and size of a lock corner-stone.

Braunston

Canals in the West Midlands

Background

Since before mediaeval times, when the Severn was one of the main trade highways of England, there has been a continuous history of inland navigation in—or rather to and from—the Midlands. In the 17th century some of the earliest attempts to improve navigation by the construction of locks were carried out on the rivers Avon, Trent, Stour and Salwarpe, though not all were wholly successful. One of the most enthusiastic and far-sighted promoters of transport by inland waterways at this time was Andrew Yarranton, a Worcestershire man. The remains of the primitive 'flash-locks' which he built around 1653 on the little Dick Brook to serve his iron furnace and forge at Shrawley may still be traced. Despite the growing industrial development of the Midlands, the seed sown by Yarranton did not immediately germinate, and it was over a century before any further progress was made. In the meantime initiative had passed to the north, where the first modern artificial waterway, independent of a natural water course, was the Bridgewater Canal, opened in 1759.

James Brindley

The engineer for this pioneering project was James Brindley, a Derbyshire millwright of ingenuity and vision. Sponsored by the ambitious young Duke of Bridgewater and supported by his resourceful agent John Gilbert, Brindley built in Lancashire a canal that excited the curiosity of the world. In the 14 years between his first involvement with inland waterways and his death, at the age of 56, in 1772, he attracted the title of 'The Father of English Canals', a title which might easily have been Yarranton's had he lived in more propitious times. Brindley's success on the Bridgewater Canal assured his reputation, and he naturally became heavily involved in other canal projects. He surveyed and superintended construction of the Trent and Mersey Canal, authorised in 1766, and reckoned by Brindley to be the first stage of the 'Grand Trunk Canal', his vision of a waterway system stretching from coast to coast, east to west and north to south. The Staffs and Worcs Canal, authorised in the same year, provided an outlet from the Midlands to the river Severn; and the Coventry and Oxford Canals of 1768 and 1769 respectively completed a link to the Thames and thus to south-east England. Brindley died with only the Staffs and Worcs line finished; but his great projects continued, and did much to encourage industrial growth in the Midlands and stimulate the construction of further canals. Ultimately the Midlands had the most intricate network of waterway connections anywhere in Britain, and even today when that network has contracted, it provides an unequalled wealth of interest for the industrial archaeologist.

Early canal development in the Midlands

The Midland canals vary enormously in character, and this is related to the topography of the land over which they pass, and also to their period of construction and the engineering skills of the time. When Brindley began on the Staffs and Worcs, the first Midland canal completed, he had no accumulated fund of experience on which to draw. As a pioneer, he was carefully feeling his way with a series of experimental features, leaving as little as possible to chance. His attitude gave this canal perhaps the most distinctive character of all.

The Staffordshire and Worcestershire Canal

Brindley's first aim was to reduce engineering works to a minimum. This he achieved by following the gentle valleys of the rivers Penk, Smestow and Stour. It was almost certainly this intention from the outset that led him to create a new canal port, Stourport, at the confluence of the Stour and Severn.

Where engineering works were unavoidable, Brindley played safe on every possible occasion. His early locks on the Staffs and Worcs, for example, had chambers which leaned outwards; it was thought that their 'battered' sides would be better able to resist lateral thrust due to frost action or clay movement; and even now his locks are less liable to damage during severe winters than the later vertical-sided ones.

His aqueducts display similar caution. The biggest and most characteristic spans the Trent at Great Haywood, only yards from the junction with the Trent and Mersey. Almost an embankment with a series of large culverts rather than a true aqueduct, its massive proportions carry not only the water but also a tremendous weight of earth and puddled clay bed, and only three low stone arches admit the flow of the river below.

Heavy lockage was avoided in several places by rock cuttings and by a couple of short tunnels at Cookley (65 yards) and Dunsley (25 yards); but at one point, the Bratch in Wombourn, Brindley encountered a sudden drop which could not be avoided by these means. He overcame the problem by building three locks, each with its own set of upper and lower gates, so close together that only four feet separated the top gates of the lower locks from the bottom gates of the ones above. The level of the intermediate lock was maintained through culverts running from side-ponds. This arrangement is unique, and one can imagine Brindley looking at what he had built and coming to the conclusion that considerable economies in masonry and timber, as well as easier working, could be achieved by using the bottom gate of one lock as the top gate of the next, in 'staircase' pattern. When he came to another sharp drop less than two miles away at Botterham, he built a double lock to this new design.

The side weirs to the locks on the Staffs and Worcs are particularly interesting. Brindley designed an ingenious experimental circular weir, with the sill taking the form of a shallow saucer, the culvert entrance being a vertical hole in the centre, the effect being that of an enormous funnel. These weirs occupy far less space than a straight weir of equal capacity, and are also less liable to jamming, as debris collects in the saucer, from which it can be readily removed. Examples may be seen at Stewponey, Awebridge and Wightwick Mill locks. It was found, however, that the increased cost of construction greatly outweighed the advantages of these weirs, and they were not used on any other canal.

Many bridges over the Staffs and Worcs Canal still retain their original oval cast-iron plates giving their names and numbers in bold lettering. Individual bridges of particular merit include number 46 (Bumble Hole Bridge), and number 109 at Great Haywood Junction. The most influential bridge design on the Staffs and Worcs, however, was a type of footbridge used on the southern section. It was of cast iron and had a cantilever form, with a division in the middle to allow the passage of the towrope, a device later adopted on the Stratford-upon-Avon Canal. None of the originals are now usable by towing horses, but several examples remain, e.g. at Falling Sands Lock near Kidderminster.

Other Brindley canals

Brindley's caution on his engineering works and his attempts to follow the contour principle, which often created an extremely beautiful, sinuous and lengthy course—but which was much cheaper to construct and maintain—are both reflected in other early Midland canals. His Birmingham Canal (1768–72) had the first long lock flight in the Midlands—20 (later increased to 21) at Wolverhampton—but its true character is better represented by the exaggerated meanderings of what are now (since Telford straightened out the canal) the Wednesbury Oak Loop, Oldbury Loop, Cape Loop, Soho Branch, Icknield Port or Rotton Park Loop and Oozells Street Loop. These were later superseded as through routes by Telford's alterations and not all are now passable. Brindley's Oxford Canal (1769–90) has also been drastically straightened north of Napton Junction, but parts of the original line survive like the Wyken Colliery Loop, Stretton Wharf Arm, Fennis Field Limeworks Branch, Newbold Arm, Barby Loop and others. His Coventry Canal (1768–90) and Stourbridge Canal (1776–9) have been little altered. The last major contour undertaking was the western section of the Wyrley and Essington Canal (1792–5), which has particularly notorious bends at Sneyd Junction and the 'Devil's Elbow' in Wednesfield.

'Second generation' canals, 1780–1820

With increasing experience, canal engineers became more ambitious, and the next generation of canals, constructed in the two decades either side of 1800, witnessed some phenomenal efforts, with canals being taken straight across increasingly difficult terrain by means of more elaborate engineering works. John Smeaton (builder of the Eddystone Lighthouse) was among the first to adopt the new approach on his Birmingham and Fazeley Canal (1784–9), which has an unusually high number of lock flights over its 20-mile course: 13 at Farmer's Bridge in Birmingham, 11 at Aston, 3 at Minworth and 11 at Curdworth, with a further 6 at Ashted on the Digbeth Branch (1799). There is also a short tunnel at Curdworth.

The Worcester and Birmingham Canal

The most interesting product of this phase is the Worcester and Birmingham Canal, authorised in 1791 to provide Birmingham with a more direct route to the Severn. This proved to be one of the most arduous and costly (£610,000) canals yet built. Apart from considerable natural obstacles, the unfortunate proprietors suffered continual embarrassment by costly disputes over water rights and exorbitant compensation demands, and it was not finally completed until 1815. It shared with the Trent and Mersey the distinction of possessing the greatest number of tunnels on any single canal line: from the north, Edgbaston (105 yards), King's Norton (2726 yards), Shortwood (608 yards), Tardebigge (568 yards) and Dunhampstead (236 yards). It was originally intended as a barge canal, so all the tunnels were built wide. Tardebigge Tunnel caused construction problems, being cut mostly through solid rock with only a small portion brick-lined. King's Norton is curious in that the north portal is quite pretentious, in strong contrast to the unadorned south portal. Edgbaston Tunnel was the only one provided with a towpath, but Dunhampstead was worked by means of handrails fixed to the wall. In the other tunnels, tugs were later used to pull the boats through.

This canal involves heavy lockage: in the 16-mile rise from the Severn at Worcester there are no fewer than 58 locks. Apart from three separate flights of six each at Offerton, Astwood and Stoke Prior, this includes the Tardebigge Flight, which with 30 narrow locks in two miles is the biggest in Britain.

In Tardebigge Top Lock it also has the deepest narrow lock in England, with a fall of 14 feet. The explanation here is that it replaced an experimental vertical lift, the first example known, designed by John Woodhouse in 1809. This lift consisted of a single wooden tank balanced by metal counterweights. But the cost of construction and maintenance of the lift proved prohibitive, and for the remainder of the descent locks were employed, the prototype lift itself being replaced by a single deep lock soon afterwards.

The Stratford-upon-Avon Canal

Financial problems also bedevilled the Stratford-upon-Avon Canal, construction of which began in 1793 from a junction with the Worcestershire and Birmingham Canal at King's Norton. By 1796 construction had reached Hockley Heath, but most of the authorised capital was spent, and a temporary terminus was made there. In 1799 work resumed and the canal was taken as far as Lapworth where, following a deviation from the route originally planned, a branch was built with one lock leading down to the Warwick and Birmingham Canal (now part of the Grand Union) at Kingswood Junction, completed in 1802. Shortage of funds again halted the project here until 1812 when the final stage to Stratford was commenced. It was completed in 1816 to the Bancroft Basins in Stratford, with a link to the Avon not originally intended and authorised only the previous year.

The only tunnel on the Stratford-upon-Avon Canal is at Brandwood near King's Norton: 352 yards long, it was built to a 16-foot width, sufficient for two boats to pass within; fixed handrails were provided for haulage. Its west portal is ornamented with a circular plaque bearing Shakespeare's portrait and a laurel spray, and flanked by two niches; the east portal also has niches and an inscription (now illegible). Much of the canal is heavily locked, with 55 locks in only 15 miles: the main groups are at Lapworth (25) and Wilmcote (11). But the chief engineering feature of the Stratford-upon-Avon Canal is its aqueducts. There is a large brick one over the river Cole on the canal's northern section, but the three most interesting ones are all on the southern section. In strong contrast to Brindley's aqueducts these are relatively lightly built, the water being contained in iron troughs. The biggest is the Bearley or Edstone Aqueduct, built by William Whitmore: 475 feet long, it crosses a road, a stream and two railways; its towing-path is slung beside the waterway like that on the first iron-trough aqueduct built in England, at Longdon-on-Tern on the Shrewsbury Canal. Wotton Wawen Aqueduct is of similar construction and date, supported on girders and brick pillars. The third and smallest, at Yarningale Lock, was added in 1834 after the original was washed away in a flood. It is a tiny aqueduct, taking the canal over the river Alne.

The Dudley Canal

The Dudley Canal is noteworthy for possessing three of the longest canal tunnels in the Midlands. The earlier was the Dudley Tunnel. Lord Dudley and Ward had begun a private canal about 1775 from the Birmingham Canal through a short tunnel to the Tipton Colliery workings, later extended with the building of the subterranean Castle Mill Basin to serve the extensive limestone quarries. In 1785 the Dudley Canal Company began to extend their original modest line by five locks at Park Head (or Parkhead) and then in 1792 through a great 2,942-yard tunnel to join Lord Dudley's tunnel at Castle Mill Basin, whence a further 196 yards of the old tunnel led back into the open. This gave a total length from end to end of 3,154 yards. Between 1805 and 1837 Lord Dudley built a further underground branch from Castle Mill Basin for some 1,277 yards to serve the limestone workings of the Wren's Nest. The specified dimensions of the Dudley Tunnel were: width 9 feet 3 inches, depth of water 5 feet 6 inches, and headroom 7 feet. Passage was by legging throughout, and much of the length is through solid rock. Strenuous efforts to restore this remarkable underground waterway system resulted in its reopening to navigation in 1973, along with the formerly impassable Parkhead locks. The same, alas, cannot be said for the even longer Lappal Tunnel (3,795 yards) on the Selly Oak Extension (or No. 2 line) of the Dudley Canal, built 1796–7. Part of it, affected by mining subsidence, collapsed in 1917 and was abandoned. Today nothing remains visible of this, the third longest canal tunnel in Britain. A third tunnel, Gosty Hill, remains on that part of the Dudley No. 2 line which is still navigable: 577 yards long, it has one solitary ventilator. There are two places within where the roof drops alarmingly in height. The fourth important tunnel is Netherton (see below).

The Warwick canals

Two further canals of this phase are the Warwick and Birmingham (authorised 1793) and Warwick and Napton (1794), both completed in 1800, both absorbed into the Grand Union system in 1929, and together opening a shorter route from Birmingham to London. There are several lock flights: 21 at Hatton, 9 at Stockton, 6 at Knowle (later reduced to 5), 6 at Camp Hill, 4 at Bascote and 3 at Calcutt. Of the several aqueducts, the most impressive carries the Warwick and Napton on three stone arches over the river Avon at Emscote. But the engineers for these two canals were less able than some of their fellows, and the Blythe Aqueduct collapsed soon after its building in 1795. One tunnel of 433 yards was built at Shrewley, but owing to a shortage of funds modifications had to be made to the original line to avoid further tunnels at Yardley, Rowington and Leamington. Another modification for the sake of economy was to join the Oxford Canal at Napton instead of crossing it at Braunston as had originally been intended.

Telford and the 'third generation' canals

The third phase of canal-building marked the peak of the canal engineers' achievement, but also coincided with increasing railway competition. The name of Thomas Telford is outstanding in this period (as was that of Brindley in the pioneering stages). Telford first appears on the scene in 1824 when the Birmingham Canal Navigations, or BCN—an amalgamation of the earlier Birmingham, Birmingham and Fazeley and Wyrley and Essington Companies—commissioned him to survey their outdated and overloaded Birmingham—Wolverhampton main line. This had remained virtually unimproved since its construction except for the replacement of Brindley's wasteful 491-foot Smethwick Summit in 1787 by a new summit built by Smeaton on the 473-foot 'Wolverhampton' level. The top three locks of Brindley's flights of six at Spon Lane and Smethwick had then been abandoned, and three new locks added parallel to the surviving Smethwick three to supplement them.

Telford's modernisation of the BCN

Telford's recommendations were executed between 1825 and 1838. A new feeder reservoir at Rotton Park and the straightening of the line between Birmingham and Smethwick came first. Then a completely new line was begun from the bottom of Spon Lane locks, parallel to Brindley's cut, but on the 453-foot 'Birmingham' level rather than the 473-foot level, via Dudley Port, rising to rejoin the old line by three new locks at Tipton. At the end of 1829 Telford made the great cutting, 70 feet deep, through the hill at Smethwick on the 453-foot level: the three parallel summits of Brindley, Smeaton and Telford at different levels on the same slope are a unique feature here.

Telford's Smethwick cutting was spanned by the great Galton Bridge, a single iron span of 150 feet, cast at the Horseley Ironworks in Staffordshire. It was then the largest canal bridge in the world; it has now been closed to traffic for its own protection, while beside it two brand-new canal tunnels have been constructed. (Comprehensive road-building required that the canal cut-

tings on the Birmingham and Wolverhampton level should both be covered over for a distance of about 100 yards each, leaving room for spacious canal tunnels with new roads on top.) Other notable structures of the BCN include the Stewart Aqueduct, carrying the Brindley line across the Birmingham Level to the top of Smeaton's reduced flight of Spon Lane locks, and the superb cast-iron Telford aqueduct which carries the Engine Arm from Smeaton's 473-foot level over the 453-foot level. This branch, built 1789–90, took its name from the first Boulton & Watt steam engine bought by the canal company to pump water up to the Smethwick summits; the engine itself is now in retirement at the Birmingham Museum of Science and Industry. A third aqueduct, the Ryland Aqueduct, carried Telford's line over the Dudley Port Road. But this was replaced by a new concrete structure in 1968 to allow the road below to be widened.

The last major re-alignment of the Birmingham Canal main line was completed in 1837 and cut off the Wednesbury Oak Loop between Bloomfield and Deepfields junctions by a broad tunnel 360 yards long, with twin towpaths, through Coseley Hill. In 1836 the Gower Branch provided a further link between the Birmingham and Wolverhampton levels by the three Brades locks, the top two of which formed the only staircase formation in the entire BCN.

By 1839 the whole line from Birmingham west to Aldersley Junction (where it met the Staffs and Worcs Canal) had been improved to the new standard, 40 feet wide, with twin towpaths throughout. Twin-arched bridges such as that below Tipton Factory locks are characteristic of the 'new' canal, as is a dead straight course running alternately through deep cuttings such as Smethwick, and on high embankments, such as that east of Dudley Port.

Oxford Canal improvements

Similar straightening operations took place on other canals. The Oxford Canal Company was forced to improve its competitive position by straightening out its route north of Braunston, so during 1829–34 Telford was commissioned to execute a series of short cuts, amounting virtually to a new waterway which drastically shortened Brindley's original circuitous route. A 250-yard tunnel with twin towpaths replaced the old Newbold Tunnel; the old loop and tunnel at Wolfhampcote were replaced by an embankment, entailing a change of site for Braunston Junction (the original junction was the entrance to the present boatyard). Brinklow Aqueduct was widened and made into an embankment; and a new iron aqueduct was built near Brownsover. Where the old loops were retained for the sake of their village wharves the new towpath crossed over via graceful Horseley Ironworks bridges, contrasting with the older brick bridges.

Trent and Mersey Canal

Further improvement of the BCN

In 1836 the Lodge Farm Loop of the Dudley Canal was by-passed by the new 75-yard Brewin's Tunnel, which was opened out into a cutting some years later; other loops at Dudley Wood and Bumble Hole were similarly cut off. Elsewhere, completely new canals were still being built around this time. The Birmingham and Warwick Junction Canal (now part of the Grand Union system) was opened in 1840, linking the Warwick and Birmingham to the Birmingham and Fazeley Canal. It is so straight that seven successive road bridges can be seen in line under the arch of the first; the five Garrison locks and Nechells Shallow Lock bring it to the level of the Birmingham and Fazeley Canal at Salford Junction. Almost opposite is the entrance to the Tame Valley Canal, opened the same year; this is even more modern, being deep and wide, with twin towpaths, long straight stretches and alternate embankments and cuttings. Both were built to avoid bottlenecks: the former bypassed the Ashted and Aston flights, saving 17 locks; the latter route, via the 13 Perry Barr locks, provided an alternative to the desperately congested Farmer's Bridge Flight. The Rushall Canal (1847) is similar with its long pound below the second Rushall Lock running dead straight for over a mile. So too were the Bentley Canal (1843) and (outside Birmingham) the Droitwich Junction Canal (1853), both now derelict.

Netherton Tunnel

Amongst the greatest engineering feats of this period was the Netherton Tunnel, built by the BCN company in 1855–8 as a bypass to the narrow and usually congested Dudley Tunnel. The last canal tunnel built in England (with the exception of the two rather different tunnels now completed—as mentioned above), Netherton was also the most sophisticated. Like Coseley and Newbold tunnels, it was given twin towpaths throughout and was wide enough to allow two-way working—indeed, with a width of 27 feet at water level (of which each towpath occupied 5 feet), a centre water depth of 6 feet, and a headroom of nearly 16 feet, it had the largest bore of any English canal tunnel. It was well ventilated, with seven airshafts. Moreover, it had a lighting system, worked first by gas, later by electricity; the remains of the turbine which produced the power are still to be found just outside the northern portal. A greater contrast with Brindley's rough rock-cut short tunnels or the claustrophobic Lappal or old Dudley Tunnels could hardly be imagined.

The Cannock Extension

The last important canal built in the Midlands was the Cannock Extension, opened between 1858 and 1863 to connect the BCN with the developing Cannock Chase coalfield. Its straightness and blue brick bridges are typical of the railway age. It is now closed off beyond Norton Canes, mining subsidence having destroyed most of the rest, including the Churchbridge locks linking it with the Hatherton Branch of the Staffs and Worcs Canal.

The Grand Union Canal modernisation scheme

One final important development on the Midland canals before nationalisation in 1947 was the absorption of the three Warwick canals in 1929 by the new Grand Union Canal Company. This company embarked on a government-backed programme of improvement in the 1930's, including bank reinforcement and piling (much of it is marked with the date), and the widening of the canal to take 14-foot barges. All the old narrow locks between Calcutt Bottom Lock and the top of the Camp Hill Flight were converted to weirs, and may still be seen alongside the new broad locks. On the Knowle Flight six locks were replaced by five; and at Bascote two separate locks were replaced by a staircase pair. Near the 'Rose and Castle' pub at Braunston may still be seen the entrance to the basin formerly used for transhipment from barges to the narrowboats working on the northern Oxford Canal. All the lock paddles on the new locks were built with an enclosed housing, which makes them easier to operate and less dangerous. By this time, however, the heyday of commercial traffic on the canals had passed, and the improvements failed to produce the hoped-for increase in trade and revenue.

What to see

We should now look more closely at some of the features which make up the landscape of the Midland canals. The style of different periods and different companies makes for an enormous variety, and even now on composite waterways such as the Coventry Canal, Grand Union and BCN, it is still possible to distinguish sections built under different companies at different dates.

BRIDGES

Bridges make a convenient starting-point. Major bridges normally included the towpath in their span, but this facility was often denied to footbridges because of the expense of the extra span. The ingenuity of the canal engineer was well tested by the consequent problem of passing the towrope round the bridge without detaching it from either the towing horse or the boat, particularly where the towpath itself changed sides.

Split bridges

One answer was to build split bridges, as tested by Brindley on the Staffs and Worcs Canal, and adopted and elaborated elsewhere. On the Stratford-upon-Avon Canal the carriageway was carried on two cast-iron brackets, each projecting towards the other from brick abutments, failing to meet by about an inch. They have integral iron handrails, each supported by a lattice of paired saltires. Many examples remain, as at Kingswood and Yarningale. A very similar type with plainer handrails is found on the Stourbridge Canal. A curious variation found on the Worcester and Birmingham involves a single cantilever instead of a divided bridge, consisting of a wooden platform, usually with handrails, heavily weighted or otherwise anchored to the bank side, so that the unfixed end was raised 2–3 inches off the ground, allowing the towrope to pass through the gap. Only one example, at Lock 33 at Tardebigge, is in its original condition, although a bridge similar in principle—if not in design—is to be found at Tipton Factory locks, on the BCN.

Lifting bridges

An alternative solution was the drawbridge, where the horizontal platform is swung upwards by about 45 degrees. The simplest type is the rolling lift-bridge, pivoted by a toothed segment of cast iron, which was used by Brindley on the Oxford Canal. The platform is counterbalanced by projecting beams fixed directly to it, which, when the bridge is open, lie in a horizontal plane, and, when it is closed, rise accordingly. The platform itself is sometimes flat, sometimes shallowly arched, with handrails mounted on either side. The water channel narrows to a width of 7 feet at the crossing point to reduce the weight and cost of the structure. Similar bridges appear on the Stratford-upon-Avon Canal, as at Lapworth. Another type of canal drawbridge, found on the Stratford-upon-Avon line at Solihull Common, has balance beams mounted on stout uprights above the platform, to which they are connected by chains and rods.

Another alternative was the swing- or turn-bridges used on the Grand Union, where the platform was pivoted on the bank side and moved horizontally into a recess.

Roving bridges

The roving or turnover bridge, enabling the towpath to change sides or cross over a junction, including an arm of the towpath under its span, was widely employed. There are many good cast-iron examples on the BCN, often bearing the Horseley Ironworks marks. Two particularly elegant examples, with a wider span than most, occur at Tame Valley Junction. Another Horseley-cast bridge is the graceful arch of 1820 spanning the Oxford Canal at Braunston Turn; more severe, but still elegant, is the bridge dated 1836 at Hawkesbury Junction.

A particularly curious footbridge occurs near Fazeley: access is gained by spiral stairways housed in squat castellated towers on either bank. This ornamental form was the whim of a local landowner, at a time when the use of follies in landscape gardening was at its height.

LOCKS

Locks are another feature of canal scenery possessing more interest than may at first appear. Although almost all in the Midlands are more or less of standard dimensions—around 72 feet long by either 7 feet or 14 feet wide—there are plenty of variations in details like the design of paddles, gates and the chamber itself. It is also interesting to see how the canal engineers, faced with the problem of ensuring adequate intermediate water supplies between locks in very steep flights, excavated every square yard of available surface area to form as large a 'reservoir' as possible. Farmer's Bridge and Aston Locks on the Birmingham and Fazeley Canal are a good instance of these; so is the top flight at Lapworth on the Stratford Canal.

Sometimes single locks in flights stand out. The second lock of the Wolverhampton Flight on the BCN main line has a single bottom gate instead of the pair found on all the others: Brindley originally built a flight of 20 with the standard bottom pair of mitre gates, but his bottom one was deeper than the rest and very wasteful of water—so a dozen years later this extra lock was added above it following the design then favoured by the Company. The eight Walsall locks, on the other hand, all have single bottom gates except No. 6, which has a pair of mitres. The replacement of the Grand Union locks has already been mentioned. Yet another altered flight is Black Delph on the Dudley Canal, locally called the Nine Locks although there are only eight: a new flight of eight replaced the original nine in 1858 after serious subsidence, re-using the top and bottom locks of the original flight, and leaving the abandoned old chambers still visible alongside the new.

Individual locks of great depth sometimes occur: Tardebigge Top Lock on the site of the lift has already been noted. Another is Blowers Green Lock, built 1893–4 on the Dudley Canal to replace the lower pair of the Park Head flight of five.

Stop locks

Many locks near a junction have the express function of protecting the water resources of the older navigation by ensuring that any transfer of water occurring on passage of a boat is favourable to it. The change in level at such locks is usually only a few inches, and sometimes nothing at all. The best-known example in the Midlands is perhaps at Worcester Bar in Birmingham, where for many years the Birmingham Canal refused to allow the Worcester and Birmingham to make a direct junction, dividing the two waterways by a narrow 'bar' of masonry across which all goods consigned from one canal to the other had to be transhipped; eventually this was replaced in 1815 by the present stop lock. Other examples may be found at Warwick Bar where the Digbeth Arm meets the Grand Union; Brockmoor Stop Lock, now derelict, where the Pensnett Fens Branch met the old Stourbridge Extension; and Autherley Stop Lock where the Shropshire Union leaves the Staffs and Worcs Canal. The stop lock at Hawkesbury Junction is still in place (there is a change in level here), but at Marston Junction, just a few miles away, the lock is out of action now.

LOCKS

The most unusual example is King's Norton Stop Lock on the Stratford-upon-Avon Canal, erected to preserve the water rights of the Worcester and Birmingham Canal Company. It is of guillotine type, with the gate designed to be raised and lowered vertically in guides forming a frame over the canal. Chains attached to the gate pass over pulleys mounted on top of the frame, and from thence to an operating winch and compensating weights. This machinery still exists, but it now performs no function and is locked in position.

Lock cottages and toll houses

Lock cottages vary greatly in style: several on the old Droitwich Canal affected Dutch architectural features. The most individual, however, are the single-storeyed barrel-roofed cottages on the southern section of the Stratford-upon-Avon Canal, contrasting with the more prosaic red brick type on the northern section.

Tollhouses are also of interest, and can be found at many canal junctions, including Autherley, Lapworth and King's Norton; there is also one at the former Braunston Junction (next to the boatyard) although the stop lock has been removed. The octagonal design used on the Staffs and Worcs Canal (examples remain at Stewponey and The Bratch) seems to have been copied by the BCN Company, judging by the one that survived until very recently near Tipton Junction. (Other surviving BCN tollhouses can be seen at the top of Walsall and Farmer's Bridge flights of locks.) The BCN has narrows or gauging stops by almost every junction, where boats' cargoes were gauged for toll purposes.

Basins and wharves

Canal basins and wharves may be found all over the canal system. Gas Street Basin, hemmed in by the industrial buildings of central Birmingham, creates a quiet haven unsuspected by the traffic thundering unseen across Broad Street only yards away, and contrasts vividly with the surviving part of the Bancroft basins in the centre of the tourists' Stratford, now shorn of all its industrial character to form an ornamental lake in a riverside park. The LNWR, who controlled the BCN after 1846, promoted 26 railway interchange basins to foster traffic between the canalside factories and their railways; one remains near Horseley Fields Junction, another at Great Bridge on the Walsall Level below Ryders Green locks. Other short limbs of the BCN, like Baskerville Basin, Gibson's Arm, Newhall Wharf and Suffolk Street basins in central Birmingham, exist no more and are virtually forgotten.

Canal-related industrial archaeology

Canal construction and industrial growth were closely related, and it is natural that in an area so densely interlaced with waterways there should be an enormous wealth of all kinds of sites to interest the industrial archaeologist. Many sites form landmarks from the canalside: the great Langley Maltings on the Titford Branch of the BCN, for example, or the last surviving conical glass kiln at Wordsley, visible from the 16 locks on the Stourbridge Canal. But other important early industrial sites retain little to see, including Pensnett Chase, the scene of Dudley's attempts (now known to have been successful) to smelt iron with coal a hundred years before Abraham Darby; and Darlaston, where John Wilkinson adapted a Boulton & Watt steam engine to provide the blast for a coke-fired iron furnace in 1785, thereby ending the industry's dependence on water power and paving the way for the enormous expansion of the Black Country. Close to the former site was the Round Oak steelworks, almost the last local survivor of the industry, which is remembered only by a plaque and a pub called the 'Fiery Holes'.

Tramways, the precursors of the railways whose competition eventually killed so many canals, are represented at Stratford: hard by the Bancroft Basin is a brick tramway bridge across the Avon, and a wagon preserved from the Stratford and Moreton Tramway, which operated from 1826. The railways faced many of the natural obstacles which had beset canals, and it is interesting to see the Tardebigge locks on the Worcester and Birmingham Canal paralleled by the equally famous Lickey Incline on the Birmingham and Gloucester Railway. Outstanding railway stations include Curzon Street in Birmingham, original 1838 terminus of the London and Birmingham Railway, with an imposing Doric arch entrance, which has outlived its much more famous counterpart at Euston as well as the original buildings of two of the other great Birmingham termini. The classical façade of Worcester Shrub Hill is also of note.

Mines and quarries

The remains of many early mines may be seen in the Black Country, Cannock Chase and Coventry areas. The remains of Cobb's engine-house, whose steam pump fought flooding problems in several nearby mines for many years, towers over the southern end of Netherton Tunnel. Salt working was important at Droitwich and Stoke Prior, and remains of the salt works and canal arms serving them may still be seen here. (Both coal and salt working caused subsidence, so that lowered ground levels and crazily leaning buildings are a prominent feature of these districts.) Limestone quarrying was an important extractive industry around Dudley, and from the spectacular Seven Sisters quarry on the Wren's Nest Hill a spiral stairway of 240 steps led to the underground basin of the great Dudley Canal Tunnel.

The canals of the West Midlands feature much that is of great interest to those who like to explore old industries, trades and communication systems. There is much to see, and happily it takes little more to indulge this growing hobby than an alert observation and plenty of energy. It is certainly surprising how easily one can find and identify the industrial 'relics' described above.

Gas Street Basin, looking towards Farmer's Bridge

Fradley Junction

Canals in the East Midlands

Trent and Mersey Canal:
Fradley to Derwent Mouth

This is the eastern section of the Trent and Mersey Canal, one of the earliest of the great waterways designed to connect industrial areas and seaports. The canal starts at the river Trent with 14-foot-wide locks, to enable the wide 'Trent boats' to work up as far as Burton-on-Trent, but from Burton northwards the locks are narrow. Work on this section of the 93-mile-long canal was in progress by July 1766, soon after the passing of the Act, and it was opened from Derwent Mouth to Great Haywood on 24 June 1770, although the whole line from Shardlow to Preston Brook was not opened for through traffic until 1777.

THINGS TO SEE

Fradley Junction

This is typical of the small settlements which sprang up where important canal junctions were made. Such settlements were usually centred, as here, around a canalside inn, and a group of cottages for boatmen and canal maintenance workers. Stables for the towing horses were also usually incorporated into the settlement, and at Fradley there are canal workshops—still very much used.

Alrewas

Here the canal merges with the river Trent for a hundred yards: the Trent enters from the north side and leaves over a weir on the south side of the canal. Navigationally this can be a hazard, especially in time of flood, but it helps the water supply of the canal.

Burton-on-Trent

Dallow Lane Lock is the southernmost narrow lock on the Trent and Mersey, for the canal has wide locks from Burton to the junction with the river Trent near Shardlow. A short distance below this is Horninglow Basin, where a few of the original warehouses survive. East of Horninglow, an aqueduct carries the canal over the river Dove.

Swarkestone Junction

Here the now-abandoned Derby Canal entered the Trent and Mersey from the north; a short section at the junction survives, and is used for boat mooring. The former Derby Canal Company's old toll-house still stands, and is now the headquarters of the Swarkestone Boat Club. In the fields between this building and the nearby Trent, traces of the Derby Canal's link with the river may be seen.

Shardlow

One of the finest surviving examples of a canal port. The old village of Shardlow lay away from the canal, and a new village grew up near the intersection of the Trent and Mersey Canal and the turnpike road from Derby. The oldest building, Corn Mill No. 2, is dated 1780, and most of the other commercial buildings appear to date from the next quarter century. Apart from the warehouses, there are some fine buildings, formerly the residences of canal merchants. Near the latter, on the towpath, may be seen the cast-iron milepost from which distances on the canal were measured. It is dated 1819.

River Trent:
Derwent Mouth to Trent Lock

The Trent was a great trade route from early times, but, partly through natural deficiencies and partly through mismanagement by earlier administrators, little serious attempt was made to realise its potential until the latter part of the 18th century, when pressure from the Trent and Mersey Canal Company ultimately led to an improvement scheme being sanctioned in 1783. The scheme was not an ambitious one and the section between Trent Lock and the junction with the Trent and Mersey Canal was finished by the end of the year; probably the greatest improvement was the provision of a towpath, hitherto lacking. A few years later, a cut and lock were constructed at Sawley. The work was completed by 1793 and was shortly afterwards followed by the building of a second (parallel) lock at Sawley as part of the major improvement scheme authorised in 1794.

THINGS TO SEE

Like many river navigations, the Trent has little of interest to the industrial archaeologist, although at Sawley the two locks (the outer one recently restored and re-opened for use) and the flood lock are interesting. Along the towpath may still be seen some of the double gates which allowed the boat horse and the boy leading it to pass through, while preventing stock in the fields from doing so.

The Erewash Canal

The proposal to build a canal to improve communication between the Nottinghamshire/Derbyshire coalmines and the Trent was prompted largely by the canalisation of the river Soar to Loughborough, opening up the prospect of a good market for coal from these pits not only to north and east Leicestershire, but to Leicester itself. An Act to authorise the making of the Erewash Canal was passed in 1777. From the first, links with the Soar Navigation Company were strong, the Clerk of the latter company being also Clerk of the Erewash. John Varley was appointed Engineer, and the first section of the new canal was opened in 1778, the whole being open to its terminal point at Langley Mill by the end of 1779; but Varley had got himself into trouble, both engineering and administrative, and was dismissed in 1780. The canal was successful in building up a considerable coal traffic and even retained a fair degree of prosperity after the coming of the railways had given it direct competitors for the trade. However, trade on the Erewash Canal slowly declined, and it was finally bought for £15,702 by the Grand Union Canal Company in 1931.

Trent Lock to Loughborough (the old Loughborough Navigation)

Although Leicestershire has its own coalfield, poor transport facilities prevented sufficient exploitation of its resources to satisfy the needs of the county town, and several attempts were made before the Canal Age to obtain supplies from north of the county. The river Soar, which flows through Leicester, was not originally navigable for commercial boats, but since it joins the Trent where the latter passes quite near to the Nottinghamshire/Derbyshire coalfield, it was natural that schemes to make the river navigable should be devised. The first successful project, however, was a more modest one: it was to make navigation possible between the confluence of the Soar and the Trent and the town of Loughborough, using the natural channel of the river as far as possible, but making an artificial cut from the river to the town itself. An Act was passed to sanction this in 1766, but, having taken the advice of Brindley, the Commissioners empowered to carry out the work decided to take no action, and it was left to a new group of promoters, mainly Loughborough men, to revive the scheme. In 1776 they obtained an Act giving them powers to make the river navigable to a point in Loughborough near to the turnpike road from Leicester to Derby. The Navigation was opened to Kegworth in 1777, but by that time it was clear that it was likely to attract more trade than had originally been envisaged (owing to the promotion of the Erewash Canal), and William Jessop, then

on the threshold of a most distinguished career as a canal engineer, was called in. He advised a number of improvements, aimed at making the navigation capable of bearing a heavier traffic, and these were accepted. Navigation to Loughborough began in 1778, though Jessop's modifications were not completed until 1780. Within 10 years, the Company was paying a dividend of 20 per cent, and its trade grew tremendously after this, as new navigations were opened to continue the line south from Loughborough. Even after railways entered into competition with it the Loughborough Navigation continued to pay reasonably well, and, although it never again achieved the amazing prosperity of its great years, neither did it become penniless and semi-derelict. It was bought for £11,595 by the Grand Union Company in 1931.

THINGS TO SEE

Mills

Navigation companies were often on bad terms with the watermills on their line, since each side was trying to get all the water it wanted for its own purposes, usually to the detriment of the other. The Loughborough Navigation and its mills were no exception, and in the end the Navigation Company had to buy two of the mills, Zouch and Kegworth, to prevent further disputes. Zouch mills remain a most impressive example of the massive structures justified by the power of a harnessed river.

Kegworth

Just north of the village is the site of a gypsum wharf. Trade in this material, which was used for making plaster for building, was quite extensive. At Kegworth, the navigation leaves the course of the river to pass through a flood lock, but there was a wharf serving the village on the old river course.

Loughborough

The junction of the Leicester Navigation and the Loughborough Navigation is marked by the 'Chain Bridge', so called because in the days when the two companies were independent, a chain was kept across to prevent boats from passing from one to the other without paying toll.

Loughborough to Leicester (the old Leicester Navigation)

The success of the Loughborough Navigation increased the existing demand from the citizens of Leicester that the line of navigation should be extended to their town. There was solid support for this in the town itself, but unfortunately there was powerful opposition outside it. The coal owners of west Leicestershire, who already had difficulty in maintaining a worthwhile trade with the county town, did not relish the prospect of Derbyshire coal coming to Leicester more cheaply than their own product, and as they were also influential members of the county aristocracy, they were successful in preventing the promoters of the Leicester Navigation scheme from getting an Act to permit this project being carried out. It was not until 1791 that the promoters succeeded in buying off the Leicestershire coal owners. To do this, they were forced to agree that, in order to allow the Leicestershire mines to compete on equal terms with Derbyshire, they would cut a branch canal from the Leicestershire coalfield to Loughborough as well as making the main line from Loughborough to Leicester. This branch, known as the Charnwood Forest Canal, or 'Forest line', because it ran through Charnwood Forest, was an extraordinary thing: the waterway ran from Thringstone to Nanpantan (near Loughborough), with a branch to Osgathorpe, but at the western end there were tramways (horse-operated light railways) to the collieries and limeworks, while at the eastern end a similar tramway connected the water level, perched up on the hills of Charnwood, with the basin of the Loughborough Navigation, down in the valley. The Act authorising the construction of these two lines was passed in 1791. There was little difficulty in making the 'River line' (Loughborough to Leicester), but the engineer, William Jessop, had much trouble with the 'Forest line', with the result that the former was ready first, and was opened for navigation on 21 February 1794. Coal, however, was not permitted to pass along the line, this being forbidden by the Act until Leicestershire coal could travel along it as well – in effect, not until the 'Forest line' was opened. This did not happen until October of the same year, when a boatload of coal from the Leicestershire collieries passed along the line, its cargo being taken down the tramway to Loughborough, and so on by boat to Leicester – followed by the first boat carrying Derbyshire coal. This was symbolic, for little more traffic passed down the 'Forest line', the coal trade being monopolised by the Derbyshire pits. A reservoir was built to feed the 'Forest line' in 1796, but it burst in 1799 causing great damage, and, although it was rebuilt, this was the final blow. The Charnwood Forest Canal went out of use completely.

The Leicester Navigation never made anything like the profits of either the Erewash or the Loughborough Navigation. Nevertheless, it was a solid concern, and did a great deal to accelerate Leicester's industrial development by bringing cheap coal in large quantities to the town. Like the other canals of the so-called 'Leicester line', it suffered from railway competition in the 19th century, and, after a long period of decline, during which the Company tried to make up for its falling traffic-receipts by investing in land in Leicester, the canal was sold to the Grand Union Company in 1931 for £48,126 10s 0d.

THINGS TO SEE

Although based on the course of the river Soar, there are several deviations. The first section of the canal, from its junction with the Loughborough Navigation, is an artificial cut known as 'the Loughborough Cut'. It joins the Soar at Pilling's Lock, near Barrow-on-Soar, only to leave it again shortly afterwards to avoid Barrow Mill. At Cossington, there is a major departure from the river course, when the navigation leaves the Soar to join its tributary the Wreake, rejoining the former by a lengthy artificial channel ('Sutton's Cut', after an early trader on the line) to Thurmaston; this was forced on the Company by the owner of Wanlip Hall (through the grounds of which the Soar passed) who refused to allow the river to be used as a navigation on his property. At Belgrave, the main channel of the Soar is left in order to take the navigation through Leicester to West Bridge.

Other boatmen's inns

'The Boat', Loughborough, served a wharf nearby, and until recently cottages for boatmen and canal workers stood alongside it. 'The Navigation', Barrow-on-Soar, served the navigation and the adjacent mill, which ground gypsum in its later years. This inn was originally owned by the Leicester Navigation Company. On Sutton's Cut is the 'Hope and Anchor', originally the house of the wharfinger here (it was known as Barkby Wharf). Near the northern end of Sutton's Cut, on the offside, is a building which was formerly an inn called 'The Junction', after the junction with the Melton Mowbray Navigation nearby; this wharf was Syston Wharf.

Mountsorrel

At Mountsorrel the navigation is crossed by a magnificent red-brick bridge, built in 1860 to carry the railway branch line from the Mountsorrel granite quarries to the Midland Railway's main line at Barrow. This stone was in great demand for road metalling, etc., and the navigation company itself built up quite a flourishing trade in it. The wharves where boats took on their cargoes can be seen near to the railway bridge Alongside the lock at Mountsorrel was the 'Duke of York', now renamed the 'Waterside Inn' and extensively rebuilt, but still presenting its original façade to the waterway.

Leicester to Market Harborough (the old Leicestershire and Northamptonshire Union Canal)

Just as the promotion of the Loughborough Navigation had helped to create a demand for a southward extension of the waterway to Leicester, so the Leicester Navigation aroused hopes of carrying the line still further, and a scheme was mooted in 1792 for a navigation from Leicester to Market

Harborough. The first few miles were to follow the course of the river Soar, but after that the entire canal was to be artificial. The plan was adopted, but before steps could be taken to carry it out, the situation was completely changed by the appearance of another project, for a canal from London to the Oxford Canal near Braunston, in Warwickshire. As a result, the promoters of the 'Harborough Navigation' altered their plans, and at a meeting in Market Harborough it was agreed to continue their canal beyond that town to join the new London to Braunston canal—the Grand Junction, as it was called. In this form, the former Harborough project, by now re-named the Leicestershire and Northamptonshire Union Canal (and later to become part of the Grand Union system), was authorised by an Act of Parliament in 1793: it was to consist of a main line from Leicester to Northampton (where it was to join the river Nene as well as a branch of the Grand Junction), via Market Harborough. Work began at the Leicester end, but there was trouble almost from the start. England was at war, and prices were rising, so that the original estimates soon became quite inadequate. There was trouble with the engineering, too. Jessop had been called in for the preliminary survey, but he was too busy to take on the position of Engineer and the post went to John Varley, who got into trouble here as he had on the Erewash. In laying out the 880-yard tunnel at Saddington (one of four tunnels planned for the line), Varley omitted to take elementary precautions for checking accuracy, with the result that when work on the tunnel was well under way, it was found to have bends in it which would make it impassable by boats. There was naturally a great deal of fuss, and an independent engineer was brought in to report, but eventually the defects were remedied. By now (1797), however, it was quite obvious that there was no hope of reaching Northampton on the money not yet called up; so the Committee ordered construction to halt when the canal had reached a minor road near the village of Gumley, and here, four miles from Market Harborough, at an isolated spot which became known as Debdale Wharf, the canal terminus remained for several years. After their experience at Saddington, the Committee were no doubt concerned with the next obstacle just south of them at Foxton, where a 1,056-yard tunnel was planned. By the time they were ready to resume construction, they had decided to avoid this by altering the line, taking the canal to Harborough by a circuitous route through Foxton village, and they obtained an Act in 1805 to allow this. Work began, but once more they found that the expense was greater than they had expected, and by the time their canal was approaching Market Harborough they had decided not to construct the rest of the line beyond that town. The final section to Harborough was opened on 13 October 1809, and the Union, or Old Union Canal,

as it was popularly known, never extended further.

THINGS TO SEE

West Bridge, Leicester

The Old Union Canal made a junction with the Leicester Navigation a short distance north of this. The point of junction is marked by the letters UN (Union Navigation) cut into the stonework of the towpath edging, on both the side and upper surfaces.

The New Cut, Leicester

As part of flood prevention works undertaken by Leicester Corporation in the latter part of the 19th century, the old meandering channel of the Soar between West Bridge and Aylestone was partly replaced by a broad, straight channel nearly a mile long, terminating at a new lock (Freeman's Meadow) which replaced two locks on the abandoned channel. It was opened in February 1890.

Aylestone

Here the Old Union Canal left the Soar, the rest of its line to Market Harborough being artificial. Near the junction may be seen the stone bridge over which coal for Leicester was brought by pack-horse, and alongside it the brick canal bridge.

Kilby Bridge

This was established in the earliest days of the canal as a centre for local trade and as an operational base for the line. Alongside the 'Navigation Inn' are two of the Company's houses; the smaller was for the lock carpenter, the larger for the surveyor (the engineer in charge of the canal). Immediately south of Kilby Bridge there are the remains of the industrial workings which grew up on the banks of the canal.

Debdale Wharf

The canal's terminus from 1797 to 1809. The inn (now a private house), wharfinger's cottage, and ruins of the wharf can still be seen.

Foxton to Norton Junction (Grand Union Canal)

The decision of the Union Company not to extend their canal south from Market Harborough was a blow to the Grand Junction Canal Company, which had looked forward to gaining much trade along the 'Leicester line', to and from Leicester itself, and from the Nottinghamshire/Derbyshire coalfield. Some of the Grand Junction promoters therefore determined to sponsor a scheme for an independent canal to join the Union Canal with the Grand Junction Canal. The project was known as the Grand Union Canal (not to be confused with the much later Grand Union Canal formed by an amalgamation of canals in 1929, although in fact the canal under discussion did eventually form part of the 'new' Grand Union). As finally decided by the Engineer, Benjamin Bevan, the new canal was to leave the Union at Foxton, climb the hill by a flight of locks, and follow a level course for 20 miles before locking down to the final summit level of the Grand Junction Canal, which it joined at Norton Junction, just north of Long Buckby locks. Three tunnels were planned, at Husbands Bosworth, Crick and Watford (Northants), although it proved possible to eliminate the last by re-routing. Some anxiety was felt about the water supply (since the boats entering or leaving the canal at either end would cause a loss of water to it) and capacious reservoirs were planned at Naseby, Sulby and Crick. The Company obtained its Act in 1809, and work started, but trouble was experienced in several places, especially at Crick, where the rock formation proved so faulty that Bevan was forced to abandon the original line and find a new one. However, progress was quite reasonable, and the canal was opened on 9 August 1814. There was now a direct waterway link between London and the East Midlands, and on the very first day, two Pickford's fly-boats (express passenger boats) made the journey to Leicester.

Neither the Old Union nor the old Grand Union was commercially successful: both had been too expensive to construct (the Old Union cost over £200,000, the Grand Union nearly £300,000), and the growing competition of the railway system ate into their revenues. The Old Union was helped by having surplus funds which it lent at interest on the security of property in Leicester to approved borrowers, but all the Grand Union's 'nest egg' was absorbed when there was a serious fall in Crick tunnel in 1867, the canal being closed for several weeks. The Old Union had an even more spectacular disaster in 1865, when a section of the embankment at Smeeton Westerby collapsed, draining the pound. In 1894, however, the Grand Junction Canal Company bought both, with a view to developing coal trade between Nottinghamshire and London. They dredged the whole line to Leicester, and installed the famous inclined plane at Foxton, opening the latter for traffic in 1900. The attempt was a failure, however: the traffic did not increase, and after 10 years the inclined plane was closed, as it was costing more to run than the canal was earning. Being part of the Grand Junction, the two canals became part of the amalgamated Grand Union Canal on its formation in 1929.

THINGS TO SEE

Foxton

The locks here are arranged in two 'staircases' of five each, with a passing pound between them. An unusual feature is the presence of large side ponds; these do not work upon the principle of the ordinary side pond, as each takes water from the lock above and passes it to the lock below, but the object is the same: conservation of water. To the east of the locks is the arm constructed to allow boats access to the inclined plane of 1900, and remains of the ramp and the base of the engine room are to be traced between this and the locks. On the ramp, a pair of counterbalanced steel tanks, each big enough to contain a pair of narrowboats, moved up and down, one descending as the other ascended, so that boats, once floated into the tanks, could be raised or lowered in 12 minutes.

Crick

Near the village is a canal tunnel almost a mile long, said by some to be haunted. There is no path over the tunnel: towing horses used to leave the canal at Crick Wharf (where the present boatyard is) and go right round by the village before rejoining the canal at the south end of the tunnel.

Husbands Bosworth

From the horse road over the 1,166-yard tunnel can be seen the upcast mounds marking the site of the working shafts from which the tunnel was excavated.

Welford

At the head of the navigable feeder bringing water to the canal from Welford, Sulby and Naseby reservoirs is a characteristic canal settlement; the former George Inn, now a restaurant, is a good example of a canal inn, built in the early 19th century. There are also cottages, warehouses, the remains of lime kilns, and a small dock, all at the canal terminus.

Watford (Northants)

There are seven locks here, four of which are in a staircase: these have large side ponds, like Foxton. The original line of survey was changed here, hence the sharp curve in the descent. Standing back from the west side of the canal, near the A5, is the former toll collector's house. As this was inconveniently far from the canal an office was built for him beside the second lock of the flight. Note the unusual footbridge at the bottom lock—its blue bricks smack of the railway age.

Gayton (Northampton Arm)

The lock house has the overhanging eaves typical of the early 19th century. Under Bridge No. 4 may be seen early stone railway sleeper-blocks, used to edge the towpath. There are several drawbridges on this branch; they were cheaper to make than brick or stone bridges, and were placed where less important paths or accommodation crossings were required. The North-ampton Arm was opened in 1815, replacing the original tramway that the canal company had laid down between Gayton and Northampton.

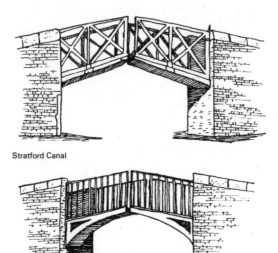

Stratford Canal

Stourbridge Canal

Worcester and Birmingham Canal

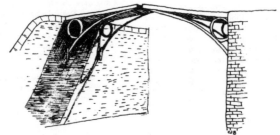

Trent and Mersey Canal

Cantilever canal bridges

The navigable canals
of the Midlands

On the following pages are set out all the navigable canals covered in this book. The maps are at a scale of 2 miles to 1 inch, and are clear and uncluttered to show as fully as possible the road network on either side of the waterways. This will help you to track down by road any particular spot on the Midlands canal network, and to follow any or all of the canals by car—from end to end, if you wish. Locks, tunnels and boatyards are shown on the maps; the last are marked by the symbol Ⓑ and their name and address are given on page 21.

Full details of all towns, villages and features of interest along the way, as well as canalside pubs, are given in the four Nicholson's Guides to the Waterways, which are published by the British Waterways Board.

Lock

(6) Lock flight and number of locks

Tunnel

Worcester and Birmingham canal from the river Severn to Kings Norton junction.

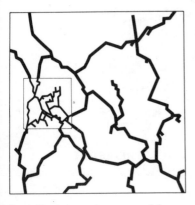

**Stratford upon Avon canal from
Kings Norton junction to
Stratford.**

**Birmingham and Fazeley canal
from Farmers Bridge to Fradley
junction including part of the
Coventry canal.**

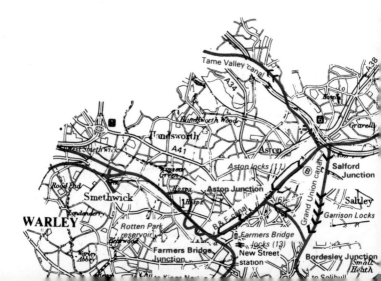

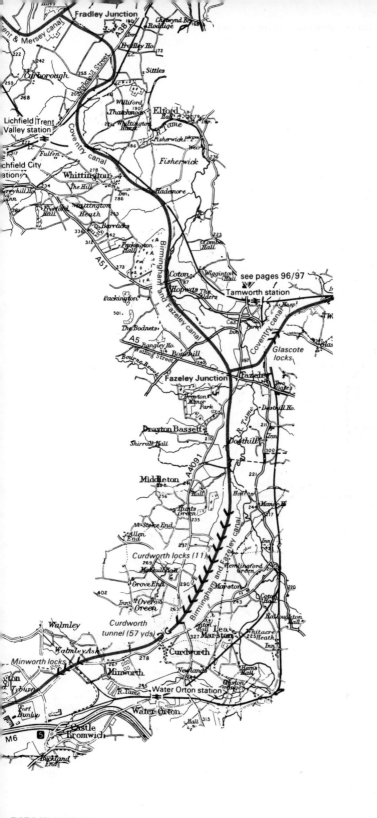

Fradley Junction

Chetwynd Br
Roddige

A38

Fradley Ho.

Curborough

Sittles

Lichfield Trent
Valley station

Williford
Thatchmoors

Elford
Hall

R. Tame

Inn

Whittington
Hrse.

Fisherwick P'r P'

Weir

Lichfield City
station

Fisherwick

Whittington

The Hull

Inn

Hademore

Barracks

Wiggington
Hall

see pages 96/97

Freeford
Hall

Whittington
Heath

Coton

Tamworth station

Packington

Coombes
Hall

Hopwas

The
Alders

Coventry canal

A51

Packington

The Bodnets

Hosp

A5

Rangley Ho.

Bonehill

Glascote
locks

Watling Street

Bourne Bro.

Fazeley Junction

Fazeley

Two
Gates

Drayton
Manor
Park

Dosthill Ho.

Drayton Bassett

Shirrall Hall

R. Tame

Dosthill

Inn

A4091

Middleton

Hall

Inn

Hall

Manor

Hunts
Green

Stoke End

Allen
End

Inn

Birmingham and Fazeley canal

Curdworth locks (11)

Hemlingford
Green

Marston

Grove End

Coton
Hall

Over
Green

Houghton
Hall

Walmley

Curdworth
tunnel (57 yds)

Lea
Marston

Whitacre
Heath

Inn

Wabmley Ash

Curdworth

Minworth locks

Newlands

Hams
Hall

Minworth

Tyburn

R. Tame

Water Orton station

Water Orton

Fort
Dunlop

Hall

M6

Castle
Bromwich

Buckland
End

BIRMINGHAM

Trent and Mersey canal from Great Haywood junction to Stretton.

Trent and Mersey canal from Great Haywood junction to Stoke on Trent.

Staffordshire and Worcestershire
canal from Great Haywood
junction to Tettenhall.

Staffordshire and Worcestershire canal from Tettenhall to river Severn.

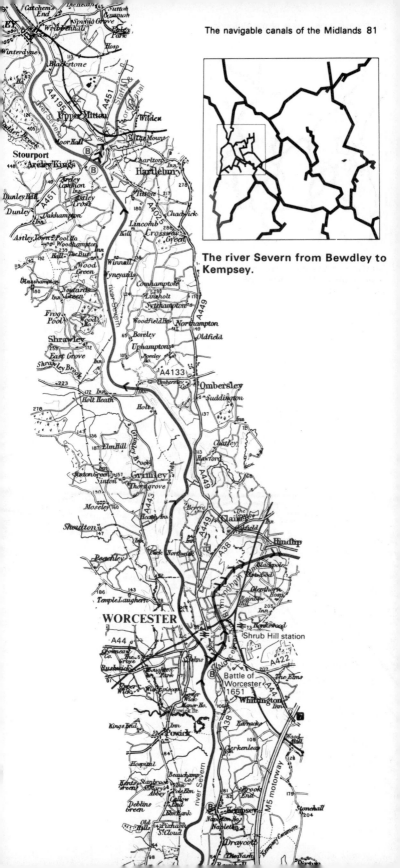

The river Severn from Bewdley to Kempsey.

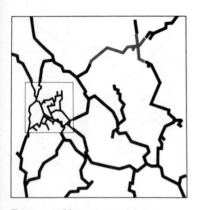

Trent and Mersey canal from
Stretton to the junction with the
river Trent at Derwentmouth,
and Trent Junction.

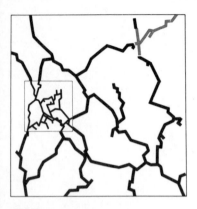

River Trent from the Trent and
Mersey canal at Derwentmouth to
Morton, including the Beeston canal
and the Nottingham canal
deviations.

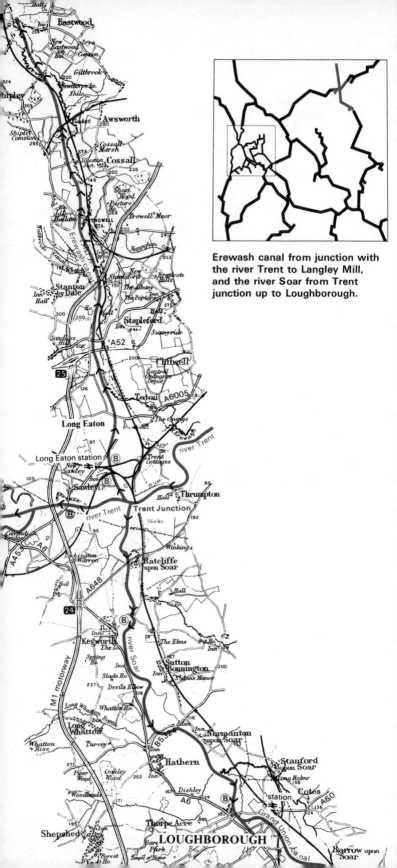

Erewash canal from junction with
the river Trent to Langley Mill,
and the river Soar from Trent
junction up to Loughborough.

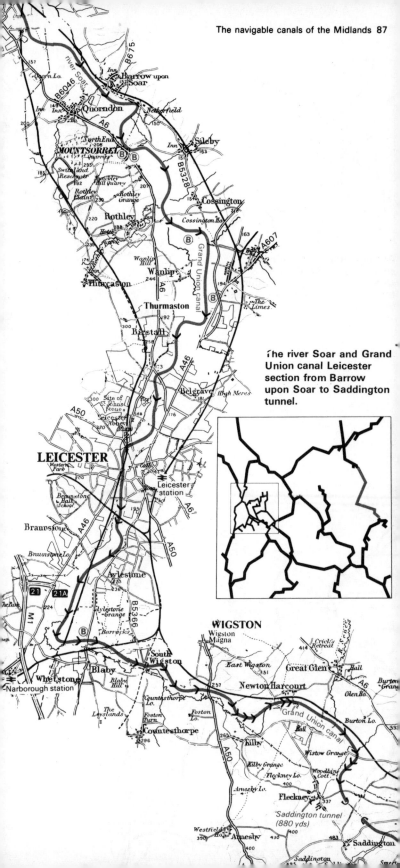

The river Soar and Grand
Union canal Leicester
section from Barrow
upon Soar to Saddington
tunnel.

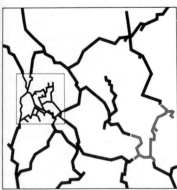

**Grand Union canal Leicester
section from Saddington tunnel
to Norton junction, including the
Market Harborough arm, and the
Welford arm.**

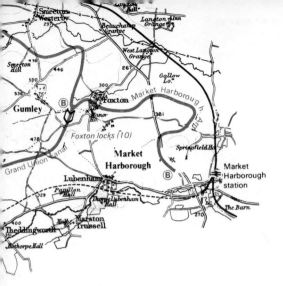

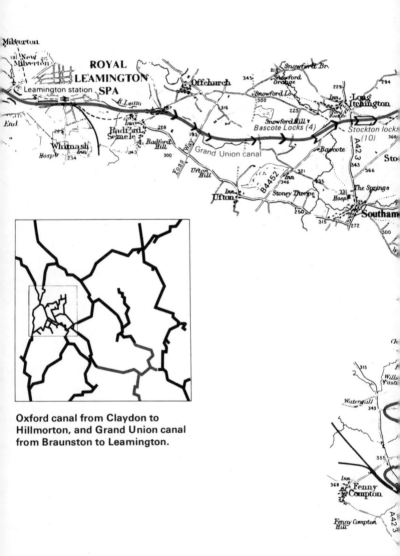

Oxford canal from Claydon to
Hillmorton, and Grand Union canal
from Braunston to Leamington.

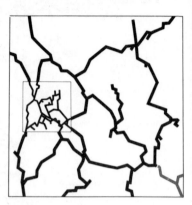

Grand Union canal from Norton junction to Stoke Bruerne and the Northampton arm.

Near Lapworth, Stratford-upon-Avon Canal

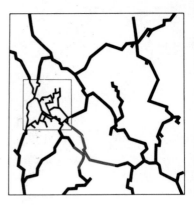

**Grand Union canal from
Leamington to Tyseley.**

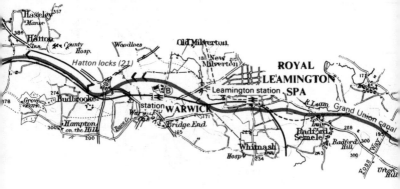

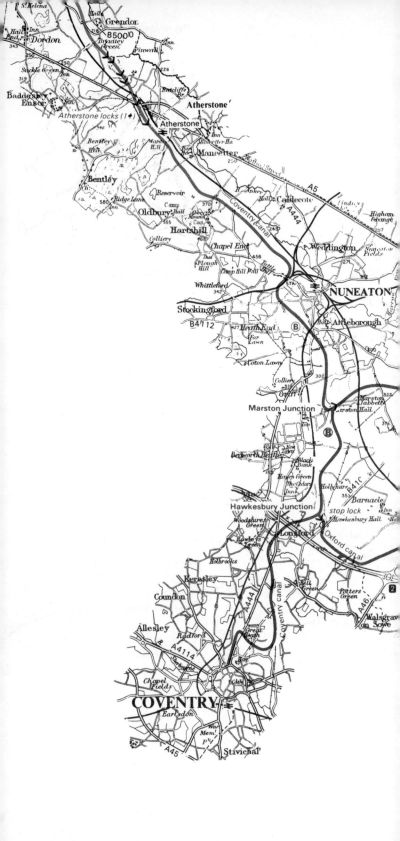

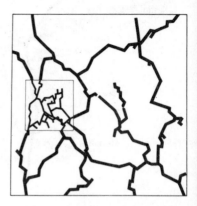

Oxford canal from Hawkesbury junction to Rugby. The Coventry canal from Coventry to Atherstone.

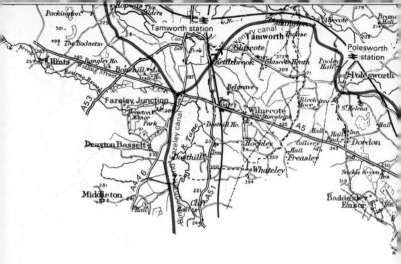

Coventry canal from Coventry to Fazeley junction.

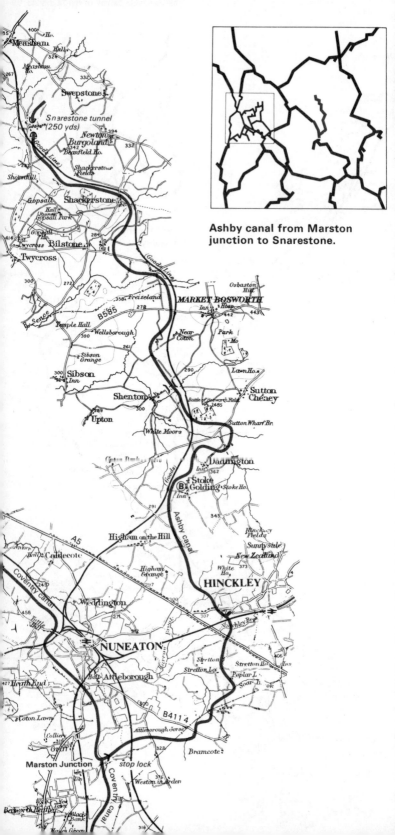

Ashby canal from Marston junction to Snarestone.

Norbury Junction

The BCN network

to Nantwich and
the North West
(see book 2)

to Great Haywood and the Trent & Mersey
Canal (see book 2)

Cannock Ⓑ

Cheslyn Hay

Shropshire Union Canal

Staffordshire & Worcestershire Canal

Essington

Ⓑ Autherley Junction

Alders ley Junction Ⓑ

21 Wolverhampton locks

Wyrley & Essington Canal

6 Bentley locks

Ⓑ Wednesfield Jnc

Bentley Canal

WOLVERHAMPTON

Staffordshire & Worcestershire Canal

Horseley Fields Junction

Birmingham Canal

Bilston

Wednesbury Oak loop

Walsall Canal

Deepfields Junction

Coseley Ⓑ

BWB Bradley
Workshops

Coseley Tunnel (360 yards)

3 Factory locks (20')

8 Ryder's Green locks (45')

Factory Junction

Tipton Junction

Dudley Port Jnc

Birmingham

Wolverhampton level

Albion Jnc

Dudley Tunnel (3,172 yards)

DUDLEY

3 Brades locks (20')

3 Park Head locks (20')

Park Head Junction

Netherton Tunnel (3027 yards)

Oldbury Old

Fens Branch

Blower's Green lock

Bumblehole
Branch

Windmill End Junction

The Sixteen locks (145')

Dudley Canal No 1

8 Delph locks

Brierley Hill

Dudley Canal No 2

Gosty Hill Tunnel (55 yards)

Stourbridge Canal

Stour bridge Arm

Wordsley Junction

Coombeswood
Basin

Stourton Junction

STOURBRIDGE

Ⓑ to Stourport and the South West
(see book 3)

Halesowen

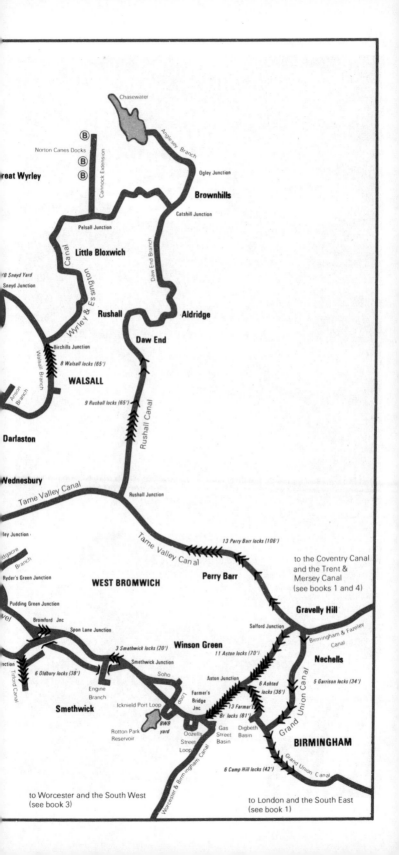

Chasewater

Norton Canes Docks

Great Wyrley

Cannock Extension

Anglesey Branch

Ogley Junction

Brownhills

Pelsall Junction

Catshill Junction

Little Bloxwich

Daw End Branch

WB Sneyd Yard

Sneyd Junction

Canal

Wyrley & Essington

Rushall

Aldridge

Daw End

Birchills Junction

8 Walsall locks (65')

Walsall Branch

WALSALL

9 Rushall locks (65')

Anson Branch

Darlaston

Rushall Canal

Wednesbury

Tame Valley Canal

Rushall Junction

ley Junction

dgacre Branch

Ryder's Green Junction

Pudding Green Junction

WEST BROMWICH

Tame Valley Canal

13 Perry Barr locks (106')

Perry Barr

to the Coventry Canal
and the Trent &
Mersey Canal
(see books 1 and 4)

Gravelly Hill

Bromford Jnc

Spon Lane Junction

Salford Junction

Birmingham & Fazeley
Canal

3 Smethwick locks (20')

Winson Green

11 Aston locks (70')

Nechells

5 Garrison locks (34')

unction

Tilford Canal

6 Oldbury locks (38')

Smethwick Junction

Soho

Aston Junction

6 Ashted
locks (36')

Engine
Branch

Icknield Port Loop

Loop

Farmer's
Bridge
Jnc

Grand Union Canal

Smethwick

Rotton Park
Reservoir

BWB
yard

13 Farmer's
Br locks (81')

Oozells
Street
Loop

Gas
Street
Basin

Digbeth
Basin

BIRMINGHAM

Worcester & Birmingham Canal

6 Camp Hill locks (42')

Grand Union Canal

to Worcester and the South West
(see book 3)

to London and the South East
(see book 1)

An old canal junction on the fringes of the Black Country

Natural history

Stretches of water always add to the natural history interest of an area, and the canals of the Midlands provide a varied and fascinating hunting ground for the naturalist. It is obviously not possible to cover each area individually, nor indeed to mention all the many different species of wildlife that abound, but local Natural History Societies and Naturalists' Trusts are always willing to help those in search of knowledge.

Enquiries regarding Natural History Societies should be addressed to the Council for Nature, c/o The Zoological Society of London, Regent's Park, London NW1 4RY and for Naturalists' Trusts to the Society for the Promotion of Nature Reserves, The Manor House, Alford, Lincolnshire.

The British Waterways Board publishes a free list of nature trails by the waterways. Copies from: Melbury House, Melbury Terrace, London NW1 6JX.

WORCESTERSHIRE

The county of Worcestershire is for the naturalist probably the most interesting area in the Midlands. Its geographical position has given it a wide variety of flora: there are plants from southern England, such as clematis, woolly thistle, stone parsley, wood spurge and grass vetchling; northern intruders like wood cranesbill, oak fern, giant bellflower, sweet cicely and bay willow; others from the west such as Welsh gorse, hemlock, water dropwort and wall pennywort; and greater burnet, saxifrage, fen rush and white bryony from the east and south-east.

As far as birds are concerned, Worcestershire lies far enough west to have dipper, grey wagtail, pied flycatcher and buzzard. Southern species such as nightingale, nuthatch, marsh and reed warblers can all be found here. However, wood lark, redbacked shrike and stonechat seem to have ceased breeding—although the last-named is still seen occasionally. To offset this, waterfowl such as the pochard, ruddy duck and collared dove have all started nesting recently. The corn bunting has changed its status from a rare species to one breeding in many places, and the hobby has bred several times since 1965. In most counties the wild service tree appears to be a rare species, and mainly southern in its range. However, it is present in many woods and hedges, while some specimens are of a fair size—up to around 70 feet tall.

The Worcestershire Trust for Nature Conservation now has over a dozen nature reserves in the county, but as some of these are habitats for uncommon or threatened species, only members can have access. Users of the waterways of the Midlands who visit Worcestershire regularly may well wish to become members of the Trust. They

should write to the Secretary: Mr A. W. Wells, Fox Hill, Ullenhall, near Henley-in-Arden, Warwickshire.

Of the reserves, Broadmoor Wood, Beaconwood, Randan Wood and Newbourne Wood are all good examples of woods across the northern part of the county. The Devil's Spittleful at Kidderminster is a pleasant stretch of heath and birch. Hewell Lake, near Redditch, and Upton Warren Pools, between Droitwich and Bromsgrove, are very good for waterfowl. Eades Meadow and Thorne Meadow, at Hanbury and Inkberrow respectively, are old unploughed meadows unusually rich in wild flowers, some of which are now becoming rare. Most of these come in the category of 'sites of special scientific interest' as defined by the Nature Conservancy, and there are plans afoot to increase the numbers of designated areas.

By comparison, the county is lacking in nature trails. The best known is on the Trust reserve at Ravenshill Wood. There is also one at Kingsford Country Park, north of Kidderminster, which was opened to the public in 1972—the first Country Park in the county.

Droitwich is probably familiar to botanists because of its saline (salt-loving) plants. Unfortunately recent developments have adversely affected many of these, but wild celery, dittander, brookweed, wild parsley and a few others still survive in the original site. Sea milkwort is now more likely to be found along the nearby Worcester and Birmingham Canal. Several others have recently established themselves on the Upton Warren reserve. A series of pools have formed here following subsidence after brine extraction, and these pools, with a local worked-out gravel pit, have become an excellent area for bird-watching throughout the year. Canada goose, great crested grebe, tufted duck and redshank breed regularly and ruddy duck have done so at least once, but the chief interest is the great variety of passage migrants and wintering ducks. Great skua, American pectoral sandpiper, avocet and temminck's stint have all been seen here at least once, while ruff, greenshank, common and curlew sandpipers, dunlin and ringed plover are frequent visitors. Garganey nested here in 1945 and still visit the pools in most years.

Westwood Pool, just west of Droitwich, has two rare aquatic plants. One of these, the ribbon-leaved water plantain, was for some time found nowhere else in Britain but has recently been found in Lincolnshire. The other, one of our two tiny waterworts, grows only under water. Both successfully survived a long period during which the pool was almost dry. Westwood Pool is also good for birds, with occasional visits by Slavonian and black-necked grebes, black terns and bearded tits. It is used as a gull roost in the winter, being especially favoured by lesser black-backed gulls. Pochard bred here in 1967 and a dead mink was found on the road by the pool two years ago.

For well over a century, local naturalists have successfully battled to preserve Hartlebury Common (216 acres just south of Stourport). Just after World War I, there was a proposal to make it into a golf course, which greatly perturbed the naturalists of the day. However, it survived this threat and various others, including a proposal for an atomic power station. In 1867 Mr Edwin Lees enumerated over 40 different uncommon plants which flourished there, including 20 different species of the sedge family. In the very hot summer of 1911, the common was devastated by several heath fires; but when the local naturalists visited it again in 1913 they found to their delight that its 'classic' plants were again flourishing, and to this day the common still retains most of its original wild species. After centuries of abuse by brick-workers, gipsy encampments, heath fires, power stations, herb gatherers, picnickers and depositors of unwanted hardware, it deserves a botanical V.C.!

The common lizard survives on the common, and in favourable weather there are numerous butterflies: gatekeeper, small copper, small heath, skippers, meadow brown, small tortoiseshell, brimstone and comma are all likely to be seen. Dragonflies and damselflies hover about the pools.

The light sand soil, peculiar to this area of Worcestershire, is rich in certain types of plants such as shepherds' cress, knawel, small cudweed, haresfoot and common birdsfoot, buckshorn plantain and moonwort. Some of these have been described as saline plants, but it is merely the very light sand providing conditions similar to some coastlines and not salt, as at Droitwich, that provides a suitable habitat here. The light soil also makes a suitable home for many aliens: some of these do not last long,

but one of them, bladder senna, seems to be holding its own, despite frequent picking of its attractive flowers. Gorse and heather are the commonest plants, with some birch and oak. A small bog remains, and several small pools, where heath spotted orchid, cotton grass, bogbean, marsh cinquefoil, marsh pennywort and various sedges grow. The light soil also suits many insects, especially tiger beetles, burrowing bees, wasps and ants. The latter provide plenty of food for green woodpeckers. Meadow tree pipits, linnet and whinchat nest here, but wood lark, red-backed shrike and stonechat have gone. A great grey shrike may be seen occasionally in winter.

Several other areas of light sand exist round Kidderminster. Heather and gorse are common on some of these. In some places tree lupin is well established and another alien, gallant soldier, first appeared here. There are dramatic outcrops of sandstone in places and these are often adorned with the spikes of wall pennywort. Toothwort is fairly common in a few places. Fly honeysuckle has been known at one site for at least 70 years, and hornbeam is frequent in a nearby wood.

Although the Severn drains most of Worcestershire, it is only below Stourport that the valley is wide enough for the scenery of the river plain to be different in aspect from that of the adjacent countryside. This plain is liable to flooding. There are a fair number of depressions close to the river, the result of extracting soil for making bricks in the past. All have been abandoned now and provide very good sites for plants. Some still hold a fair amount of water and all are wet to some extent. Riverside plants such as meadow-rue, meadow-sweet, purple loosestrife, angelica, black mustard, great yellow cress, meadow cranesbill, comfrey, hemlock and reed grass are most in evidence. Most of them are not confined to these sites but flourish all along the river.

Large stretches of the Clent Hills (between the Worcester and Birmingham and Staffs and Worcs canals) are covered with bracken and rosebay willowherb, and there is plenty of gorse. There are some woods with climbing corydalis, dark mullein and ivy-leaved crowfoot. Oak is colonising the open parts, much of it of the Turkey variety as well as common oak. Further south the Randan and Chaddesley Woods are a nice example of mainly sessile oak, partly on basic clay and partly on acid sand, and the finest wild service tree is found here. Tutsan, violet and broad-leaved helleborines, herb paris, small-leaved lime, dogwood, orpine, bilberry, hard fern, mountain buckler fern and some alder buckthorn are also to be seen.

These woods are rich in insect life. Over 30 different butterflies and many moths have been noted here, including leopard, goat, lime and eyed hawk moths, while the death's-head hawk moth has been spotted twice quite close by. The common ground-hopper and the oak bush-cricket occur here, and six species of shield bug. During a period of tree felling there was an unusual concentration of timber beetles—15 species of longhorns and many weevils. A small herd of fallow deer is now resident in the Clent area and has spread southwards to some extent. Other mammals from this area include common, pigmy and water shrews, dormouse, wood and yellow-necked mice, bank and field voles, noctule, whiskered and natterer's bats, as well as badger and fox. The birds include all the woodpeckers, nuthatch, tree-creeper, all the woodland warblers, six species of tit, redstart, tree pipit and woodcock.

The following areas of Worcestershire have been selected as being of particular interest to the naturalist; at the same time they provide an example to the canal user of the wide variety of wild life that abounds near the canals and rivers of the county.

The Staffordshire and Worcestershire Canal between Dunsley and Wolverley

To the west of the Staffs and Worcs Canal lies the historic area of Kinver Edge. Kinver Edge and Blakeshall Common were for many decades favourite hunting grounds of Victorian naturalists. The rock dwellings excavated into the red sandstone around Wolverley and Kinver have always been a source of speculation and interest; in 1911 members of the Worcestershire Naturalists' Club found dusky crane's bill, shining crane's bill and meadow saxifrage. It is very improbable that any of these survive in the area today, but strangely enough the mountain crane's bill seems to be holding its own in the county. It can often be found on the verges in country lanes that have not been too enthusiastically scraped by the roadmen's machines. Canal users may find it in the vicinity of sandstone cuttings, which it seems to favour.

The western banks of the Severn between Stourport and Worcester

Shrawley area

Between Astley Burf and Holt Fleet lies the little valley of the Dick Brook, which is a very interesting area for both naturalists and archaeologists. There was a mediaeval iron industry along the Dick Brook with forge and furnace sites which have been excavated in recent years.

Another good spot is Shrawley Wood; Carleton Rea, who was in his day the foremost authority in the whole country on the higher fungi, reckoned this the best wood in the country for agarics; many good specimens are still to be found, as are flowering plants and small-leaved lime. Shrawley Wood and Lower Astley Wood are private property, but a number of interesting walks can be taken along the public footpaths shown on the 1-inch O.S. Map, some close to the Severn and some further afield. A pleasant path leads from a lane south of the Dick Brook bridge via Glasshampton Monastery to the village of Astley. The giant bellflower was once quite common in this area, but has now retreated, although the nettle-leaved bellflower is still occasionally seen.

Worcester and its vicinity

A botanical walk in the city of Worcester itself may seem an improbable pleasure, yet there are things of interest to be seen by the observant naturalist. In winter the redpolls and siskins frequent the alders along the Severn banks quite close to the Cathedral, and on the floodplain meadows, among the many black-headed and herring gulls, there is occasionally to be seen a great black-headed gull.

There are two trees of some historic interest to botanists in the city: one is a specimen of the black pear of Worcester, which figures in the city's coat of arms. The fruit was favourably commented on by Queen Elizabeth I during her visit to Worcester, and derives its name from its dark russeting. The specimen growing just inside Cripplegate Park close to Worcester Bridge was planted by the late Duke of Windsor, who as the Prince of Wales opened the park in 1932.

The other tree is the whittypear, or sorb tree, not a true pear at all but one of the *Sorbus* family. It stands in College Green, on the south side of the Cathedral. Although not yet a very large tree, it must be over 60 years old, as this species does not bear a crop of its tiny green 'pears' until it reaches that age. It is slow-growing and long-lived; the leaves resemble those of another *Sorbus*, the rowan or mountain ash, but the bark of the whittypear trunk is much rougher and more fissured.

Plants, like human beings, are given to travelling: in recent years the Oxford ragwort, one of the veteran tourists of the vegetable kingdom, has again arrived on the banks of the Severn. This plant achieved notoriety a few years back when it spread from the Botanical Gardens and colonised Christ Church Meadow at Oxford rather too enthusiastically. It was quite absent from the urban scene in Worcester until a few years ago, when it apparently decided to travel along the railway embankments from Oxford to Worcester, and is now established in various nooks and crannies about the city. Perhaps its Latin name *Senecio squalidus* may not seem to commend it, but in fact the '*squalidus*' refers to its stiff, branched stems.

The Worcester and Birmingham Canal between Tardebigge and Worcester

From Tardebigge to Hanbury Wharf on the Worcester and Birmingham Canal there is some very pleasant countryside with many unspoilt country lanes which are ideal for walking. Good walks can also be taken from several points along the canal south of the old Salt Works (Stoke Works) to Piper's Hill

Common, or Dodderhill Common as it was formerly known. This is a surviving piece of the ancient forest of Feckenham, and one of the most charming pieces of woodland in the county. There is an area of beechwood here which is not common in Worcestershire, and this has a good variety of fungi in autumn. In the north-west corner is a pool where several varieties of dragonflies and damselflies can be seen in the appropriate season. Bird life is always plentiful, and the wood warbler and blackcap can be heard in May and June.

The flight of locks at Tardebigge, with the nearby tunnel and reservoir, are of course classic canal structures, and the surrounding countryside is tranquilly English. Stoke Prior's 12th-century church is particularly fine, and is only a short walk from the canal. From Shernal Green there is a pleasant walk from the canal to Bow Brook at the Shell Ford, where the horned pondweed has been recorded. Walking quietly in the lanes around here on weekdays, one may see lapwings wheeling over the fields, a pair of courting partridges on the laneside verge, a weasel shepherding her family across the road, or even a shrew dashing into the hedge.

THE BIRMINGHAM AND FAZELEY CANAL AND THE COVENTRY CANAL

These two waterways have been closely linked ever since they were built. For right back in 1790, when the Coventry Canal Company was cutting a new waterway link between the Oxford Canal near Coventry and the Trent and Mersey Canal at Fazeley, it became apparent that they would not get much further north than Fazeley. So the Birmingham and Fazeley Canal Company, who were clearly relying on the completed link for most of their trade, built the first five miles for them, and the Grand Trunk Canal Company, who owned what is now called the Trent and Mersey Canal, built the rest. The Coventry Canal Company later bought this section back, but the former 5-mile length remained part of the Birmingham and Fazeley. The Coventry Canal thus has a disjointed length of waterway—and has remained in this state ever since. So the two canals still have this unusual interdependence, and they have many other features in common—including even aspects of the natural history that is formed on or near them.

The Birmingham and Fazeley Canal

This canal leaves Birmingham via many locks, passing under 'Spaghetti Junction' on the way. After Minworth, the city gives way at last to open countryside, and the canal follows the Tame valley, with its conspicuous gravel extraction works. Over the four seasons of the year, and through the many moods of nature, in fair and in rough weather, much interesting wildlife is to be seen both in and along the canal.

The gravel pits, set in the river terraces around Bodymoor Heath, extend to well over 100 acres of deep fresh water. Indeed, some of the workings go almost to the canal. For the past 20 years or more they have become a haven for flocks of waterfowl. Wintering duck comprise mostly mallard, teal, wigeon, tufted duck and pochard, and goldeneye sometimes reach or even exceed 30 in number in the winter. Several pairs of great crested grebe take up residence in spring, where they display ceremoniously and adopt breeding territories in the reedy margins. The bare stony shores are visited by various wading birds at passage migration times, amongst the most frequent being green sandpiper, ringed plover and dunlin. There are also visitors more unusual inland: oyster-catcher, wood sandpiper, greenshank and others. Curlew, with their wild exciting calls, redshank and lapwing breed regularly in the water meadows between the river and the canal. There is a scheme to develop a water park in this area.

Many uncommon spiders inhabit the edges of the gravel pits, and a very small *Linyphiid* spider is numerous beneath certain patches of shore weeds. This is the only site in Warwickshire where this species is known, and it has been recorded from only a few other places in Great Britain. A good deal of plant and animal life worthy of note which has colonised the sandy and gravelly explosures is to be found here, and so some acid heathland flora is now developing. Fly-ash from local power stations is being brought in to fill some gravel pits, in order to restore the land to agriculture.

Most lengths of the canal are enlivened in summer by dragonflies flitting over the water and landing in the reeds. The most frequent here are the brown aeshna, with wings like opaque gauze, two common blue damselflies, the common ischnura, and a few red-bodied dragonflies. Dragonflies spend the early stages of their lives as aquatic creatures and probably it is the organisms from the canal that have populated the newer stretches of water such as the nearby gravel pits. Here on a recent winter's day, when biting frosts brought a sparkling appearance to the canalside vegetation, a stoat was observed to cross from one side of the canal to the other by slithering over the ice and swimming the intervening gap of chilly water.

North of Bodymoor Heath, the canal leaves Warwickshire for Staffordshire. Situated mainly between the 200-foot and 250-foot contours, it falls just below 200 feet near Drayton Bassett. Locks and bridges hereabouts possess some good plant life. Several lime-loving mosses show up in bright green patches especially around water level.

Encrustations of lichens grow slowly on the tops of old walls, extending perhaps a millimetre or two in a year. The plant body, or thallus, consists of two different organisms, a fungus and an alga, growing together in intimate association. They are useful indicators of atmospheric pollution, and those existing in this district are mainly tolerant of or resistant to a large amount of atmospheric pollution. However, there are signs that the air has been generally becoming cleaner in the last few years.

Now, low-lying water meadows extend on either side of the canal, the neutral grassland comprising such common and well-known grasses as cocksfoot, timothy, meadow foxtail, rye grass and creeping fescue, with some sweet vernal grass in damp places. Large flocks of lapwings and golden plover resort to the adjoining fields from September to March. They evidently prefer to feed on arable land, particularly fields which have yielded potatoes as their summer crop. Often lapwings are referred to as 'peewits' or 'green plover', and the golden plover as 'whistling plover'. In spring, before they depart to breed on the northern moors, a proportion of the golden plover develop their full breeding plumage with black patterns on their undersides.

Dosthill Quarry

South of Fazeley, a landmark to the east of the canal is Dosthill Quarry, or Round Hills, as the hilly area is known locally, occurring at an elevation of about 260 feet above sea level. Some places have been worked at Dosthill where the rocks are known to consist of Camptonite Intrusions into the Cambrian Stockingford Shales. The Camptonite, or Dioritic Sills, are rocks of the Cambrian period, about 500 million years old. The outcrops, after working, have developed interesting plant life. Dosthill Quarry became flooded with water in the 1930's, and the rocks, after weathering over many years, have given rise to rich soil conditions. A number of limestone-loving, or calcicolous, plants are to be found at Dosthill Quarry, including milk vetch, musk thistle, rest harrow and burnet saxifrage. A pretty species of larger birdweed, with pink flowers, also grows at the quarry, along with other colourful wild flowers like mullein, lady's bedstraw, musk mallow, greater scabious and welted thistle. Amongst the grasses is early hair grass which has taken root on the bare ground, and there are uncommon spiders which have also colonised the stony wastes. One is a wolf spider, which catches its prey by running in fast pursuit and pouncing.

In recent years scrub has extended around the quarry and it now has quite a well-wooded appearance with 30- and 40-foot oaks, elms and birches, and a horse chestnut which presents a very pleasing sight in May with its white candelabra-like flowers in bloom. A pair of badgers has been noted in the area in recent years.

Near the canal and the river Tame the poisonous plant of the umbellifera family, hemlock water dropwort, is scattered in places along the water-courses. There are several kinds of pondweed, with broad-leaved pondweed probably the commonest: curled pondweed, perfoliate pondweed, fennel pondweed, horned pondweed and the introduced Canadian pondweed all thrive in close proximity. Spiked water milfoil puts forth, above water level, its little spikes of flowers with ruby-red petals and yellow anthers; its feathery leaves weave daintily, gently swaying under the water.

Near the curious canal bridge at Drayton Bassett is Drayton Manor, which was the abode of the Victorian Prime Minister Sir Robert Peel, founder of the police force; it is now a zoo and pleasure park. The grounds are well wooded with long-standing native and exotic deciduous and coniferous trees. A small group of pools at the manor include a duck decoy which was in use at the turn of the century. A nature trail has been set out, focusing attention on the woodland life, birds, insects, mammals and plants to be found living there.

The wide floodplain of the Tame valley is in the neighbourhood of the canal, and floodwater occasionally reaches the roadways. Beside clumps of reeds and rushes, several kinds of sedges grow along the canal banks; great pond sedge and tussock sedge are prominent. Wrens are typical inhabitants of the rank herbage lining the canal, busily seeking insect food in the leafy stems. Small plots of reeds are taken over by reed buntings to accommodate their nests. In places the summer migrant sedge warblers and reed warblers break into song; their cradle-like nests are built in the reeds.

Hopwas Wood

Nearing Hopwas, 2 miles west of Tamworth, the Birmingham and Fazeley Canal and the river Tame almost come together. Boulder clay is left behind and the canal traverses sand and gravel beds at Hopwas and sandstones with pebble beds. There are a large number of different kinds of native deciduous trees and shrubs in the wood, adding character and colour to the dense blocks of dark green conifers. On the hill stand fine oaks and sycamores, and winter visiting redpolls feed on the seed of the graceful silver birches. In summer these same trees occasionally hold the nests of redstarts.

A wealth of woodland birds can be observed from the canal towing path. The alders lining the canal banks attract parties of siskins in winter, and in summer there are breeding green woodpecker, great spotted woodpecker, woodcock, blackcap, garden warbler, and numerous willow warblers and chiff-chaffs, and many other birds in the broad-leaved trees, the Scots pines, larches and other conifer trees. Nightjars and wood warblers have declined in recent years.

Amongst the earliest of the wild flowers to come into bloom are dog's mercury, often out in January or February, and coltsfoot, followed in March by lesser celandine, wood anemone and moschatel which is also called 'town hall clock', then golden saxifrage, bluebell, wood-sorrel and enchanter's nightshade, and hosts of other wild flowers as summer advances. Bilberry is one of the shrubs present, the food plant of the green hairstreak butterfly which is observed at times. Marsh marigolds (also known as kingcups or May blobs) occur by the banks of the canal and create deep-yellow patches. Several badger setts are occupied each year. There are a number of spiders of the woodland, and many small *Linyphiid* spiders may be found in the leaf-mould.

To the north of Hopwas Woods and Tamhorn Park the canal passes through boulder clay again. Pondweeds are apparent in some density and, again, broad-leaved pondweed which has translucent leaves. Pondweeds thrust their flowering spikes above water level for pollination purposes. Water-starwort species and water milfoil also grow in the canal, but only a little water crowfoot is to be found as it is rather unusual in the local canals. Floating water plantain has survived here for a dozen years, but it has not been found in flower. The water weeds harbour an abundance of insect larvae, and midge larvae or red chironomids are numerous. Sedges are spread along the canal banks, hop sedge in one or two places, and also the tufted sedge which has the alternative and very apt name of graceful sedge.

There is good, fertile farming land on each side of the canal, but the Tame valley sand and gravel beds are being exploited at the present time: extraction is going on between Tamworth and Lichfield and the landscape is being drastically altered. Now some of these new gravel pits are showing as expanses of water, and attracting waterfowl and aquatic wildlife; increasing numbers of wading birds scurry along the waterlines. Mallard and moorhen adults often appears with broods of young in quieter lengths of the canal.

Pairs of mute swans frequently breed along part of the canal here, at intervals of a few miles from each other. They have varying success. A few years ago a pair of swans successfully reared a large brood of nine cygnets in this area, but obviously those nesting in more built-up areas come in for more disturbance and their success in breeding is correspondingly less.

Stonewort, a non-flowering plant, is a curiosity here in the canal; it is brittle and requires a good amount of calcium carbonate, as do the shelled animals. Ramshorn snails are plentiful in the canal, as are several kinds of snails with whorled shells. There are also a good many aquatic beetle larvae, such as the voracious diving beetle, and dragonfly nymphs with their 'masks' which they extend to catch their prey.

Caddis-fly larvae crawl on the canal bed, different species constructing their larval cases with different materials—sand grains, small stones, or vegetable matter. Between Fazeley to Hopwas and beyond, on still summer evenings, just before dusk, swarms of small black caddis flies may be encountered. These have been identified as the 'black silverhorns' of the fly fishermen. Kingfishers often hunt here, and water voles are resident.

The Coventry Canal

A stretch of 15 miles or so of the Coventry Canal, from just north-west of Nuneaton to the east and south-east of Tamworth, goes through mainly gentle rolling countryside in Warwickshire, and up to the county boundary with Staffordshire. The plant and animal life found here is generally similar to that typical of southern and south-eastern England.

Near Hartshill, Oldbury and Mancetter the countryside is hilly, at a height of about 300 feet to 350 feet above sea level. Outcrops of Camptonite or Diorite rocks have been quarried here, for use in road metal and concrete aggregates. A number of limestone-loving wild flowers and mosses exist at and around the quarries. Deadly nightshade has survived for many years at one quarry area. Mancetter is, incidentally, the Roman settlement of Mandvessednum, a site of considerable archaeological importance.

Wooded scenery and mature parkland follow the route of the canal which runs past Hartshill Wood and Purley Park to Atherstone, where it is close to the picturesque setting of Merevale Hall where a few small pools nestle. There is much woodland life here to absorb the naturalist. Bentley Park Wood is a site of special scientific interest and contains a large tract of the sessile oak. However, the common oak is the typical tree of the river valleys in this district. (The sessile oak has acorns without stalks and leaves with long stems, while the common oak has acorns with long stalks and leaves with very short stems.)

North-west of Atherstone the canal continues its journey through mainly open, pastoral land, quite intensively farmed. Rich water meadows occur in the Whittingdon-Grendon area, and the canal runs almost side by side with the river Anker, where grass snakes have occasionally been found. Yellow wagtails flit in the wet meadows in the summer months and, with pied wagtails often in attendance, they avidly snap up flies from around grazing dairy herds. The local woods are the breeding places for a selection of 'tree-loving' birds, and the oaks, birches, alders and pines are visited in winter by parties of goldcrests, redpolls and siskin, with roaming bands of four or five kinds of titmice, which may be joined by a tree creeper.

At Atherstone locks the canal drops to roughly 200 feet above sea level. Duckweeds are widely distributed on the surface of the water here, and the reeds include reed sweet grass with stripe smut fungus prevalent on its leaves. On close examination, a variety of insect life can be seen to be sheltered there. The waterside vegetation is visited by orange tip and green-veined white butterflies: eggs of these species are laid on plants such as hedge garlic and lady's smock. The canalside herbage brings to it other butterflies such as small copper, meadow brown, small heath, large skipper, peacock and small tortoiseshells, usually only in small numbers. The china mark moth may also be seen; it is an unusual moth, having an aquatic larval stage. Several kinds of willows line the canal and river sides, mainly goat willow and sallows. There are also crack willows, and osiers which were formerly regularly pollarded, their shoots being much used for basketry work.

Several opencast coal-mining sites have been worked in the Polesworth-Shuttington area, but they have been restored to agricultural use, mainly pasturelands of the neutral grassland type. Now, between 10 and 20 years after restoration of the land, a number of interesting wild flowers have reappeared, including spotted orchids on one or two former opencast sites. The vegetation is diverse on the carboniferous soils in these parts, but the soils display little in the way of lime-loving or acid-loving plants. Water in the canal is slightly alkaline, and there is river alluvium in a narrow belt along the Anker valley.

Alvecote Pools

Mining subsidence from deep mine workings has caused pools to form around the river Anker and the canal in the Alvecote neighbourhood. Although some subsidence took place earlier, most of the land subsided between about 1940 and 1960. The largest pool is of 36 acres, one of three large pools in the course of the river. Today the pools cover about 125 acres of shallow fresh water. Local naturalists began careful study of the wildlife of the pools in 1946. In 1955 the area became a site of special scientific interest; in 1959 Alvecote Pools Nature Reserve came into being after informal agreement between the National Coal Board, farmers and other interested parties, and the area is now managed as a nature reserve by the Warwickshire Nature Conservation Trust.

After extensive study of the natural history of Alvecote Pools for more than 25 years, perhaps the following figures may help to indicate the wealth of wildlife which has colonised the pools. A total of 175 species of birds are known, 80 species have nested there; 350 species of beetle have been identified; 126 species of spider; 150 species of lepidoptera (moths and butterflies); 84 species of land and water bugs; 450 species of flowering plants and ferns, and more than 100 species of mosses and liverworts.

The electrified London–Glasgow railway runs along Alvecote Pools and the canal is situated close to the railway here. The land between the railway and canal, Pooley Fields, contains much of the biological importance of this nature reserve. At Pooley Fields there are a few pools of up to five acres in extent, reedbeds, much scrub development and natural tree regeneration, and waste ground including colliery spoilheaps. In 1963 a nature trail was set out at Pooley Fields, along the old Miners' Path, one of the first nature trails in Great Britain, and the disused Methodist chapel at Alvecote was converted into a field studies centre. (The nature trail guide is available from the Warwickshire Nature Conservation Trust, County Museum, Warwick.) The educational reserve at Pooley Fields, close to the Coventry Canal, has been much used by schools and students since 1963. No doubt much of the plant and animal life which has colonised these recent subsidence pools has originated through the presence of the canal. In or on the canal, whirligig beetles gyrate, and pond skaters reside on the surface of the water; the water spider constructs its 'diving bell' under the water, and several species of water boatmen swim around. Dragonfly and caddis larvae are numerous along the bed of the canal, and many water snails attach themselves to the aquatic vegetation. Great pond snails may be found in the canal, about 2 inches in length.

Freshwater mussels dwell on the muddy canal bed; pea shells, orb shells and others including the zebra mussel and water scorpions lie in the waterside vegetation. Crayfish were frequently found in the canal up to 20 or so years ago, but they are much rarer now. There is good coarse fishing, and the canal is a popular angling venue. However, from 1967, roach in particular suffered many casualties, probably through disease, and they have been recovering only slowly.

In the Alvecote area, water voles and occasionally water shrews may be seen disporting themselves in the canal or scampering in and out of the waterside vegetation. Frogs and toads are also found, but they are rather less plentiful now than they used to be. Small numbers of common newts also settle down in these waters, or, out of the breeding season, can be found hiding away under stones on dry land. Airborne insects over the canal and nearby pools are much sought after by swifts, swallows and martins. In late summer hordes of swallows and sand martins line up on overhead wires near the canal, and thousands roost in reedmace and reedbeds in the valley, before departing for their winter quarters in South Africa. Pairs of reed buntings, sedge and reed warblers nest in the canalside reeds, also grasshopper warblers whose peculiar 'reeling' song has been likened to the unwinding of an angler's reel. Mute swan, mallard and moorhen may nest here too and bring up their families on the abundant freshwater insect life in the canal.

Near Alvecote Bridge grow wild flowers such as nodding and tripartite bur-marigold, gipsywort, yellow cresses, water mint, and the semi-aquatic fool's watercress and lesser water parsnip. There is a luxuriant growth of water-weeds, and some uncommon pondweeds are amongst them. Species of water starwort, water milfoil and the neat and bushy hornwort are other 'aquatics' profuse in the canal. Yellow water-lilies flower well here, and freely develop their bottle-like fruit capsules.

Along the banks, particularly where canal basins exist to provide relatively undisturbed water, various wild flowers bloom during the summer: purple loosestrife, white-flowered water plantain and arrowhead, flowering rush with its gorgeous clusters of pink buds and opened flowers, and yellow flag. One will also see sweet flag, with its sword-like leaves bearing off-centre midribs, and occasionally sprouting its distinctive flower-spike which is called a spadix. In the Middle Ages leaves of the sweet flag were used to strew on floors as they provided a sweet-smelling carpet.

West of Alvecote is Amington. In 1949 an otter was found in the canal bank here in its hole or holt, and otters were occasionally met with in the Anker valley up to the middle of this century, but they have probably been absent from this area for the past 10 or 20 years. At Kettlebrook, on several occasions, carrion crows have been observed to take live fish of about 2 inches in length from the canal and devour them. Great hairy willowherb provides splashes of bright pink when in flower along the canal for a month or two in the summer. Pondweeds again are plentiful, and include the grass-wrack pondweed, and uncommon species of algae which have been found attached to the pondweeds.

Both the Birmingham and Fazeley Canal and the Coventry Canal offer many hours of fascination for the naturalist — and, indeed, for all who are interested to learn about the varied plant and animal life in these areas by quietly looking and listening.

Kilby Bridge—a canal maintenance yard

Patterns of water life in the Midland canals

Like all inland waters, canals present a wide range of both plant and animal forms, and there is always plenty to see. Although much of their water life is similar to that of still waters, there is bound to be in all navigated waterways at least some water flow, which helps to maintain aeration and nutrient supply.

The average width of a Midland canal is 30—40 feet, and its depth is rarely as much as 6 feet at the centre. The bed of the saucer-shaped canal is usually lined with 'puddled' (or kneaded) clay, to prevent any leakage of the water, and the nature of this bed naturally has some bearing upon the creatures living there, although in canals where there is little traffic the decay of canalside vegetation will produce an annual quota of black organic mud. Most canal water, being generally shallow and slow-moving, tends to warm and cool rapidly. As one would expect, more aquatic life is to be found in those stretches which are little used by pleasure craft—but even a regularly used canal is surprisingly rich in flora and fauna.

Plant life

As in most land habitats, the animals to be found are governed by the available plant life which they eat. Food is plentiful in an easily available form: the water acts as an all-round support for submerged plants, and various nutrient salts dissolved in the water can be absorbed, not only through the roots but especially through the leaves.

As a boat makes its way along the canal, even a cursory glance by its crew will reveal the presence of several distinct communities of plants. Those living in the marshy area by the bank, particularly in stretches which are little used, may include the great willow herb sometimes known as 'codlins and cream', whose rose-coloured flowers and tall growth make it so easy to recognise; the feathery creamy-white clusters of the fragrant meadow-sweet; and the lovely purple loosestrife whose tapering spires lean over the quiet waters in late summer. In some areas will be the yellow iris whose sword-shaped leaves mingle with the delicate water forget-me-not and the bur-reeds amidst the various species of rushes and sedges.

One of the commonest plants which fringes the canal bank is the swamp-loving reed grass whose feathery plumes persist throughout the winter months, forming in some places quite dense reed-beds. One may also encounter along the bank the white umbels of the water plantain and the densely packed rose-red flower spikes of the amphibious bistort, its longish leaves and stems floating on the water surface.

At very broad but quiet places on canals, such as Diglis Basin on the outskirts of Worcester, or along unnavigable waterways, one comes across true aquatic plants, rooted in the mud and silt bottom with their leaves floating or even standing above the surface; the white species of water lily is probably the most common. The flowers are borne above the water and are pollinated by insects. The fruit of the white water lily sinks to the canal bottom and eventually bursts, releasing as many as 2,000 seeds, which first float for a few days on the water surface and then sink to the bottom, thus ensuring a reasonably wide dispersal.

The pondweeds are a large and diverse family, and it is difficult to distinguish one from the other. One likely to be seen in large drifts is the broad-leaved pondweed which has largish floating oval leaves. These leaves are, like those of the water lily, platforms for many aquatic creatures, and beneath them may be found the gelatinous egg masses of water snails and the curious oval cases of the larvae of a group of semi-aquatic moths called china marks.

Floating freely on the water surface are the various duckweeds, which in some areas in summer form continuous carpets of green. The 'leaves' of these tiny plants are really short pieces of flattened stem from which a single root hangs down into the water. In spring and summer, budding takes place and then new fronds arise which will eventually break away. A cover of duckweed on a canal is often an indication of a high content of organic matter in the water, where oxygen is likely to be deficient. The Midland canals tend to feature the lesser duckweed with fronds about $\frac{1}{4}$ inch across, the greater duckweed whose fronds may be up to $\frac{3}{4}$ inch across, and the ivy-leaved duckweed. This last differs from the other two in that it lives totally submerged, just below the surface.

Depending upon the amount of water traffic, a number of other truly aquatic water weeds should be encountered. The water starwort is a perennial plant with floating leaves which appear as a star-shaped formation upon the surface. Another plant, the water milfoil, has very long stems bearing large numbers of very finely dissected leaves borne in whorls—a beautiful plant when seen trailing in the water.

Invertebrate life

All these submerged weeds often represent a tiresome obstacle to the steerers of powered canal boats, but it is this aquatic vegetation which provides both food and cover for the larval forms of the many insects that delight the eye as they fly about in the summer sunshine. Feeding upon the weeds will be the grubs or larvae of various species of caddis flies, which build around their soft bodies a housing of weed fragments, small sticks, sand and even tiny shells. These caddis larvae are often called caddisworms. Their case-like homes are built up on a silken envelope which the larva spins before fixing to it the various particles. Each group of species seems to construct similar cases, inside which they are theoretically protected from many enemies; but in fact water birds and fish will often swallow the whole case. Pupation takes place inside the case, but the pupa is unlike those of moths, for when the adult insect is ready to emerge, the pupa bites its way out of the case and swims or climbs to the water surface. The caddis fly emerges crumpled from the pupa case (which acts as a raft), but its wings expand and dry very quickly.

Dragonflies must be the best-known insects frequenting the canals. Their brilliant body colourings and shining membraneous wings are a common sight in summer. There are two main types likely to be encountered: the less frequently seen hawk dragonflies and the much smaller and more delicate thin-bodied 'Demoiselle' dragonflies. Watch out for the pairing habits of the damsel flies, as the smaller ones are sometimes called. The male and female fly in tandem, the male clasping the female at the back of her head by his abdominal appendages. Sometimes the male will hold on to a reed whilst the female partly submerges to lay her eggs. Some species, however, drop their eggs willy-nilly over the water whilst flying. These eggs hatch into nymphs which are active throughout the year, climbing sluggishly amongst the submerged vegetation, or lurking on the canal bottom, their dull brown colour rendering them inconspicuous. They feed upon anything which moves and possess a unique false jaw—a so-called 'mask' which is normally folded back beneath the head but is shot forward when prey comes within reach. The victim is then secured by claws on the mask, pulled back to the mandibles, and slowly eaten. Most of the smaller damsel flies only take a year to reach maturity; those of the hawk dragonflies may take two years.

During May and June large numbers of cumbersome-looking insects will be encountered clinging to bushes and all kinds of vegetation alongside the canal banks. These are alder flies, about an inch long, with long antennae and dull, heavily veined wings, which when at rest are kept folded over the back like the roof of a house. When emerging from their pupae they often crawl about the herbage in large numbers. They are very loth to fly, and even when they do it appears to require such effort that they drop down quickly on to the nearest object. The females, larger than the males, lay medium-brown cigar-shaped eggs, cemented together in masses on reed stems or leaves. From these eggs hatch tiny larvae which wriggle their way to the water where they develop to adulthood. The larval stage lasts almost two years and is spent crawling in the muddy canal bed. When fully grown, in March or April, the larva is about an inch long, cylindrical in shape and brown in colour. The thorax has three pairs of legs, but the abdomen bears seven pairs of jointed structures, which are gills enabling the creature to absorb the oxygen which is in short supply so close to the canal bottom. Throughout its life the larva of the alder fly is carnivorous, seizing with its powerful mandibles any creatures it may encounter.

Also moving along the mud bottom will be the canal scavengers, the multi-legged water skaters sometimes called water-lice or hog skaters. These are extremely common, clambering amongst the plants or amongst the decaying material on the canal bed. Their bodies are flattened from back to front and they have a superficial resemblance to the wood-lice found sheltering beneath bark or stones on the land. They feed upon all kinds of decaying organic matter and spend the whole of their lives in the canal.

On sunny days, numerous creatures are likely to be found living, moving, and feeding upon the water surface of the canal. A number of insects have become specially adapted to this exclusive life upon the surface film. In sheltered stretches the dull black, long-legged pond skaters, or water-striders, will be seen sliding rapidly over the surface. These are predatory insects, which feed upon living and dead insects that happen to fall into the water. Much smaller, and much more fragile, is the tiny water-measurer which may be only $\frac{1}{2}$ inch long, and so incredibly thin that one wonders how all its internal organs can be accommodated in a hair-width of a body. Unlike the much more robust water-strider, the water-measurer picks its way slowly over the surface without making any impression upon the water film at all; despite its own minute size it feeds upon other tiny creatures to be found amongst the vegetation and on the water surface.

A number of other water insects are to be found beneath the water surface. One such creature, the long water scorpion, sometimes called the water stick insect, is common in the Worcester and Birmingham Canal. Its thin brown body may be up to 2 inches long, and with its long thin breathing tube may measure $4\frac{1}{2}$ inches. This rather awesome creature climbs down a reed and waits motionless below the surface, breathing through a long hollow tube like a diver's snorkel until it grabs its prey between its prehensile forelegs, which fold up in scissor fashion like those of a praying mantis. Two other free-swimming insects will be encountered: the well-known water-boatman and the less known, but more common, lesser boatman. The former gives itself away by floating to the surface in order to push the tip of its abdomen through the surface film and thus replenish its oxygen supply. This true boatman of the canals swims upside down and the body, keeled along the back with long fringed oar-like hind legs outstretched at the ready, bears a striking resemblance to a tiny boat. The water-boatman will feed upon any living creature it can attack, and will not hesitate to tackle the young sticklebacks with which the canals abound. The lesser water-boatmen are similar in appearance but may be readily distinguished by their flatter backs and blunter abdomens, and they do not swim on their backs. They spend most of their time in shallowish water at the canal bottom and have to swim to the surface to renew their air supply.

One may often see a heron fishing for the freshwater mussels that abound in the muddy canal bottom, and numerous broken-open shells of the swan mussel lying discarded on the canal bank. These are bivalve molluscs: their shell consists of two valves, hinged along one edge by an elastic ligament. Swan mussels filter food particles from the water and are entirely aquatic. Mussels like a muddy but firm bottom, which is probably why they are so common in many stretches of the canal system. The larger species live half buried in the mud, through which they clumsily plough their way by means of a tongue-shaped foot. Sometimes many of the swan mussels are deposited on the banks of canals by dredging operations, and one can watch their slow arduous movement as they strive to get back into the water. Some of the larger mussels filter several pints of water every hour to extract both the oxygen and the various food particles that may be present. Such a mollusc is useful in an aquarium provided it does not die and decompose. Swan mussels have separate sexes: the females lay eggs into special brood pouches inside the gills, and the males eject their sperm into the water so that it is sucked into the siphons of the female, thus fertilising the eggs. The eggs hatch into a mussel larva called a glochidium which, although it has a bivalve shell, is less than $\frac{1}{2}$ millimetre across when released into the canal water. There the glochidia float about until they come into contact with a fish, to which they anchor themselves, usually on the fish's gills, which grow around the mussel larva like a cyst. Inside, the larva obtains its nourishment from its unfortunate host. Minnows and three-spined sticklebacks are often to be seen with these swellings. After a few months the enlarged young mussels drop from their hosts to become independent on the canal bottom.

Like land snails, water snails require a certain amount of calcium for their shells. It therefore follows that the hardness or softness of the canal water will greatly influence the numbers and species of the freshwater molluscs. Undoubtedly the commonest to be found in the Midland canals will be the tiny Jenkins Spire shell which rarely grows much more than $\frac{1}{4}$ inch in length. Not far from Worcester the attractive nerite is found, an almost globular shell about $\frac{1}{2}$ inch high and up to $\frac{3}{4}$ inch long, varying in colour from yellow through brown to black, but always with irregular pink or purple blotches. It has a reddish-brown operculum (gill cover), like the saltwater winkle, which is only seen when the mollusc is lifted from the water. Related to the nerite and much more common, especially where the canal banks have been strengthened with limestone blocks, are the freshwater winkles. These are large snails with shells over $1\frac{1}{2}$ inches in height and of a greenish-brown colour, with three distinctive brown spiral bands running around each whorl; the operculum is hard and horny. Unlike most other freshwater snails, which are hermaphrodite, this species has both males and females. The females lay eggs which are retained in the body after fertilisation until the embryos have fully developed, when the young snails are released into the water. Other snails likely to be found are the great pond snail, the wandering snail and very occasionally the great ram's horn.

Vertebrates

Among smaller fish, the three-spined stickleback and the lively little minnow are both common in the canals. Whereas the male stickleback becomes resplendent in his scarlet breeding colouring during spring, the male minnow, as well as having reddish patches near to his mouth, appears during early summer with the doubtful embellishment of white tubercles upon head and back. These appear similar to the growth caused by the various odd-looking fish-lice as they bore into the flesh of their hosts—who are mainly minnows, sticklebacks, tench and bream. These lice are common in canal waters, especially during July and August, when they may often be found swimming amongst the various duckweeds whilst waiting to attach themselves to an unsuspecting fish.

Water voles, sometimes called water rats, are harmless rodents, and being very timid only indicate their presence by a splash into the water and a few ripples. They are unlike rats in that they have small ears, blunt faces and short tails, and feed mainly upon water plants. Look for the rushes and other waterside plants that have been bitten off, as well as the small footprints in soft mud. The tell-tale evidence of fish partly eaten and left on the canal bank will surely be the work of the introduced American mink, which is already on the increase from its strongholds in the South Midlands.

and fish thrive in or by the water in rural canals, and many of them in urban canals too. Some of them are so small or inconspicuous that you would never normally notice them; but everything mentioned above can be easily found by anyone who takes the trouble to look. So next time you're walking along a canal towpath, just remember to tread carefully. There's a whole world of wild-life around you. Happy hunting!

Atherstone

Canal feeder reservoirs and their bird life

Canal feeder reservoirs are of major importance as habitats for wild birds and some are of outstanding ornithological value. Belvide Reservoir, Lower Bittell and Earlswood Lakes are designated by the Nature Conservancy as sites of special scientific interest.

Perhaps the most important of these three is Belvide Reservoir (known until a few years ago as Bellfields Reservoir), on the Shropshire Union Canal near Brewood. This reservoir, which feeds the canal, is situated at the northern end of a ridge of fairly high ground, 375 feet above sea level. The surface of the reservoir covers 186 acres, with a brick-faced dam approximately $\frac{1}{2}$ mile long at the eastern end. The shore is low and grass-covered, backed by a low bank which surrounds the whole reservoir. When the water level is low, extensive areas of mud are revealed and, occasionally, shingle banks appear. Thick hawthorn hedges and a small wood on the northern side give the area a rural peacefulness that even the close proximity of the A5, which passes within yards of the north-western corner, cannot spoil. Belvide is one of the few remaining large areas of water in the Midlands that is not sailed upon or extensively used by anglers, and, being relatively undisturbed, has in recent years been shown to support a great variety of birds. Like all sizeable waters Belvide has no doubt attracted birds, particularly wildfowl, since it was completed in about 1830, although interest in birds was not as widespread then as it is today and no records have been preserved.

In the winter months common duck such as mallard, teal, wigeon, tufted duck and pochard collectively number 2,000 or more. Less usual species such as pintail gadwall are quite frequently noted in small numbers, and visits of scaup, smew and merganser are almost annual. The handsome goosander is present throughout the winter and flotillas of up to 40 or more can be seen, Belvide being one of the few places in the Midlands where one can be virtually guaranteed a sight of this bird. Wild swans and geese appear periodically; the rarer members of the grebe family are seen each year, and, less frequently, a great northern diver or red-throated diver is to be found. A large number of gulls roost at Belvide, and a 'blizzard' of several thousand black-headed gulls, herring gulls and lesser black-backed gulls makes an impressive sight as they wheel and turn against the background of a winter sky, gathering to roost. During most winters the rarer glaucous and Iceland gulls, visitors from the Arctic, can be identified. Although

Belvide is notable for its wildfowl in winter, the spring and autumn migration periods often provide great excitement for bird-watchers, especially when water has been drawn off to replenish the canal, revealing stretches of mud. Under these conditions unusual and interesting wading birds are to be seen, and rarities in recent years have included such species as avocet, black-winged silt and pectoral sandpiper. Belvide also offers cover for nesting birds, and the grassy areas surrounding the reservoir provide nesting sites for mallard, tufted and shoveller duck, red-shank, lapwing and reed bunting.

Some 5 miles to the east along the A5 are situated the Gailey reservoirs. These comprise two stretches of water known as Gailey Upper and Lower reservoirs and an adjacent smaller stretch of water known as Calf Heath Reservoir. The Gailey reservoirs supply water to the Staffs and Worcs Canal and, like Belvide, offer a quiet retreat for wildfowl, in spite of their proximity to the M6 and A5 roads. One of their most important features is the heronry, which is situated on a small island almost in the centre of the Lower reservoir. The number of pairs of herons present has, in recent years, averaged 35. These reservoirs tend to attract fair numbers of diving duck such as pochard and tufted duck since these waters do not have any shallow sloping shoreline to encourage surface feeding waterfowl; consequently other species like wading birds, which prefer shallow water or muddy fringes, are not often seen.

Apart from herons, the most notable birds to be seen at Gailey are probably cormorants, which are fish-eating species more usually associated with coastal waters; yet each winter as many as 30 or more roost on the trees of the island where the herons have their summer home.

Just off the A5 between Cannock and Brownhills lies Cannock Reservoir, now renamed Chasewater. This 260-acre stretch of water was impounded to maintain the level of the Birmingham Canal Navigations. The reservoir has two dams, one at the eastern end and one round the south-west side. The pool's exceptionally clear waters are fed by two small rivulets, countless springs and extensive seepage through the Bunter gravel beds which form a major part of the surrounding hills. It is one of the few places in the Midlands where one can regularly see such specimens as scaup, long-tailed duck, scoter, eider and merganser. It has many other unusual species to its credit, and such improbable birds as corys shearwater, little auk and hoopoe have been seen in recent years.

Some interesting passerines (birds that perch) are also regularly seen around the reservoir; species such as stonechat, snow bunting and corn bunting are common, but the area is most notable for the annual resident winter flock of twite. These are small birds usually found on soil heaps and embankments. Chasewater is a regional recreation centre for water sports and other activities. Consequently, its list of breeding birds is now a relatively short one, and such species as mallard, lapwing, curlew and redshank, which favour the type of terrain that surrounds the reservoir, no longer breed there. Staffordshire's canal feeder reservoirs are the best for bird-watchers, but two other such reservoirs are of major ornithological importance in the Midlands area, one in Worcestershire and the other in Warwickshire. The Worcestershire waters are situated on the Worcester and Birmingham Canal 10 miles south of Birmingham, and just south of the King's Norton Tunnel. There are three reservoirs: Upper Bittell, which covers 80 acres, Lower Bittell (22 acres) and Cofton (11 acres), just under the ridge of the Lickey Hills. The reservoirs are all fed by the headwaters of the river Arrow, impounded to supply the Worcester and Birmingham Canal. Bittell reservoirs have attracted the attention of ornithologists for many years past, and some of the rare birds in the Chase collection in the Birmingham Museum are from Bittell.

As with other reservoirs in the Midlands, Upper and Lower Bittell have been extensively watched in recent years, and an impressive list of birds has been noted. Only part of Upper Bittell is accessible by public footpath, and Lower Bittell has no public access at all. Thus the wildlife there has a considerable degree of protection.

The other canal feeder reservoirs of ornithological import are to be found in Warwickshire, about 8 miles south of Birmingham, and are known as Earlswood Lakes. Consisting of three stretches of water totalling 72 acres, they were constructed around 1800 in order to supply the Stratford-upon-Avon Canal, which runs just to the north. Over the years a variety of wildfowl has been observed at these waters, although only in small numbers, for Earlswood Lakes have never supported large colonies of duck. Lack of shorelines does not encourage wading birds, although these do appear from time to time.

There are several smaller canal reservoirs such as Tardebigge in Worcestershire and Napton in Warwickshire which have also provided interesting records of birds at times, but it is those major waters referred to earlier that are so important to the birds of the Midlands.

Great Haywood Aqueduct, Staffs and Worcs Canal

Bird life of the Trent and Mersey canal

The region of the Trent valley around Burton-on-Trent and Derby lies on one of the principal bird migration routes across the country, and the gravel pits in the Sawley-Shardlow, Clay Mills and Branston area attract many interesting and unusual birds. Across the river from Branston gravel pits (2½ miles south-west of Burton-on-Trent) lies Drakelow Wildfowl Reserve, containing gravel pits and fly ash pools which the Central Electricity Generating Board, with the co-operation of local ornithologists, have turned into a reserve, complete with a nature trail in nearby woodland. (The nature trail booklet is available from the Public Relations Dept, Central Electricity Generating Board, Midland Region, Hashicks Green Road, Shirley, Solihull, Warwicks.) These areas are all closely watched by local ornithologists and in terms of variety and numbers of birds to be found here they represent one of the most worthwhile birdwatching sites in the Midlands. The Trent and Mersey Canal runs right past all the places named below.

Dabchicks (little grebes) can be seen along the whole length of the canal; they breed amongst the reeds and overgrown vegetation. The nest is usually well hidden—a rotting mass of vegetation often very close to the water—because grebes are primarily water birds and only come to the land in order to nest. The grebe is very shy and if disturbed it will submerge immediately and make for the nearest cover. The beautiful great crested grebe with its unmistakable summer plumage—dark double-horned crest and reddish-brown neck—can only be seen on the gravel pits at Clay Mills (just northeast of Burton-on-Trent), Branston and Drakelow. It is a wonderful sight in spring to watch their striking courtship display. The nest on which the grebe lays her clutch of eggs consists of a tangle of floating water-weed and other aquatic vegetation. The young hatch out after approximately 28 days and immediately take to the water, although while they are very young they are carried on their parents' back for much of the time. The birds are usually migratory and move to larger waters, such as Eye Brook Reservoir in Leicestershire and, to a lesser extent, Staunton Harold Reservoir in Derbyshire. In winter they lose their reddish-brown colour and are generally black on the head, back and wings, and white elsewhere. Occasionally these birds can be seen on the river Trent near the start of the Trent and Mersey Canal at Derwentmouth.

There are no longer any heronries in the Trent Valley, but herons can still be seen standing silently in the marshy ground waiting for unsuspecting prey. They can also be seen flapping over the canal, especially in the Clay Mills-Willington area and also around Shardlow and Sawley from July onwards, when breeding birds and their young disperse. In 1968, on a patch of marshy ground surrounded by willow thicket near Shardlow, purple heron, cattle egret and bittern were seen, but these were all visitors to the area.

October to April is the best time to see wildfowl: Shardlow and Sawley are very good for viewing teal, and sometimes up to 100 of these beautiful little ducks can be seen. Similar numbers of wigeon can be seen, drawing attention to themselves with their distinctive whistling call. The common mallard may nest in the area, and pintail, shoveller, gadwell and garganey have also been noted, the last usually between late March and May. When the river floods and large expanses of water are left, diving birds such as tufted duck and pochard frequent the area in small numbers, and the expanses of water also attract Bewick's swans to this part of the valley. Since 1968 flocks of up to 35 wild swans have spent from January to late March in this area. These are doubtless birds starting their return migration to northern Russia, possibly after having spent part of the winter in southern Ireland or at the Wildfowl Trust grounds at Slimbridge, near the Gloucester and Sharpness Canal.

Clay Mills, Egginton No. 7 gravel pit (near the canal between Burton-on-Trent and Willington), Branston gravel pit and Drakelow Wildfowl Reserve all attract up to 200 tufted duck. There are similar numbers of pochard from September to March, and many a quiet hour can be spent watching the mixed flock. Tufted males are easily identified by their black plumage and white flanks, with a conspicuous tuft on the back of the head. Male pochard are identified by their red head, black breast and grey body, the female being drab and brown. Tufted duck can be seen during the summer, some pairs attempting to breed, whereas pochard are migratory and are not seen in summer. Goldeneye, another migratory species, can usually be spotted in small numbers amongst the diving ducks. Up to 500 teal and smaller numbers of wigeon have been seen in the Clay Mills area, whilst goosander is another speciality of this area, mainly from December to March. Eider and long-tailed duck, both species of sea duck rarely seen inland, visited Clay Mills gravel pits

Emscote

during 1971. Small numbers of Bewick's swans can also be seen during the winter.

A pair of mute swans is a common sight on any part of the canal, but with increased use of this waterway by pleasure boats, nesting has not been very successful recently. Coot and moorhen are frequently to be seen all along the canal, although the moorhen tends to be somewhat shy. Sometimes Canada geese can be spotted, although they are usually heard first, their 'honking' call being most distinctive. Flocks of up to 200 can be seen at Clay Mills and Drakelow.

Owing to the recent increase in pesticide pollution, the only bird of prey likely to be seen along the canal is the kestrel. This species is again on the increase, partly because modern trunk roads like the A38, with their extensive grass verges, attract the small mammals on which this species feeds, and the sight of a kestrel hovering virtually motionless with rapidly beating wings and tail outspread as it searches the ground below for its prey is once again becoming fairly common. As with most species of hawk, the male is smaller than the female and is more beautifully marked, having black spotted chestnut upper-parts and a bluish-grey head, rump and tail; the under-parts are buff with dark streaks.

Partridge are fairly common along most of the length of the canal, but they have to be looked for, and are nowhere near as conspicuous as the handsome cock pheasant. The large hen pheasant is very drab in colour, but try to spot her when she is incubating her large clutch of eggs, perhaps hidden in the towing-path hedge, when the excellence of her camouflage becomes obvious. Wading birds tend to like marshy and wet areas, but large numbers of lapwings can be seen in the ploughed fields and rough grazing land along the canalside. One of the finest sights of spring is a lapwing tumbling and twisting in its display flight. Nesting starts in early April, and as soon as the young hatch they can move from the nest—usually just a scrape in a ploughed field lined with grass stalks. Flocks start to build up again in June and can be seen anywhere along the canal. Lapwings provide an advance warning of a hard winter as they tend to move south in huge numbers before its onset.

Golden plover often associate with lapwings in winter, and the fields between Willington and Clay Mills are one locality favoured by this species. With their breeding plumage of black cheeks, throat and under-parts, and golden brown upper-parts, they are a most beautiful sight; the birds assume this plumage from March onwards.

Three other species of waders can be found at various times: the curlew, with its long curved bill and distinctive call, usually spends the summer in suitable haunts along the valley, but is unfortunately becoming scarce—although Drakelow has a fairly large roost of this species during summer and early autumn. In winter, snipe can be seen along the canalside, especially in hard weather when the marshy ground is snow-covered and hard with frost. Redshank also breed at some sites throughout the year. Their distinctive call and sharp eye, which spots intruders before any other species, aptly gives them the name 'the warden of the marshes'.

Common sandpipers can sometimes be seen feeding by the side of the canal, and rarer species like black-tailed godwits have been seen near Shardlow and Aston-on-Trent. The gravel pits at Willington, Egginton No. 7, Clay Mills, Branston and Drakelow are favoured spots for little ringed plover, which usually appear in late March and depart again in September. These areas attract such species as ringed and grey plover, jack snipe, bar-tailed godwit, green and wood sandpiper, spotted redshank, greenshank, turnstone dunlin, sanderling and ruff. Such rarities as little stint, curlew sandpiper, temminck's stint and avocet have been noted at Clay Mills and Drakelow Wildfowl Reserve.

Many people think of gulls as being confined to coastal areas, but over recent years the birds have become increasingly attracted to the many inland rubbish tips and sewage works to be scavenged, and to the growing number of large reservoirs for roosting and bathing. Any one of the five common species of gull, namely great and lesser black backs, herring, common and black-headed gulls can be seen flying over the canal—the last two actually feeding on the canal. Black-headed gulls are present all year round although they do not breed (they need a cliff habitat for this), whilst the other four can usually be seen from August to April. Rarer species such as the kittiwake have been seen at the confluence of the rivers Trent and Derwent, and glaucous gull, the big white gull of the Arctic, at Drakelow Wildfowl Reserve. Cormorants can also be seen flying over the area, and were fairly numerous from September to December 1970.

Whilst going through Shardlow by canal, keep an eye open for the collared dove; this species was only seen in this country for the first time in the mid-1950's. Their distinctive call—a triple 'coo-coo-coo'—can usually be heard in this area. Wood pigeon can also be seen along the canal, and during winter some large flocks build up to feed on any available field. Stock doves are more local but can be spotted in the Shardlow and Clay Mills areas. The migratory turtle dove seems to be getting scarcer, and now it is only on the sewage works at Clay Mills that it can be found with reasonable certainty during the summer.

Owls, not usually seen during the day, can often be heard at night calling from cover. The tawny and little owls are the species to listen for. The barn owl may be seen as a ghostly white form at dusk or may be picked out by its long eerie shriek, and the tawny owl may be recognised by its well-known 'hoot'.

Although Weston Cliff and the woods which lie just across the river Trent used to ring to the 'yaffling', laughing call of the woodpecker, today it is rarely heard. The green woodpecker in particular is becoming very scarce. Great spotted woodpeckers are slightly more common and have been noted at Shardlow, Weston Cliff and several other spots along the canal.

The hedgerows and vegetation bordering the canal begin to come alive at the end of March as the small birds start nesting. Blue and great tits are common, but coal tits have to be looked for. Willow tits can be seen at any time of the year, usually in small numbers, and occasionally a small party of long-tailed tits can be seen moving along the hedgerow, with their undulating flight and long tails, mainly black and white plumage and distinctive 'zee-zee-zee' call. When the young are fledged they usually form small mixed parties, and during the winter goldcrests can often be found with them.

The month of April is taken up with the passage of summer migrants; sand martins are usually among the first to reappear, and can be seen hawking insects over the canal. These birds tend to breed in the banks of gravel pits and the river Trent. Swallows usually appear about mid-April and make a lovely sight swooping over the surface of the canal. From late July onwards the young can be seen perched on branches or bushes waiting to be fed by the adults. House martins with their distinctive white rump are to be seen from late April, and nest under overhanging eaves by the side of the canal at Shardlow. Swifts can be seen from the beginning of May: it is captivating to see a party of screaming swifts performing aerobatics. They are the first to depart, leaving in August, whilst sand martins leave by mid-September and swallows and house martins linger on into October. The flocks of swallows and martins which perch on telegraph wires before leaving for their long journey to Africa for the winter are a sight characteristic of late summer.

Another early migrant is the chiff-chaff, which can be heard singing its own name repeatedly – 'chiff-chaff, chiff-chaff'. They can be seen from late March and care has to be taken to distinguish them from the very similar willow warbler. Both are marked with dark greenish back wings and crown, yellowish tinged breast and flanks and white under-parts. The best method of identification is by voice: the willow warbler's song is a series of wistful descending notes, somewhat more tuneful than the chiff-chaff's monotonous call. Any patch of reeds or thick vegetation by the side of the canal may turn up a sedge warbler; a continuous jumble of notes often gives it away, with its clear white eye stripe and streaking on back, mantle and crown. Reed warblers are usually to be found in reed beds and are

not very common, although birds may be seen and heard on passage. At one time whitethroats were very common, but since 1969 numbers have declined drastically, and they are now very scarce. When travelling along the canal, if a sound like a fishing reel is heard from some thick clump of bushes, it is likely to be a grasshopper warbler. Other species of warblers that may be seen are blackcap, garden warbler and lesser whitethroat.

Wheatear is another early migrant en route for the moorlands of the north, and may be seen flashing its prominent white rump and tail base. Whinchats come through the area from late April and may be seen perched on top of bushes or plants. The male is more prominently marked than the female and has a distinct white eye stripe, dark cheeks, streaked brown upper-parts, and rusty-brown throat, breast and under-parts. Cuckoos are more likely to be heard than seen, mainly from mid-April onwards; they lay their eggs in other birds' nests, picking on such species as the robin and the hedge sparrow which are commonly seen along the canal.

Spotted flycatchers can often be seen from early May, busily living up to their name. They make regular sallies from their perches on branches and fences in search of flies, returning to their perch to devour their catch. 'Spotted' refers to their streaked breast and throat, the upper-parts being grey-brown and the under-parts greyish-white. From early April it is worth looking for yellow wagtails along the banks of the canal, marked by a beautiful flash of bright yellow breast and under-parts. They tend to stand and bob and wag their tail up and down; late September sees them departing for warmer climes. Pied wagtails are with us all year round, recognisable by their black and white plumage. Also to be seen here are the meadow pipit, common all along the canal, and the much rarer water pipit, which is gradually increasing as a wintering species in this country. Pipits are common at Clay Mills and Drakelow. Skylarks are also very common and their lovely songflight is a feature of any good day in March or April.

From October to April the fieldfare and redwing can be seen searching for food on the fields by the canal. Again Shardlow is a good area for these, especially the willow scrub near Derwent Mouth Lock. The fieldfare is the size of a mistle-thrush but is easily identified by its blue-grey head and rump, combined with a chestnut back and distinctive 'chack-chack' call. Redwings are the size of the song thrush, but are distinguishable by the combination of the white eye stripe and reddish flanks and underwings. During October and November the distinctive call of redwings, a thin piping 'seep', can be heard at night.

Chaffinch, greenfinch, goldfinch, bullfinch and linnet can all be seen alongside the canal; a charm of goldfinches feeding on thistle heads is a particularly lovely sight. In winter their northern cousins siskin and red-poll may be seen, especially in alder trees. A typical bird of the canalside vegetation is the reed bunting, the male looking very elegant with his black head and throat, white nape and streaked brown back and wings. The under-parts are white with streaks on the flanks, and the tail is brown with white outer tail feathers. Corn buntings are indigenous to this area; their call has been likened to the jangling of keys.

Thus there is an enormous variety of birds to be found in this part of the Trent valley—particularly, of course, at the gravel pits mentioned above and at Drakelow Wildfowl Reserve. This abundance of bird life is perhaps surprising, for the Trent valley is well populated, and busy road and rail routes run along it. But the birds clearly thrive on their particular habitats in the region and this part of the Trent valley continues to be excellent bird-watching country.

Bratch Locks, Staffs and Worcs Canal

Great Haywood

Canal walks

Towpath walking has many attractions. The canal towing-paths were constructed to enable horses to pull the boats before the days of engines. Today, they provide scope for delightful walks. Some of the paths are overgrown and eroded, and strong shoes are desirable. The scenery has qualities different from the rest of the countryside, resulting from the construction and subsequent use of the canals, and nature has worked on man's creation to produce an unusual effect. Wildlife, in the form of both animals and plants, abounds all along the line. But the human mark is apparent everywhere and round each bend is a piece of history: perhaps some feature of early engineering, or a cottage that was once a boatman's inn.

A Midland Red bus timetable showing all the local bus routes is a useful asset, for even the most experienced 'canal rambler' can get caught out, or wet through at times. As well as strong shoes, light rainwear and a small haversack are recommended. Polythene bags are invaluable for protecting maps and sandwiches; a large one is useful to sit on in damp conditions.

The Stratford-upon-Avon Canal

Where the A435 leaves Birmingham's outskirts, it crosses the canal at Millpool Hill beside the Horseshoe Inn, which was built to capture the custom of both the casual traffic on what was then a quiet road, and the trade of the canal. From here to where it enters the river Avon in Stratford-upon-Avon, this canal is a walker's dream. The banks are dotted with cattle, old cottages and canalside inns. It is particularly enjoyable to walk this canal in the late autumn, when the hips and haws are out and the blackberries still hang, although one should not be tempted to pick them since, according to ancient lore, the devil puts his foot on them come the first days of October.

At Lady Lane Bridge is a large and thriving boat club, boatyard and moorings, and here the feeder comes in from Earlswood Lakes. These three reservoirs, with a total water area of 72 acres, are fed from the waters of the Spring Brook. Near the canal, they are well worth a visit and are much used by yachtsmen, fishermen and bird-watchers. Pleasant, quiet walks can be taken around the lakes, and rights-of-way run into the ancient Earl's Wood, where there is a nature trail. (Trail guide available from The Museum and Art Gallery, Congreve Street, Birmingham 3.)

A little further along is the fine National Trust property of Packwood House, standing within easy walking of the waterway (see page 143). Nearby is Baddesley Clinton's moated manor, one of the finest houses of this type in England. Try to find time to visit the church with its plain Norman font and interesting windows—particularly the east window. The font is fitted with a locking staple, a relic of the times when fonts were locked against the fear of witches stealing the baptismal water—evidently worth its weight in gold for spell-weaving!

Henley-in-Arden is worth exploring for its varied architecture: the ancient cross, church, guildhall and great high motte and bailey of the castle of Peter de Montfort. Lovely old buildings grace Wootton Wawen, including a famous old inn and the church, sometimes described as three churches in one, with the famous 'Saxon Sanctuary' under the tower. There are traces of the old monastic fish-ponds, and the river Alne flows through at a picturesque spot. The canal crosses the A34 here on a sturdy iron aqueduct; there is an attractive modern boatyard, a basin and a pub at this point.

At Temple Balsall is the ancient church of the Knights Templar, built on several levels to suit the degrees of this knightly order which, having acquired great riches, fell into trouble and was finally disbanded. The church has been lovingly restored. Here also are the great almshouses, excellent examples of the architecture of their time.

At Lapworth a short linking canal goes from the Stratford-upon-Avon Canal to the Grand Union Canal. An interesting diversion can be made from here to the church in Rowington village—about 2 miles southeast along the towpath of the Grand Union. The two old parish chests in the church were operated by three locks, the keys held respectively by the priest, the priest's warden and the people's warden: opening the chests required all three to be present. Rowington church also contains a 15th-century stone pulpit—a rarity, since pulpits were not used much before the Reformation.

The Worcester and Birmingham Canal

The walk over King's Norton (Wast Hill) Tunnel following the track of the boat horses is interesting, with the ventilating shafts for the long tunnel peeping above the earth. South of the tunnel are the great canal reservoirs of Upper and Lower Bittell, with yachts on the former and bird-watchers with their binoculars trained on the latter. The canal does a little twisting and turning before reaching Alvechurch. Now serving as a commuter village to both Redditch and Birmingham, the centre, on both sides of the A441, still contains much that is old and beautiful. There was a grange of the Abbots of Worcester here, of which moat traces remain. The great church sits high on its hill and is well worth a visit if only to inspect the tomb of an unknown 14th-century knight, for his effigy is clad in a suit of armour that was only in use for five years—from 1345 to 1350.

At Tardebigge many pleasure boats are clustered about the old wharf buildings at one end of the canal tunnel. Tardebigge Church is set on the hillside above the canal, and in the churchyard there is a seat from which to admire the view; beautiful traditional carving can be seen in the classical figure of a weeping woman by Chantrey. The present church, with its windows and delicate interior wall colouring, replaced a much older edifice. Nearby is Hewell Grange. Now a remand home, this was once the seat of the Earl of Plymouth: the Plymouth family owned the manor of Stanwell near Windsor but, in 1542, Henry VIII forced them to exchange it for Hewell and the surrounding estates.

Not far from Tardebigge Wharf the canal begins to descend the great Tardebigge Flight of 30 locks, passing the tree-lined feeder reservoir and reaching Stoke Pound, Stoke Works and Stoke Prior. Here is a very early experiment in planned villages: John Cobbett made a fortune from the brine springs of Stoke Prior and made good use of his money by building a model village for his workers. Here also is the 'Boat and Railway' inn: it clearly owes dual allegiance to the two rival transport systems that flank it. Less than 2 miles further on one can leave the canal either by delightful deep lanes or fieldpaths pointing eastwards to Hanbury Hall, which is under the care of the National Trust (see page 144). Hanbury Church, perched high on the hill, has a lovely old cross (note the shell fossils in its pillar). It was once the spot where travellers, about to enter the fearful depths of Feckenham Forest, prayed for safe keeping.

Below the ancient salt way near Hadzor, there is a wide area of interest to explore. Half a mile westwards is Hadzor College, a Roman Catholic establishment with the old and interesting Anglican church in its grounds. Hadzor also has a beautiful Catholic church with a window dedicated to St Richard, who miraculously restored the flow of the salt wells at Droitwich when they had dried up. Droitwich itself—once the Salinea of Roman times—ranks as one of our oldest settlements, and from it radiate ancient salt ways. Salt was vitally important in early times for salting down the cattle which had to be killed off as winter approached, since the growing of winter cattle feed was unknown. In later times it was transported by canal.

Just above Tibberton and below Oddingley, the canal makes a westward sweep.

The district to the east of the canal has some lovely half-timbered houses: Crowle Court, 2 miles by lane or 1½ miles by fieldpaths from Tibberton, and Huddington Court, nearer to Oddingley, are two good examples. Many of these old houses have one or more hiding holes to shelter a priest.

The Staffordshire and Worcestershire Canal

From the great basins beside the river Severn at Stourport, the canal leads off to the north along the Stour valley. A corridor of warehouses introduces the old-established carpet-weaving town of Kidderminster. There is a short tunnel here.

From Cookley, where the canal negotiates a little tunnel under the main street, fieldpaths or lanes lead to Kinver: here is a great high stretch of tree-clad hills with caves, now a Country Park. At Stewponey is the junction with the Stourbridge Canal. On the Staffs and Worcs Canal, walking should be confined to the west side where narrow lanes and tracks lead across to Enville Common and, further north opposite Swindon, Highgate Common. Although the canal is now flirting with the so-called 'Black Country', one would never realise it, and to the west, wide areas of interesting walking country laced with fieldpaths and bridleways can be explored.

Further north, beyond Autherley, the canal loses its isolation, being crossed by several main roads and railways, while around the Penkridge area the M6 motorway follows the canal closely, so this is no place for a quiet walk. North of Acton Trussell the motorway moves off to the west, but the best walking countryside is a few miles on, beyond Stafford. Here the canal joins the valley of the river Sow, but the busy railway which accompanies it does not spoil the valley's attractiveness. There are few roads in this relatively secluded valley and the best route to follow is the canal towpath itself, which is carried by a low, heavy aqueduct over the river near the village of Milford.

If you continue walking east along the canal you will reach Tixall, where the waterway opens right out into an artificial 'wide'. On the hill is Tixall Gatehouse, all that remains of a former Elizabethan building, and straight ahead is another aqueduct—over the river Trent—and Great Haywood Junction, where the Staffs and Worcs Canal meets the Trent and Mersey.

The Shropshire Union Canal

The Shropshire Union passes through pleasant walking country, with quiet bridleways and fieldpaths on either side. Over the Roman Road (A5) by Belvide Reservoir, through Wheaton Aston, Church Eaton, Coton and High Offley, many interesting walks can be taken from the towpath. There is a particularly good one by bridleways just past Knighton to the vast area of Bishop's

Wood; a trip, if one explores the woodland, of 8 miles there and back to the canal.

Birmingham and Fazeley Canal

At Curdworth, the outskirts of Birmingham have been left behind and there is some delightful walking country to be explored. Curdworth itself is interesting and the old church should be visited. North of the little damp tunnel in Curdworth is Bodymoor Heath: the great complex of lakes formed from old quarry workings are quite close to the canal. Many types of water birds can be seen here. Kingsbury, a little over a mile east from the towpath, has another interesting church.

A mile westward from the canal, reached by a fine old lane, is Middleton, with the remains of its old hall. Through Fazeley, the canal then runs neck-and-neck with the river Tame for a space, passing the wide expanse of Hopwas Wood to link with the Coventry Canal.

The Trent and Mersey Canal

About 4 miles from Fradley Junction, westward along the Trent and Mersey Canal, is the Ridware country. The name seems to denote 'river folk', and the whole district is splendid walking country. A couple of miles westward from the towpath at Rugeley, where the former Armitage Tunnel has been opened out, one can become immersed in the vastness of Cannock Chase which was once a Royal Forest. Richard I, needing money for his crusades, sold much of the area to the Bishop of Lichfield. Only kings could own hunting forests, so the place lost its royal title and became a chase. Cannock Chase covers 30,000 acres and several days are really needed to explore it thoroughly. Deer can often be sighted, and the breathtaking beauty of Spring Slade with its crystal-clear brook draws walkers from all over the Midlands. An information post in Milford village gives details of walks and nature trails in the Chase. At the south end of the Chase is the big canal-feeding reservoir of Chasewater which is much used for water recreation.

Through industrial Burton-on-Trent, the north-western side of the canal affords numerous short excursions into the countryside, especially around Egginton where the rivers Dove and Hilton run through the flatlands.

Canal walks in Leicestershire

The canals in Leicestershire run through an area of peaceful, unspoilt countryside which provides many pleasant towpath walks. There are several canals within easy reach of Leicester. The Ashby Canal to the west of the county winds its way through some very attractive countryside which will probably soon be better known because of two developments close by. One is the railway museum at Shackerstone Station, the other the improvement of public access to the site of the Battle of Bosworth, between Shenton and Sutton Cheney.

The Grantham Canal, which runs from Nottingham to Grantham, cuts across the north-eastern corner of Leicestershire. The Grantham Canal Society is working hard to develop it as a public amenity and at the same time maintain its character. Unfortunately most of the road bridges over it have been culverted to eliminate humpbacks, for the benefit of motorists but at the expense of canal architecture and any future through traffic on the waterway.

The Grand Union Canal's Leicester line is naturally the best known waterway to Leicester people. It comprises what were formerly the Loughborough Navigation, the Leicester Navigation and the Union Canal. The last was built to join the first two to the Grand Junction, and was the final link in a through-way from the Thames to the Trent. The whole line is now called the Grand Union Canal. One can either walk along the towpath all the way from Leicester to Foxton and then follow either the Welford or the Market Harborough Arm, or one can start at South Wigston or Kilby Bridge. Not all bus services are good, so check with Midland Red beforehand. It is better to vary the route, using public footpaths and bridleways to fit in with bus services, or plan a circular walk if using a car. Buses to South Wigston *are* frequent.

1. For the first walk alight at Canal Street in South Wigston, walk the length of the recreation ground, and a few yards along Countesthorpe Road is the canal. Follow it left; the second lock, after $\frac{3}{4}$ mile, is known as Double Rail Lock; the old lock gates with two handrails have gone. The second rail was added after a woman was drowned using this crossing. There is still a public right of way over the canal here on the path from Wigston to Countesthorpe. Unfortunately the vast new housing estate at Little Hill, Wigston, has cut the path short, north of the railway line.

Soon Kilby Bridge is reached. A centre of population grew up here with the coming of the canal. Three locks further on is Turnover Bridge where the towpath changes from one side to the other. This was at the insistence of the Countess of Denbigh who owned the Wistow estate when the canal was planned. Although six locks have already raised the water 50 feet since leaving South Wigston, the winding course and a look at the map will show that the builders of this canal generally tried to follow the contours to avoid the expense of locks and tunnels. This point is the highest part of Tythorn Hill. A little further along, three locks take the canal up to the village of Newton Harcourt. A path from the keeper's cottage leads into the village over a bridge spanning the railway.

Leave the towpath at the next bridge to see Newton Harcourt Church, opposite the Manor House. Then continue away from the canal to the bend in the lane. Through a gate on the left a path goes off to Wistow Church, which is reached by crossing a footbridge over the stream. In the field to the right of the church is the site of a mediaeval village. Beyond the church is Wistow Hall, and along the road, right, is a triangle of open field where, in summer, the farmer's wife sells bedding plants and refreshments. Return to the church, cross the footbridge again and take the path that bears right towards a long spinney of trees beyond which the canal may be joined once more. Turn right and follow the canal for $\frac{1}{2}$ mile as far as the end of the spinney. At this point the river Sence is crossed by a small aqueduct. Here also a path goes left, down the embankment, across the stream and under the railway; then after a couple of ploughed fields that call for careful map reading the way into Great Glen is easy. A new major road is proposed to by-pass the village and save it from the ravages of the present A6 trunk route.

2. The A6 beyond Oadby is not as well served by public transport as the Wigston area, but Glen Gorse is easily reached from Leicester. Ask the bus conductor for Gorse Lane; cross the dual carriageway carefully and follow the Old Mere, a rough track running by the golf course. After about $\frac{1}{2}$ mile turn left along a footpath which leads to Newton Harcourt. One may either divert to Wistow again or this time follow the towpath on past the Sence Aqueduct. A little beyond is Crane's Lock, from where a path goes left to Great Glen. A few hundred yards on some of the water in the Burton Brook passes under the canal, for there is an automatically operated feeder into the waterway. The stream is dammed and the water is diverted down a side channel, but there is a sluice gate to allow part of the brook to follow its normal course.

Not far on, the Kibworth–Wistow road crosses the canal by Kibworth Bridge, and the towpath changes sides again. The farmhouse close by was once the Navigation Inn—a common name for hostelries alongside waterways. Just beyond, Second Lock and Top Lock lift the canal to the summit level of the original length of the Union Canal, which terminated at Debdale Wharf. The scenery around here is good, except for a conglomeration of pylon lines. The bridleway from Fleckney to Smeeton Westerby is pleasant. It crosses the canal by a bridge; the raised ground just beyond on the left is the earth that was excavated when the tunnel ahead was dug.

Around the corner, Saddington Tunnel comes into view. The towpath ends here, but a track leads along the top of the tunnel. The boatmen used to unhitch their horses, which would make their way along the track to the other end, while the men lay on their backs on special boards and 'walked' along the roof the $\frac{1}{2}$ mile through the blackness. This was known as 'legging'. If a horse arrived at the other end of the tunnel before the 'leggers', it would be tied up in a stable; some of these 'tunnel stables' can still be seen today.

As the track above the tunnel climbs slightly a view opens up ahead over the rolling hills of south Leicestershire—Fernie Hunt country. Part way over the tunnel, the Kibworth-Saddington road crosses the track. Saddington is worth a visit, but there is a better way, so continue with the canal for the present. At the end of the tunnel one will find that the towpath has changed sides yet again. A little further on the Smeeton-Saddington road is reached. Turn right here for a very attractive climb up to Saddington—and steep too!

In the village, turn left along the Gumley path which starts at the bend near the chapel and goes downhill, crossing several streams. Ahead rises Smeeton Hill, also known as Gumley Hill. After the third footbridge turn right to follow a banked path to a rough road. Continue right, uphill, until reaching Saddington Reservoir, which stores water for the canal. Sometimes one can watch the sailing dinghies of the British Transport Yacht Club. This is also a good spot for wild birds, but to view them go back and follow the road past the boathouse. After a few hundred yards there are plenty of gaps in the hedge on the right leading on to the marshy fringe of the reservoir. It is a wonderful place, wild and lonely, often enhanced by a slight mist.

The road continues, flat at first, soon very steeply, to a gated junction near Gumley, a most attractive village among woods and hills. Return by the rough road to the outflow from the reservoir into the canal feeder. Now go back to the third footbridge on the path from Saddington and then turn right to cross a fourth bridge. Straight ahead is the feeder, which is in effect a mini-canal. At this point there is an interesting old sluice gate, held up by ratchets, for regulating the flow.

The feeder winds above the little valley of the Mowsley Brook. The footpath to Smeeton Westerby makes its way down the same valley, keeping between the brook and the feeder for three fields, but it is more interesting to follow the feeder, diverting at each fence to the stile closer to the brook. Farm tracks cross the feeder and in the third field one of these bridges carries a path that goes to the canal and on to Smeeton. Either follow the path which forks left to cross the brook at the very foot of the canal embankment, or stay with the feeder to its confluence with the canal, then turn left along the canal to the spillway, or overflow. This is where the bank burst in 1865 when the reservoir could not hold all the rain of a wet English summer. From the spillway descend the steep wooded bank to the brook where it runs through a culvert in the embankment. In wet weather it rushes along here at quite a pace. The path continues along the foot of the embankment until a track leads to the right under a small aqueduct. The path climbs up towards Smeeton and soon a choice of routes presents itself. One can either go into Smeeton or pass it and go on to Kibworth to catch a bus to Leicester.

3. Another time, one can take the bus or go by car to Kibworth and return to the bridge by which the path from Saddington crosses the feeder. This time vary the route between Kibworth and the canal, in order to walk **up** the Mowsley Brook valley, seeing it in another way. It is a very beautiful valley, surrounded by hills, dominated at one end by the canal bank and at the other by the reservoir dam. After re-visiting the reservoir, return to the drop gate and cross the feeder by the footboard, to follow the Gumley path, which leads over Smeeton Hill. The view is good, but on a misty day one may as well use the rough road. At the top of the hill take the right fork to Gumley Church. There is a second steep hill to climb in order to reach the village, but it is worth it. Follow the twisting road through Gumley as far as the telephone kiosk and turn left down the green track which is the start of the path to Foxton. On the left Gumley Wood spills down from the hill; this is south Leicestershire at its best.

The canal is not far away, and is crossed by a footbridge. Turn right along the towpath, and a short distance ahead is the junction with the Market Harborough Arm. Overlooking the junction, almost towering above it, is the magnificent flight of Foxton Locks. Cross the humped bridge to the main line of the canal, then walk up the locks. There are several footbridges: go up one way and down the other, comparing the views at the different stages. The two sets of five locks carry the canal up 75 feet, and at the top is the keeper's cottage. The rough, hilly, overgrown land opposite the cottage is worth exploring, but with care, especially when the ground is wet and slippery. The derelict brick and stone work is the remains of the inclined plane lift that was built at the close of the last century to by-pass the flight of locks. (Full details of the inclined plane are given on page 7). Dense undergrowth has covered the site since the plane was dismantled, but part of the slope has now been cleared and explorers can easily find the masonry of the bare slope. Boats approached the lift by a short stretch of canal from the Market Harborough Arm. This is crossed a few yards along by the bridle road which runs from the bottom lock to the outskirts of Foxton village. It is now a little backwater used for moorings.

Head now towards Foxton either along the Market Harborough Arm towpath or by the bridle road. In the village, take the path from North Lane, where occasionally buses run to Leicester on Saturday; this goes across the fields to Debdale Wharf. Careful map-reading is needed. Debdale was the terminus of the canal from Leicester from 1797 to 1809, when the route was extended to Market Harborough. Nearby was Debdale Wharf Inn. At the road turn left to cross the canal to a gate on the other side of the road and follow a clear track. This is the old road to Smeeton Westerby where

it is called Debdale Lane. After one field it humpbacks its way over the canal and continues downhill. Half a mile on, it crosses a stream, and just beyond, at a stile, a footpath leads across flat country to Kibworth, where a Midland Red bus goes back to Leicester.

4. When next at Kibworth, walk to Smeeton and then go the whole length of Debdale Lane, thus climbing **up** to the canal, which seems to make it more impressive. Follow the towpath to Foxton Locks, then take the footpath west to Laughton some 2 miles up a valley. This is a peaceful little place which, like Gumley, seems to be approached only by paths and gated roads. Follow the Theddingworth road south. In less than a mile the edge of the Laughton Hills is reached where there is a truly outstanding view across to the Hothorpe Hills in Northamptonshire. Walk from here down to the main line of the canal below. Descend to the towpath and follow it to the right, into the delightful scenery of the Leicester Avon valley, with more tunnels, locks and reservoirs. Returning by towpath to Foxton Locks, you can choose for yourself whether to make for Kibworth or follow the Market Harborough Arm.

The latter, after 2 miles, leads to Gallow Hill bridge, near which is a wharf; once a coal depot, it is now a glue factory. The tall chimney can be seen from many miles away, and the smell of the animals' bones detected from almost as far! From here to the centre of Market Harborough it is about 2 miles by road, but nearly 4 by canal. The waterway terminates at the edge of the town, at the boatyard close to the A6 road. Buses run from Market Harborough to Leicester more or less every hour on Saturdays, but on Sundays there are only three in the whole day.

Having covered nearly the whole length of the Grand Union in south Leicestershire, work out other variations yourself, and remember the canal north of the city: visit Birstall 'Backwater', the weir at Sileby Mill, the towpath between Barrow-upon-Soar and Loughborough, and, on the Nottinghamshire border, Zouch Mill, the Devil's Elbow and Trent Lock. Using footpaths and bridleways, one can easily work these into circular rambles or loops based on the regular bus route between Leicester and Loughborough.

The Grantham Canal (now disused and unnavigable) is less visited and so more peaceful, but the towpath is overgrown in places. There are not so many locks, but in doing without them the canal meanders through some excellent countryside: the Nottinghamshire Wolds and the Belvoir escarpment on the south are especially attractive. From Leicester a car is necessary to make the most of this strip of country and the walks that it offers. The Grantham bus is quite useful for the eastern end of the canal.

It is worth enquiring at a good bookshop

about suitable maps. The 1-inch sheet 133 is quite helpful, but in order to use some of the footpaths and bridleways that cross the canal, $2\frac{1}{2}$-inch maps are necessary. The reference numbers of those required are: SP49/59, SP69/79, SP68 and SP78. The second and third are the most useful; the last two will soon be part of a more economical double sheet SP68/78. The new double sheets show rights of way in green where the information is available; on the 1-inch map they are printed in red. The $2\frac{1}{2}$-inch maps give other important details, especially field boundaries. Further information regarding the public rights of way, shown on the latest editions of the 1-inch and the $2\frac{1}{2}$-inch O.S. maps, can be obtained by writing to the Footpath Secretary, East Midland Area, Ramblers' Association, 35 Lymington Road, Leicester LE5 1LT.

There are innumerable sights on the canals of Leicestershire that one may return for again and again: a boat making its lazy way along the canal or patiently coping with the climb at Foxton; a lock-keeper whose family have inhabited the cottage for three long generations; engineers repairing the lock gates; anglers seemingly making no progress, others at the moment of unexpected success; the bailiff emptying a bucket of fish into the water to replenish the stock; graceful swans admiring themselves in the water (to be respected during the nesting season, for the drake is a dutiful husband and father); hissing geese which tell you that you have no right to be there; pigs digging themselves into the mud on the opposite side of the canal during a heat wave; a fox skulking away across nearby fields; or a heron soaring over the trees to its high nest or to the margin of the reservoir.

Man made the canal for economic reasons, but nature took over as much as she was allowed. Between them they created a new world which we are only just beginning to appreciate: none better than the observant walker.

Angling on the Midland canals

The fishing rights on most of the Midland canals are owned by the British Waterways Board. Many of the Board's fisheries are leased to angling clubs and associations, although most operate their lengths on a day-ticket basis for non-members. The Board also sell day tickets and fishing permits from boats on certain lengths and reservoirs. A River Authority rod licence is usually required in addition to a fishing permit: it is essential to obtain this licence **before** starting to fish. The following is a list of current angling arrangements on the Midland canals; information regarding club addresses is available from British Waterways Board, Melbury House, Melbury Terrace, London NW1 6JX. The numbers refer to the map.

CANAL & LOCATION	ANGLING CLUB
Ashby Canal	
1A Orton Bridge 1 at Marston to Dratleys Bridge 11 at Burton Hastings	Coventry & District AA
2 Dratleys Bridge 11 at Burton Hastings to Friestons Bridge 20 at Wyken	Hinckley & District AA
3 Friestons Bridge 20 at Wyken to Dadlington House Road Bridge 32	Leicester & District ASA
1B Dadlington House Bridge 32 to Bridge 45 at Congerstone	Coventry & District AA
Coventry Canal	
1C Coventry to Bulls Head Bridge at Polesworth	Coventry & District AA
5 Bulls Head Bridge at Polesworth to Fazeley	Tamworth WMC
6A Whittington Brook to Huddlesford Junction	Birmingham AA
7A Huddlesford Junction to Junction with Trent & Mersey Canal at Fradley	British Waterways Board
North Oxford Canal	
1D Braunston Junction to Willoughby Wharf Bridge 85	Coventry & District AA

CANAL & LOCATION	ANGLING CLUB
8A Willoughby Wharf Bridge 85 to Hillmorton Wharf Bridge 73	Rugby Federation of Anglers
9 Hillmorton Wharf Bridge 73 to Bridge 70 at Hillmorton	Rugby British Legion AS
8B South End of Newbold Tunnel to point 630 yards south of Bridge 34 (All Oaks Wood)	Rugby Federation of Anglers
10 Point 630 yards south of Bridge 34 to Bridge 30	Courtaulds AC
11 Bridge 27 (Johnsons Bridge) to Hawkesbury Junction	Hawkesbury AS
Grand Union Canal (West of Braunston)	
1E Braunston Junction to Napton Junction	Coventry & District AA
12 Calcutt Locks to Junction Bridge, Warwick	Royal Leamington Spa AA
13 Saltisford Basin, Warwick	Fabwell Sheet Metal Company
14 Saltisford Basin to bottom Lock 26, Hatton Flight	Warwick Productions Social Club
6B Lock 26 at Hatton to Lock 41 at Hatton; Lock 46 at Hatton to south end of Shrewley Tunnel	Birmingham AA
15 Between north end of Shrewley Tunnel and Bridge 62 at Rowington	Charterhouse WMC
16 Bridge 62 at Rowington to Bridge 67 at Chessets Wood	Massey-Ferguson Recreation Club
17 Bridge 67 at Chessets Wood to Knowle Bottom Lock	British Legion AS (Dorridge and Packwood Branch)
18 Bridge 78 (Catherine de Barnes) to Bridge 71 (Kenilworth Road)	Coleshill & District AC

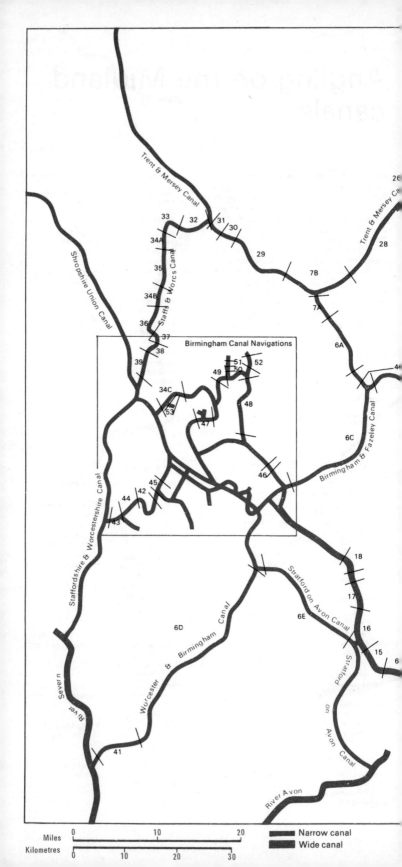

Miles | Kilometres scale: 0, 10, 20 / 0, 10, 20, 30

Narrow canal
Wide canal

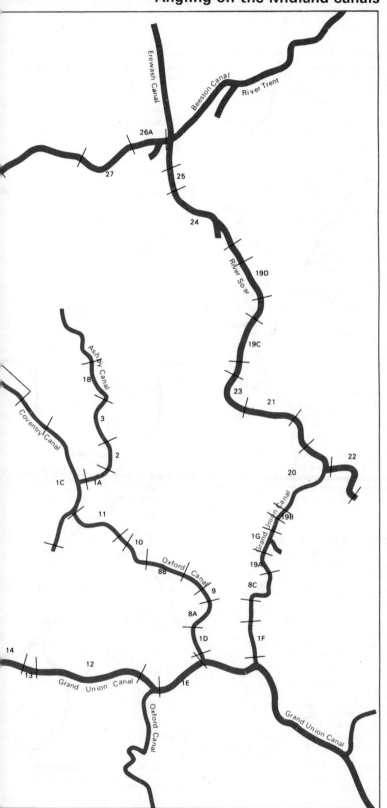

CANAL & LOCATION	ANGLING CLUB

Grand Union Canal (Leicester Line)

1F	Norton Junction to south-east end of Crick Tunnel	Coventry & District AA
8C	North end of Crick Tunnel to Bridge 28	Rugby Federation of Anglers
19A	Bridge 28 to Bridge 37, South Kilworth	Leicester & District ASA
1G	Bridge 37 to south end of Bosworth Tunnel	Coventry & District AA
19B	North end of Bosworth Tunnel to Bridge 50	Leicester & District ASA
20	Bridge 50 at Theddingworth to south end of Saddington Tunnel	Leicester Angling Club
21	North end of Saddington Tunnel to Glen Parva (Bridge 94)	Wigston AS
22	Market Harborough Arm	Market Harborough AS
23	Bridge 94, Glen Parva, to West Bridge, Leicester	Leicester Angling Society

Soar Navigation

19C	Belgrave Lock to Johnsons Bridge, Thurmaston	Leicester & District ASA
19D	Wreake Junction to Barrow Shallow Lock	Leicester & District ASA
24	Pillings Lock to Kegworth Old Lock	Loughborough Soar AS
25	Kegworth Flood Lock to Ratcliffe Lock	Long Eaton & District AS

Trent & Mersey Canal (South)

26A	Derwent Mouth to Weston Parish Boundary	Derby AA
27	Extent of Canal within Weston Parish Boundary	Derby Railway Institution FC
28	Bridge 28, Claymills, to Wychnor Lock	Burton Mutual AA
26B	Claymills to Burton Parish Boundary (R. Flame)	Derby AA
7B	Wychnor Lock to Handsacre Bridge 58	Controlled by BWB bailiffs on 'day-ticket' basis
29	Handsacre Bridge 58 to Wolseley Bridge 70	Rugeley and Brereton AA
30	Wolseley Bridge 70 to Colwich Lock	Controlled by BWB bailiffs on 'day-ticket' basis
31	Colwich Lock to Great Haywood Lock	Shugborough Fishing Club

Staffordshire & Worcestershire Canal (North) (Great Haywood Junction to Autherley)

32	Great Haywood Junction to Milford Aqueduct	Potteries AS
33	Milford Aqueduct and Roseford Bridge 94	Izaak Walton (Stafford) AS
34A	Roseford Bridge 94 to Penkridge Lock	Whitmore Reans CAA
35	Penkridge Lock to Gailey Wharf	Broomhill AS
34B	Gailey Wharf to Gravelly Way Bridge 78	Whitmore Reans CAA
36	Gravelly Way Bridge 78 to Long Molls Bridge 76	Blackfords Progressive AS
37	Long Molls Bridge 76 to Deepmore Bridge 75	E. Thomas Ltd
38	Bridge 72 to Bridge 73	Midland Aluminium AS
39	Bridge 71, Cross Green, to Autherley Junction	Provincial AA

Birmingham & Fazeley Canal

6C	Salford Bridge, Birmingham, to Whittington Brook	Birmingham AA
40	Watling Street Bridge, Fazeley, to Sutton Road Bridge, Fazeley	Fazeley Victory AC

Worcester & Birmingham Canal

41	Diglis Basin to Blackpole Wharf Bridge	Worcester & District UAA
6D	Blackpole Wharf Bridge to King's Norton	Birmingham AA

Stratford-upon-Avon Canal

6E	King's Norton to Kingswood Junction	Birmingham AA

Stourbridge and Dudley Canals

42	Nine Locks Junction to Leys Bridge	Brierley Hill BL
43	Stourton Bridge to Wordsley Bridge	Kidderminster & District AA
44	Tansey Green/ Brierley Hill Road to Fens Pools at Pensnett	Fry's Diecastings AC
45	Woodside Bridge to Bottom Lock, Parkhead Locks (Number 1 Line)	Woodside Ward AC

BCN SYSTEM

Tame Valley Canal

46	The Mile Pound, Perry Barr (Lock 11 to Lock 12)	The Barn Social Club and Institute

CANAL & LOCATION	ANGLING CLUB
Walsall Canal	
47 Forsters Bridge to Scarborough Road Bridge and Anson Branch	James Bridge Steelworks Angling Society
Rushall & Daw End Branch Canal (i.e. Catshill Junction to Rushall Junction)	
48 (Section restocked 10 January 1973 by British Waterways Board with 6,000 fish)	Whole length – approximately 7½ miles – available for match-fishing, day tickets, etc., controlled by BWB bailiffs
Wyrley & Essington Canal	
34C Alma Street Bridge to Wards Bridge	Whitmore Reans CAA
49 Freeths Bridge to Cannock Extension Junction	Wellman-Cranes Ltd AC

CANAL & LOCATION	ANGLING CLUB
Cannock Extension	
50 Pelsall Road Bridge to junction with west and east Canal at Pelsall Junction	Angling Section, Edward Street WMC
51 Jolly Collier Bridge to Railway Bridge (west and east)	Bridgetown & Allport Street Sports & Social Club
Anglesey Branch (West and East)	
52 Anglesey Bridge to Freeths Bridge	Middleton House AS
Bentley Canal	
53 Between Lock Number 6, Neachells Road, and Lock 7, Well Lane, Wednesfield	Willenhall Liberal Club

Fishing at Northampton Locks, Grand Union Canal

Houses and gardens

One of the fruits of England's past history is her heritage of grand houses and castles. Fortunately, at least for the general public, economic and social change has meant that many of these buildings can no longer be maintained purely as private dwellings, and if dukes wish to continue to sip their port they must also open their doors to the public. The Midlands have long been well endowed with such houses, although many are modest compared with the vast palaces and castles that are to be found in other parts of the country. It is clear that in this region the houses were built neither for display, nor for defence: they were built for living in.

The following is a selection of those houses and gardens in the Midlands which are open to the public. Several are owned or maintained by the National Trust: these are indicated by the abbreviation NT. It is worth bearing in mind that for members of the National Trust entry to such properties is free. Membership forms can be obtained at most of these houses or by writing to the Head Office, 42 Queen Anne's Gate, London SW1H 9AS.

DERBYSHIRE

Duffield Castle The foundations of the Norman keep of the castle of the Ferrars which was razed to the ground in 1266 by Prince Henry, nephew of Henry III. NT. *Access:* At Duffield, 2½ miles S of Belper, on W side of A6.

Ednaston Manor Brailsford (Brailsford 325). A Lutyens house with a formal garden recently redesigned with a wide range of trees, flowering shrubs and roses, including a collection of acers, sorbus, rhododendrons, azaleas, climbing and old-fashioned roses. *Garden only open certain Suns Apr to Sep 14.00–19.00. Open on other days by special arrangement. Access:* 8 miles NW of Derby; gate on A52 W of Brailsford. Trent bus service 31A.

Foremarke Hall Milton. A fine Georgian house built in 1762. Now a school. *Open daily mid to end Jun 14.30–16.30. Access:* 3 miles E of Repton, 4 miles W of Melbourne, off A514.

Kedleston Hall Derby. Probably the finest Robert Adam house in England, standing in a 500-acre deer park. Magnificent marble hall and state rooms, contemporary furniture and collection of fine pictures. Museum containing ivories, weapons and Robert Adam's signed drawings. Serpentine lake and orangery. *Open Easter Sun & Mon, then Suns from end Apr to end Sep & B. Hol Mons: 14.00–18.00. (Gardens 13.00–19.00) Access:* 4½ miles NW of Derby.

Melbourne Hall (Melbourne 2502). An 18th-century mansion, and later home of Queen Victoria's first Prime Minister, Lord Melbourne. Im-

portant collection of pictures, furniture and works of art. Famous formal gardens. 18thC wrought-iron pergola, statuary, topiary and clipped yew tunnel. *Hall & gardens open certain days from Apr to Oct. Access:* At Melbourne, 8 miles S of Derby on A514. Midland Red bus service 689.

Norbury Manor Ashbourne. One of the earliest examples of mediaeval domestic architecture (1250), now restored. *Open Weds May to Sep 14.00–17.30. Access:* 4 miles SW of Ashbourne, on B5033.

Sudbury Hall near Uttoxeter. A fine 17thC brick house. Contains plasterwork ceilings with murals by Laguerre, and some Grinling Gibbons carving. NT. *Open Apr to Oct: Wed, Thur, Fri, weekends & B. Hol Mons 12.00–18.00. Access:* At Sudbury, 6 miles E of Uttoxeter on A50 road. Potteries Motor Traction bus services, 14, 23. 90.

LEICESTERSHIRE

Ashby-de-la-Zouch Castle Mainly 14thC, with the tower added in 1474 by Lord Hastings. A Royalist stronghold in the Civil War. *Open Mar to Apr & Oct: weekdays 09.30–17.30, Sun 14.00–17.30; May to Sep: weekdays 09.30–19.00, Sun 14.00–19.00. Nov to Feb: weekdays 10.00–16.30, Sun 14.00–16.30; Access:* At Ashby-de-la-Zouch, 9 miles SE of Burton-on-Trent, on A50. Midland Red bus services 667, 668.

Brooksbury Agricultural College Melton Mowbray. Lake and water garden, demonstration plots; everything named. *Access:* 5 miles W of Melton Mowbray, on A607. Midland Red bus service 661/2.

Kirby Muxloe Castle A ruined, moated 15thC fortified manor house, built of brick. *Open weekdays only: Mar, Apr & Oct 09.30–17.30, May to Sep 09.30–19.00, Nov to Feb 09.30–16.00. Access:* At Kirby Muxloe, 5 miles W of Leicester, off B5380. Exit 21 off M1. Midland Red bus services 636, 664, L19.

Sir John Moore Junior School Appleby Magna. Designed by Sir Christopher Wren in the 17thC and later modified. Notable arcaded entrance façade. *Open weekdays 17.00–20.00, weekends 10.00–19.30. During school holidays by arrangement with caretaker on premises. Access:* 6 miles SW of Ashby-de-la-Zouch, off A453. Midland Red bus service X99.

Stanford Hall near Rugby (Swinford 250). William and Mary brick mansion built 1697–1700, with Georgian additions. Furniture and paintings; motor cycle and car museum. Experimental flying machine built by P. S. Pilcher in 1898. Walled rose garden leading to Old Forge. *Open Easter Sun to end Sep: Thur & weekends 14.30–18.00. Also B. Hol Mons & following Tue 12.00–18.00. Access:* 7½ miles NE of Rugby, off B5414; M1 motorway access between Junctions 18 and 20. Midland Red bus service 564.

Whatton House Hathern. The house dates from 1800 and contains a museum of family heirlooms. The 25 acres of gardens display flowering shrubs, 50,000 bulbs, 2,000 roses, a 100-yard-long

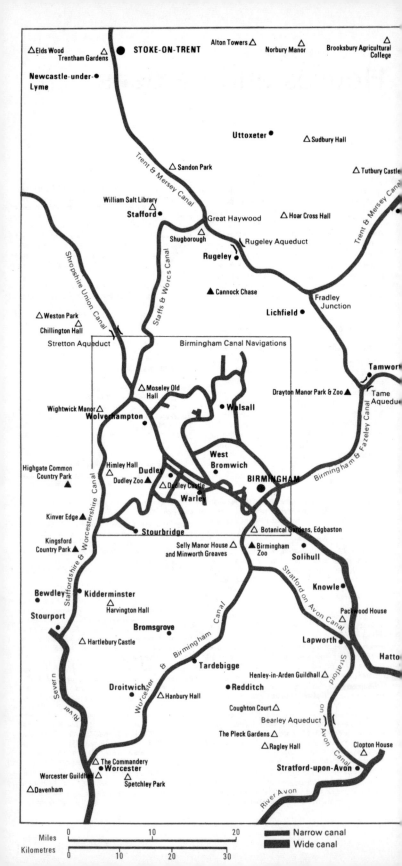

Houses and gardens

△ Duffield Castle
△ Kedleston Hall
▲ Sherwood Zoo
Ilkeston
Erewash Canal
NOTTINGHAM
Beeston Canal
Beeston
River Trent
Holme Pierrepont Country Park
Elvaston Castle Country Park △
Derby
Shardlow
Trent Junction
Foremarke Hall △
ton-on-Trent
Melbourne Hall △
Whatton House △
Stapleford Lion Reserve ▲
Loughborough
River Soar
shby-de-la-Zouch Castle △   Ashby
Moira   ● Ashby
Melton Mowbray
△ Sir John Moore Junior School
Snarestone
Ashby Canal
Bradgate Park ▲
Kirby Muxloe Castle △
LEICESTER
▲ Twycross Zoo Park
Coventry Canal
Atherstone
Nuneaton   Hinckley
Arbury Hall △
Nuneaton Zoological Garden ▲
Foxton
Market Harborough
Hawkesbury
Grand Union Canal
Lutterworth
Ford's Hospital △
t. Mary's
Guild Hall △
COVENTRY
Brinklow Arches
Oxford Canal
Stanford Hall △
venty Zoo Park △
Rugby
Hillmorton
Cottesbrooke Hall △
△ ● Kenilworth
Kenilworth Castle
Coton Manor Wildlife Garden △
Draycote Water Country Park ▲
Avon Aqueduct
Leamington
Braunston
Althorp △
△ △ ● Warwick
Grand Union Canal Napton
Lord Leycester Hospital
Warwick Castle
Southam Zoo Farm ▲
Northampton
Delapré Abbey △
Grand Union Canal
△ Charlecote Park
Oxford Canal
Daventry
Burton Dassett Hills Country Park ▲
Farnborough Hall △
△ Canons Ashby
Stoke Park Pavilions △
Stoke Bruerne
△ Upton House

△ House, garden or House & garden
▲ Country park or Zoo

herbaceous border and Oriental gardens. Fine views. *Open Easter to end Sep: Sun & B. Hol Mons 14.00–19.00. Access:* 4 miles NW of Loughborough, on A6. Buses: Barton Transport and Trent Motor Traction services.

NORTHAMPTONSHIRE

Althorp Harlestone (East Haddon 209). A house dating from 16thC, with alterations in 1670, 1790 and 1877. Splendid interior containing pictures of many European schools; historic portraits, 115-foot-long picture gallery. Large collection of Oriental and European porcelain; 18thC furniture. *Open May (Sun only), then Jun to Sep: Sun, Tue & Thur 14.30–18.00. Access:* 6 miles NW of Northampton on Northampton–Rugby road (A428). Midland Red bus service X96.

Canons Ashby A beautiful 16thC and 18thC manor house, with fine gardens. The house contains a secret chamber and retains as museum pieces the bakery, smithy and carpenter's shop. Notable long gallery and Queen Anne Room. *Open Apr to mid-Oct: Sun 14.30–18.30. Access:* At Canons Ashby, 11 miles NE of Banbury, on B4525.

Coton Manor Wildlife Garden (Guilsborough 219). An outstanding old English garden of exceptional charm and beauty. Water gardens with flamingoes, wildfowl and tropical birds. *Open Apr to Oct: Thur, Sun & B. Hols. Access:* 10 miles N of Northampton and 11 miles SE of Rugby, off A428; 2 miles from A50 via Guilsborough.

Cottesbrooke Hall A fine early 18thC house of brick, with stone dressings. Unusual large formal and wild garden; greenhouses. *Gardens shown on certain days in summer. Access:* At Cottesbrooke, 9 miles NNW of Northampton, off A50. United Counties bus service 316.

Delapré Abbey near Northampton. A 16th to 19thC house with a fine porch, built on the site of a Cluniac nunnery. Contains the County Record Office. *Open all year: Thur & Sat 14.30–18.00 (closes 16.30 Oct to Apr). Access:* On London road (A50) 1 mile S of Northampton. Frequent bus services from town centre. The Northampton Arm of the Grand Union Canal joins the river Nene nearby.

Stoke Park Pavilions Stoke Bruerne, near Towcester. Twin pavilions and colonnade built 1630 by Inigo Jones. *Exterior only on view Jul & Aug: weekends 14.00–18.00. Access:* 7 miles S of Northampton, just off the Stony Stratford–Northampton road (A508). United Counties bus services 330, 331. The seven Stoke Bruerne locks close by lead the Grand Union Canal up towards the Northamptonshire Heights.

STAFFORDSHIRE

Alton Towers Uttoxeter (Oakamoor 449). A ruined early 19thC mansion by Pugin standing in beautiful grounds, which can be viewed from model railways and aerial cable cars. *Open daily G. Fri to Oct. Access:* 4½ miles E of Cheadle, off B5032.

Chillington Hall Brewood (Brewood 850 236). The home of the Giffords since 1178, the present house dates from 1724 and 1785. Grounds by 'Capability' Brown. Associations with the flight of Charles II after the Battle of Worcester in 1651. *Open May to Aug: Thur 14.30–17.30. Access:* 4 miles SW of A5 at Gailey, and 2 miles S of Brewood. The Shropshire Union Canal is nearby. West Midlands Transport bus service 52.

Elds Wood Willoughbridge. A 200-year-old gravel quarry converted into a unique woodland garden with daffodils, rhododendrons and azaleas. *Garden always open. Access:* 9 miles SW of Newcastle-under-Lyme, on A51 between junctions with A525 and A53.

Himley Hall A large 18th to 19thC house, the ancestral home of the Earls of Dudley. Until recently a National Coal Board headquarters, it is now used as a college. *Grounds only open: daily Easter to end Oct. Access:* At Himley, 6 miles SSW of Wolverhampton, off A440. Midland Red bus service 882/5.

Hoar Cross Hall near Burton-on-Trent (Hoar Cross 224). Elizabethan-style mansion. Varied collection of arms and armour; 17th, 18th and 19thC furniture and paintings. Landscaped and terraced gardens, yew tree walks and fountains. *Open G. Fri to Sep: Wed, Thur & weekend 14.00–18.00, B. Hols Mon & Tue 12.00–19.00. Access:* 9 miles W of Burton-on-Trent, 10 miles S of Uttoxeter, 15 miles N of Lichfield. Green bus service.

Moseley Old Hall Wolverhampton (Wolverhampton 782808). An Elizabethan house, formerly half-timbered and now encased in 19thC brick. Contains interesting panelled rooms. Provided refuge for King Charles II after the Battle of Worcester in 1651. NT. *Open Mar to Nov: Wed, Thur, weekend 14.00–18.00 (or dusk), B. Hols 10.30–12.30, 14.00–18.00. No dogs. Access:* 4 miles N of Wolverhampton, midway between A449 and A460. Off M6 at Junction 11 then via A460. The Staffs & Worcs Canal is not far away. Midland Red bus service 876.

Sandon Park Great Haywood. 50 acres of flowering shrubs, lawns and wild garden. Rose gardens, kitchen garden, amphitheatre. Tulip trees, manua ash and other specimen trees. Several tall monumental columns. *Open Apr to Aug: Suns, also Mar to May 14.00–19.00. Access:* 5 miles NE of Stafford, on A51, entrance by Sandon War Memorial. The Trent & Mersey Canal runs through the village and meets the Staffs & Worcs Canal at Great Haywood Junction.

Shugborough Great Haywood (Little Haywood 388). The Hall (residence of the Earl of Lichfield) dates from 1693, with 18thC additions by James Stuart and Samuel Wyatt. Fine French and English furniture, china, tapestry and paintings. The large park contains some notable garden features including a Chinese House, a Doric Temple, the Arch of Hadrian and the Tower of the Winds. NT. *Open mid-Mar to end Sep: Tue to Sat & B. Hol Mons 11.00–17.30, Sun 14.00–17.30. Closed G. Fri. Access:* 5½ miles SE of Stafford, turn off A513 at Milford. Midland Red bus services 823, 824, 825, 826, 830. The Hall is very close to the Staffs & Worcs Canal here, where it spreads out into the attractive reeded Tixall Wide.

Trentham Gardens Stoke-on-Trent. The Hall, former mansion of the Duke of Sutherland, was demolished in 1909 except for the ballroom and orangery; these are now used as a leisure centre (concerts occasionally given in the ballroom). Beautifully laid out rose and Italian gardens. Facilities include a lake for fishing and boating, heated swimming pool, garden centre and a miniature railway. *Open daily. Access:* At Trentham, 4 miles S of Stoke-on-Trent on A34. About 1 mile W of the Trent & Mersey Canal.

Tutbury Castle (Tutbury 2129). Ruined 14thC stronghold where Mary Queen of Scots was twice imprisoned for a total of seven years. *Open regularly: summer 10.00–19.00, winter 10.00–16.00. Access:* At Tutbury, 3 miles NW of Burton-on-Trent, on A50. J. Stevenson bus services.

Weston Park Weston-under-Lizard. A fine mansion built by Lady Wilbraham in 1671 and today the home of the Earl of Bradford. Notable collection of pictures, furniture, tapestries and 17thC silver. Disraeli letters on show. Fine gardens and vast parklands by 'Capability' Brown. Three lakes, a herd of deer, and falconry displays. *Open Apr to Sep: Wed, Thur & Sat 14.00, Sun 11.00. B. Hols Sat to Tue 11.00, House 13.30. Access:* 4 miles NE of Shifnal, on A5. Midland Red bus service X97.

Wightwick Manor Wolverhampton. A 19thC house furnished with many original William Morris wallpapers and fabrics, de Morgan ware and a collection of Pre-Raphaelite works of art. Formal terraced gardens contain yew hedges and topiary, a lake, and a remarkable row of Irish yews and golden hollies. NT. *Open all year: Thur, Sat & B. Hols 14.30–17.30. Also May to Sep: Wed 14.00–18.00.* No unaccompanied children. *Access:* 3 miles W of Wolverhampton, up Wightwick Bank, A454. West Midlands Transport bus services 16, 17, Bridgnorth service. The Staffs & Worcs Canal runs close to the house.

William Salt Library Stafford (Stafford 52276). A fine 18thC town house containing a comprehensive and valuable collection of books and manuscripts concerning the county. *Open weekdays 10.00–12.45 & 13.45–17.00. Closed Mon.*

WARWICKSHIRE

Arbury Hall Nuneaton (Fillongley 40529). Originally an Elizabethan house, neo-gothic features added in 1750–1800. Fine plaster ceilings, furniture, pictures, china and glass. Family documents and letters. Parkland and landscaped gardens with many trees, some in avenues along carriage ways. *Open Easter to Oct: Suns only, also B. Hols Mon & following Tue 14.30–18.00. Access:* 2 miles SW of Nuneaton, off B4102. Nuneaton Station 3 miles; AA direction signs. Frequent Midland Red bus services. The Coventry Canal runs east of the Hall; but the network of private canals (they used to connect the coal mines on the estate to the Coventry Canal) is now disused.

Botanical Gardens Edgbaston, Birmingham. Founded over 100 years ago, with trees, flowering shrubs, plants and hot houses. Alpine garden, lily pond and aviaries. Large rock garden and several greenhouses including cacti house. *Open weekdays 09.00–dusk, Sun 10.30–dusk. Access:* Westbourne Road. The Worcester & Birmingham Canal passes through Edgbaston in a cutting, and access is difficult.

Charlecote Park Warwick (Wellesbourne 277). A fine restored Elizabethan house (1558) built by the Lucy family. Picturesque Tudor gatehouse. The house contains a museum on the first floor. The park, with fine cedars and avenues, also contains a flock of Spanish sheep and a herd of deer. NT. *Open daily Apr to Sep & B. Hol Mons 11.15–17.45. Closed Mon. Access:* 4 miles E of Stratford-upon-Avon, on the N side of B4086. Midland Red bus service 518.

Clopton House Stratford-upon-Avon. Stands in a park of which Shakespeare owned 107 acres. Home of the Cloptons for 750 years. Period furniture and Old Master collections. Shakespearian and Gunpowder Plot associations. *Open daily all year 10.00–17.00. Access:* 1 mile N of the town centre. The Stratford-upon-Avon Canal joins the river Avon in the town with an attractive basin.

Coughton Court Alcester. Mainly Elizabethan house with an imposing stone gatehouse of 1509, where the wives of some of the Gunpowder plotters awaited the result of the trial. Two mid-Elizabethan half-timbered wings form an open courtyard on the east. The rooms contain a number of Jacobite relics. The Jacobean staircase in the ball-

room was moved here from Harvington Hall. NT. *Open weekends Apr & Oct; Wed, Thur, weekends & B. Hols Mon & following Tue May to Sep 14.00–18.00. Access:* 2 miles N of Alcester, just E of A435. Midland Red bus services 148, X3, 339, R5, R8, R28.

Farnborough Hall near Banbury. A 17th and 18thC house with fine plasterwork in the hall and saloon. Terrace walk with garden temples and an obelisk. Splendid views across the Warwickshire plain towards Edge Hill. NT. *Open Apr to Sep: Wed & Sat 14.00–18.00. Access:* 6 miles N of Banbury, ½ mile W of A423. Midland Red bus service 509.

Ford's Hospital Greyfriars Lane, Coventry. A well-restored, picturesque half-timbered almshouse with an interior courtyard. Founded by a Coventry merchant in 1529. *Open daily Mar to Sep 10.00–19.00, Oct to Feb 10.00–17.00.*

Henley-in-Arden Guildhall High Street, Henley-in-Arden. A gabled, timber-framed building of 1448, restored in 1915. There is an outside staircase from the Dutch-style garden leading to the hall of the mediaeval Guild, with notable roof timbering. Many relics and town records are displayed. *Open at reasonable times on application to caretaker, Guild Cottage. Access:* 8 miles W of Warwick. Midland Red bus services 546, 548.

Kenilworth Castle Kenilworth. The massive keep dates from 1155–70, with a later Great Hall by John of Gaunt. Further additions, including a gatehouse, were made by the Dudleys during the 16thC. *Open weekdays 09.30–19.00, Suns 14.00–19.00 (summer Suns 09.30–19.00). Mar, Apr & Oct: close 17.30; Nov to Feb: close 16.00. Access:* 5 miles N of Warwick, on A46. Midland Red bus services 167, 517, 518, 537, 581, 582, 590 and 592.

Lord Leycester Hospital High Street, Warwick (Warwick 42797). A picturesque half-timbered building, founded in 1383, and adopted for its present use by the Earl of Leycester in 1571. There is a chapel dating from 1123, and a selection of historic exhibits. *Open all year: summer weekdays 10.00–18.00, winter 10.00–16.00. Closed Sun, G. Fri & Xmas. Access:* W gate of Warwick, A46. ¾ mile from Warwick Station. The Grand Union Canal skirts round the town to the north.

Packwood House Hockley Heath (Lapworth 2024). Timber-framed Tudor house, enlarged in the 17thC. Collection of tapestry, needlework and furniture. 113 acres of park and woodland; the gardens include a Carolean formal garden, and a 17thC yew garden representing the Sermon on the Mount, the trees taking the place of Jesus and his followers. NT. *Open Apr to Sep: Tue, Wed, Thur & weekend 14.00–19.00. Oct to Mar: Wed & weekend 14.00–17.00. Closed Xmas. Access:* 2 miles E of Hockley Heath, which is on A34, 11 miles SE of Birmingham. Lapworth Station. Midland Red bus service 150. Close to the Grand Union and Stratford-upon-Avon Canals.

The Pleck Gardens Alcester. 3 acres of roses, heather and rhododendrons; also a formal garden, two ponds and free-flying budgerigars. *Open daily Apr to Oct 10.00–20.00. Access:* 9 miles WNW of Stratford-upon-Avon, off B4090. Midland Red bus service 529.

Ragley Hall Alcester (Alcester 2090/2455). Built in 1680, with a splendid Great Hall by James Gibbs, featuring baroque plasterwork. Fine English and French pictures, furniture, china and works of art; also a valuable library. Gardens and park with lake. *Open daily & B. Hols May to Oct 14.00–17.30. Closed Mon & Fri. Access:* 2 miles SW of Alcester on Birmingham–Alcester–Evesnam road, A435. 8 miles from Stratford-upon-Avon. Midland Red bus service 148.

St Mary's Guild Hall Bayley Lane, Coventry (Coventry 25555). Splendid example of a mediaeval guild house, started in 1340 and completed in 1500. Restored hall, with portraits and Flemish tapestries. Minstrels' gallery. *Open most weekdays Apr to Oct 10.00–17.00, Sun 12.00–17.00 (enquiry advisable before visiting).* The Coventry Canal basin is near the town centre.

Selly Manor House and Minworth Greaves Maple Road, Bournville. Two attractive 13th and early 14thC timbered houses, re-erected in Bournville. Interesting collection of old furniture and domestic equipment. *Open Tue, Wed & Fri 13.00–17.00, or by appointment with curator, 44 Mulberry Road, Bournville. Access:* 4 miles SW of Birmingham, off A38. Near the Worcester & Birmingham Canal as it passes through Bournville.

Upton House Edgehill. Late 17thC house containing a set of Brussels tapestries, a collection of Sèvres porcelain and Chelsea figures. 18thC furniture, and a fine collection of paintings. Lawns surround the house, with a formal garden beyond terraced to a long pool at the bottom, with a series of herbaceous borders. NT. *Open May to Sep: Wed & Sat 14.00–18.00, other months Wed only 14.00–18.00 (or dusk). Access:* 1 mile S of Edgehill, 7 miles NW of Banbury, on the Stratford road, A422. Stratford Blue bus services 35 and 36.

Warwick Castle Castle Hill (Warwick 45421). One of England's finest inhabited mediaeval castles, standing on a steep rock cliff beside the river Avon. The exterior of the present castle is a famous example of a 14thC fortification, with towers and dungeons. The State Apartments contain a magnificent collection of pictures by Holbein, Rubens, Van Dyck and Velasquez. Parkland and Italian garden, laid out by 'Capability' Brown. *Open G. Fri to mid-Sep daily 10.00–17.30. Shorter hours out of season. Closed Nov to Feb.* The Grand Union Canal skirts round the town to the north.

WORCESTERSHIRE

The Commandery Worcester. A former refectory containing an interesting 15thC hall. Two 14thC columns from a former chapel are in the grounds. Headquarters of Charles II at the Battle of Worcester in 1651. *Open all year: weekdays 10.00–12.00, 14.30–16.30. Access:* In city; Shrub Hill Station ¾ mile. The Worcester & Birmingham Canal runs past its walls, and there is a lock here.

Davenham Malvern Link. Attractive garden featuring plants, trees, shrubs and alpines. *Open certain days in summer 14.00–19.00. Access:* 2 miles N of Great Malvern, off A449, Midland Red bus services X91 and 144.

Dudley Castle Extensive remains of a mainly 14thC stronghold, partly destroyed in 1647. The original Norman fortress was destroyed in 1173. Now part of Dudley Zoo and entertainments centre. *Open daily 10.00–18.00 or sunset. Access:* At Dudley, 6 miles SE of Wolverhampton, on A461. Midland Red bus service 125. The castle and zoo are right above the Dudley Canal Tunnel.

Hanbury Hall near Droitwich. A particularly fine Queen Anne house. Notable staircase and hall painted by Sir John Thornhill. Good plaster decoration in the Long Room. NT. *Open Apr to Sep: Wed & Sat 14.00–18.00. Access:* 2½ miles E of Droitwich on B4090, turn left for Hanbury Church, entrance 1 mile on left. Midland Red bus service 326. Hanbury Wharf, some way from the village, is at the junction of the Worcester & Birmingham and Droitwich Junction Canals.

Hartlebury Castle The 15th to 18thC home of the Bishops of Worcester, now restored. The 17thC north wing is now the Worcestershire County Museum (see page 153). The 15thC Great Hall was re-planned two centuries later. The library was added in 1782, and the mediaeval chapel has 18thC neo-Gothic decorations. *State rooms shown Sun & B. Hol Mons 14.00–18.00. Access:* At Hartlebury, 5 miles S of Kidderminster on A449. Midland Red bus service 315.

Harvington Hall Kidderminster (Chaddesley Corbett 267). A moated Tudor manor house containing priests' hiding places. *Open daily 14.00–18.00 or dusk, also Easter to Sep & by prior arrangement, B. Hols 11.30–13.00. Open other times by appointment with curator. Closed Mons, Fri after B. Hols, G. Fri & Xmas week. Access:* 4 miles SE of Kidderminster, ½ mile N of the Bromsgrove–Kidderminster road. Midland Red bus service 317.

Spetchley Park Worcester. Fine gardens and park surrounding an early 19thC mansion. 30 acres of trees, shrubs and plants; lake with ornamental waterfowl; red and fallow deer in park. *Gardens & garden centre open daily (except Sat) Apr to Oct 11.00–17.00, Sun 14.00–18.00, B. Hol Mons 11.00–18.00. Garden centre also open Mar weekdays 11.00–17.00. Access:* 3 miles E of Worcester, on Stratford-upon-Avon road (A422). Midland Red bus service 351.

Worcester Guildhall High Street, Worcester. A notable restored 18thC building. Paintings and armour on show in the assembly room. *Open all year: weekdays 09.00–17.00.* The Worcester & Birmingham Canal passes through the E side of Worcester.

Foxton

Places to visit in the countryside

COUNTRY PARKS

One of the recent developments in Britain's vanishing countryside is the concept of the country park—a carefully thought-out answer to the new leisure demands of Britain's increasing population. They are excellent for motorists who want to get 'out and about' and enjoy the countryside in a more enterprising way than simply eating sandwiches in a lay-by. Country parks are set up with grant aid from the Countryside Commission, a government body with special responsibility for recreation in the countryside.

DERBYSHIRE

Elvaston Castle Country Park Elvaston. Thel castle, which incoporates the remains of an earlier structure dated 1633, was built by James Wyatt in 1817. It has been adapted as the country park centre, comprising a countryside museum, field studies centre, café and general information centre. The first of the new country parks to be created, it includes 200 acres of woodland, parkland and formal gardens with some famous topiary work. There is a nature trail and reserve, and facilities for riding, cricket and camping. *Open at all times. Access:* 4 miles SE of Derby off A6 and B5010.

LEICESTERSHIRE

Bradgate Park Newtown Linford. 800 acres of mostly open parkland including a deer park and incorporating Swithland Wood. There are the ruins of Bradgate House, birthplace of Lady Jane Grey in 1537, and the remains of the tower of Old John, a folly dating from 1786. *The park is open all year,* but cars via the Newtown Linford entrance are only permitted *Wed & Thur 14.30–20.00 Apr to end Sep. Ruins open Wed & Thur 14.30–17.30 Apr to Oct. Access:* 4 miles NW of Leicester, off B5327. Midland Red bus services, 680, 632, 631.

NOTTINGHAMSHIRE

Holme Pierrepont Country Park near Nottingham. The park adjoins the new National Water Sports Centre, formed from excavated gravel pits near the River Trent Navigation. The Centre contains the Olympic Rowing Course and a water skiing and canoe slalom area, for which the park provides good views. There are various footpaths along the river Trent and by the Centre, and the park contains a nature reserve, fishing areas and a small wood. *Open daily. Access:* On eastern outskirts of Nottingham, off A52 (beside the river Trent near Holme Sluices).

STAFFORDSHIRE

Highgate Common Country Park near Wombourn. 280 acres of heath and birch woodland, containing footpaths and bridlepaths which offer good opportunities for walking, nature studies, riding and kite flying. A warden service provides information on the park. *Open all year. Access:* 5 miles NW of Stourbridge, off A449. 1½ miles W of the Staffs & Worcs Canal where it passes through Greensforge or Swindon.

WARWICKSHIRE

Burton Dassett Hills Country Park near Banbury. 94 acres of grassy upland with extensive views over rural Warwickshire. There are disused ironstone quarries, plenty of open spaces for walking and informal games, and secluded and sheltered picnic areas. *Open all year. Access:* 8 miles N of Banbury, off A41. Midland Red bus service 510.

Draycote Water Country Park near Rugby. 22 acres of open hillside overlooking Draycote Water Reservoir, providing good views of the reservoir and the activities of the sailing club. There are several good walks, and areas for picnics and games. *Open all year. Access:* 5 miles SW of Rugby, off A45. Midland Red bus services 561, 571, 576.

WORCESTERSHIRE

Kingsford Country Park near Kidderminster. 213 acres of conifer woodland and an area of scrub birch woodland. The ridge of Kinver Edge (NT) to the N extends into the park, providing excellent views. There are ample opportunities for riding with a good network of bridleways. The park provides several attractive walks, and there is a nature trail marked out; guide books available. *Access:* 3 miles N of Kidderminster, off A449. Midland Red bus service 883. The park is 1½ miles from the Staffs & Worcs Canal, at Wolverley.

Two other principal areas of great interest and beauty in the Midlands available to the public are Cannock Chase and Kinver Edge. Both are near the Staffs & Worcs Canal.

Cannock Chase Staffordshire. 10 square miles of undulating heathland and coniferous woodland, of which 1,000 acres are a motorless zone for the protection of wildlife. All the NW part of the Chase has been designated a site of special scientific interest by the Nature Conservancy, and Brocton Reserve, a reclaimed former quarry with a large stretch of water, has been established as a Nature Reserve. There are three nature trails in this area, and a warden post and information centre at Milford Common, 3 miles SE of Stafford on A513.

The Chase, famous for its ancient herd of fallow deer, contains many places of interest, including the American Cemetery, Shugborough Hall (see page 142) and the County Museum. A detailed map of the Chase showing footpaths, bridleways and vantage points, and natural scientific, architectural, historical and recreational places of interest is available from the County Planning Department, Staffordshire County Council, Martin Street, Stafford. *Access:* 4½ miles SE of Stafford, on A513. Midland Red bus services 823, 824, 825, 826, 827. The Staffs & Worcs Canal passes its NW boundary, while the Trent & Mersey Canal approaches it on the E side.

Kinver Edge near Kinver, Staffordshire. A 300-acre ridge, rising 550 feet, of heathland and woodland, owned by the National Trust and designated as a site of special scientific interest. It is an area of great landscape value, and one of its main features is the extensive views to the Clent and Lickey hills. The whole area is covered by footpaths, but riding is not permitted. There are bright orange sandstone rock dwellings on the highest part of the Edge. *Access:* 4 miles W of Stourbridge, off A449. Midland Red bus services 249, 254. The Staffs & Worcs Canal is only a mile from Kinver Edge: it flows along the valley in which Kinver is situated.

ZOOS

LEICESTERSHIRE

Stapleford Lion Reserve Stapleford Park, Melton Mowbray (Wymondham 650 & 657). Opened in 1968 as a breeding ground for African lions, the reserve has about thirty lions with a circuit for cars to drive round. There is also a small zoo with a good variety of animals, including tigers, brown bears, monkeys, exotic birds and reptiles. 35 acres. *Open 10.00–18.30 summer; 10.00–dusk winter. Access:* 5 miles SE of Melton Mowbray, off B676.

NOTTINGHAMSHIRE

Sherwood Zoo Broomhill Park, Hucknall, Nottingham (Hucknall 2425). Opened in 1968, a small, well presented and maintained collection designed for outdoor viewing only. Animals include lions, pumas, cheetahs, leopards, elephants, monkeys, antelopes, deer, cranes, ostriches and llamas. There is a large waterfowl collection, an aquarium, nocturnal house and pets' corner. Parrot shows are given in the afternoons, and pony rides on fine days. 17 acres. *Open 10.00–19.00 summer only. Access:* 2 miles N of Nottingham, on A611, 4 miles E of M1, Exit 27.

STAFFORDSHIRE

Drayton Manor Park and Zoo Fazeley, near Tamworth (Tamworth 2631 & 5421). An attractive 160-acre park, now an entertainment centre, with a zoo built in 1967 beside one of the lakes. The reptile collection includes pythons, lizards, turtles, toads and some tropical fish; the crocodilian house opposite has a 30-foot pool. The centre of the zoo has cages, aviaries and enclosures for cranes, flamingoes, parakeets, owls and waterfowl.

There is a 'big cats' area, a monkey house, a sea-lion pool, and a well-designed nocturnal house with sloths, bats and bushbabies. There are also paddocks with Highland cattle, llamas, goats, wallabies, fallow and sika deer and Jacob's sheep (four-horned). The Zoo Farm demonstrates the handling and care of domestic animals, with a model cow milking parlour (*daily demonstration 15.30*). 15 acres. *Open 10.30–19.00 summer; 10.30–dusk winter weekends. Access:* 2 miles S of Tamworth, on A4091 (off A5). Midland Red bus service 198. Drayton Manor Park is next to the Birmingham & Fazeley Canal about a mile from Fazeley Junction.

WARWICKSHIRE

Birmingham Zoo Canon Hill Park, Pershore Road, Birmingham 29 (021-472 1930). Opened in 1964, this has now been converted into an attractive small children's zoo, with cedar-wood buildings and well laid-out gardens. Designed to exhibit young animals, it also houses Dudley Zoo's collection of monkeys. There are outdoor enclosures for lions, leopards, camels, bears, kangaroos, llamas, zebras, antelopes, cranes, ostriches, storks, pelicans, emus and waterfowl; there are also gibbons, and aviaries for exotic birds. 4½ acres. *Open 10.00–dusk, Easter to end Sep. Access:* 2½ miles SSW of city, on A441. Local buses stop outside the zoo.

Coventry Zoo Park Whitley Common, Coventry (301772). Opened in 1966 to show large mammals such as lions, tigers, camels and bears. The zoo was sold in 1969, and the present owners have added leopards, rhinoceros, polar and black bears, elephants, Highland cattle and donkeys. There are also dolphins and sea lions, three aviaries which include peacocks, parrots and storks, and a pets' corner. 8 acres. *Open 10.00–18.30 all year. Access:* on SE outskirts of city, off A 423. Midland Red bus services X96, 584, 589.

Nuneaton Zoological Garden Plough Hill Road, Chapel End, Nuneaton. Opened in 1968, a small zoo on the outskirts of Nuneaton containing chimpanzees, leopards, sea lions, spotted deer and llamas. The speciality is birds and there is a collection of passerines (birds that perch) in the bird house, and aviaries containing Bateleur eagles, cockatoos, macaws, lories, lorikeets, turacos and—a rare species—a pair of Rothschild's grackles. There are pheasants and crowned cranes, and ponds for pelicans and Chilean flamingoes. There is also an elaborate tropical house. 4 acres. *Open 10.00–19.00 summer, 10.00–dusk winter. Access:* ½ mile N of Hartshill, on NW outskirts of Nuneaton, off A47. Midland Red bus service 771. Near the Coventry Canal as it passes through Hartshill.

Southam Zoo Farm Daventry Road, Southam, near Leamington Spa (Southam 2431). Originally a private collection, it became a zoo in 1966. One of the aims is to breed unusual animals to save them from extinction, and the first binturong to be reared successfully in England was bred here. Other animals include lions, leopards, pumas (all bred here), black bears, porcupines, racoons, llamas, various kinds of monkeys, Brazilian tapirs, Malabar squirrels, a cheetah, a spotted hyena and a lynx.

There are ponds for waterfowl, and other birds include Chilean flamingoes, Ceylon fish owls, vultures, eagles, hawks, pelicans, parrots, penguins, macaws and peafowl. 8 acres. *Open 10.00–dusk summer only. Access:* ½ mile E of Southam, on A425. Midland Red bus services 551/3, 596. 2 miles W of the Oxford Canal at Napton.

Twycross Zoo Park Norton-Juxta-Twycross, near Atherstone (Twycross 250). This started life as a private collection of animals, which expanded into a zoo and opened on its present site in 1963. One of the aims of the zoo is to breed species in danger of extinction, specialising in anthropoid apes and monkeys, and there are orang-utans, gorillas, chimpanzees, breeding colonies of black and white colobus monkeys, silvery marmosets and gibbons. It also contains lions, tigers, leopards, giraffes, camels, zebras, pumas, baby elephants, kangaroos and sea lions amongst other species.

There is a good collection of snakes, lizards and amphibians in the reptile house, which has a landscaped crocodile pool in the centre. The bird house and aviary contain colourful tropical birds, and there is a children's pets' corner. Summer attractions include a falconry display, chimpanzees' tea party, elephants' bath time and feeding the sea lions and penguins. 50 acres. *Open 10.00–19.00 summer, 10.00–dusk winter. Access:* 5½ miles N of Atherstone, on A444. Midland Red bus service 778.

WORCESTERSHIRE

Dudley Zoo Dudley (52401). Founded by Lord Dudley in 1937 and controlled by Dudley Zoological Society, the zoo is in the grounds of Dudley Castle (see page 144). The hill on which the castle stands was formerly used for surface limestone quarrying, and the quarries have now been made into spacious ravines for tigers, lions and bears. The aquarium, in the old crypt beneath the ruins of the castle chapel, contains over 1,100 tropical and freshwater fish.

The zoo contains a collection of over 1,200 animals, including a rare herd of Arabian gazelles, Barbary sheep, Cuban flamingos, giraffes, zebras, llamas, antelopes and camels. It is unusual in having two sea-lion pools for the purpose of breeding and rearing young. There is a children's zoo, a good reptile house, and an ape house with gorillas, orang-utans, chimpanzees and monkeys. 48 acres. *Open 10.00–18.00 or sunset, according to season. Access:* On northern outskirts of Dudley, off A459. The Dudley Canal is right underneath the zoo, tunnelling its way through Dudley Hill.

Guillotine gate, King's Norton Stop Lock

Stourport

Museums and galleries

Some of the museums listed below are of particular waterway interest, usually situated by canals; these are indicated by asterisks.

DERBYSHIRE

Derby

Derby Museum & Art Gallery Strand (Derby 31111). Museum: antiquities, bygones, ethnography, coins and medals, zoology, geology, local industries. Bonnie Prince Charlie room. An industrial section incorporating working layout of the former Midland Railway. Art Gallery: paintings by Wright of Derby, Derby porcelain, costume. *Open weekdays 10.00–18.00, Sun 14.30–16.30. Closed G. Fri, Xmas & Box.*

LEICESTERSHIRE

Leicester

Belgrave Hall Thurcaston Road (61610). Small Queen Anne house and garden. Good collection of early 18th and 19thC furniture. Also stables, coaches and agricultural collection. *Open weekdays 10.00–17.00 (Apr & Sep 10.00–18.00, May to Aug 10.00–19.00), Sun 14.00–17.00.*

Guildhall Guildhall Lane (21523). Mediaeval Guildhall and later Town Hall of Leicester. Hall, Mayor's Parlour, library, cells, fine oak panelling and a massive carved chimney-piece dated 1637. *Open weekdays only 10.00–17.00 (Apr & Sep 10.00–18.00, May to Aug 10.00–19.00). Closed G. Frl & Xmas.*

Jewry Wall & Museum of Archaeology St Nicholas Street (22392). Remains of 2ndC Roman Baths and the Jewry Wall can be seen, also two Roman mosaic pavements in situ. *Open weekdays 10.30–19.00, Sun 14.00–17.00. Closed G. Fri & Xmas.*

Leicester Museum & Art Gallery New Walk (26832-3-4). 18th and 19thC English paintings and watercolours. Also modern paintings. Ceramics gallery. Archives and geology. *Open weekdays 10.00–17.00 (Apr & Sep 10.00–18.00, May to Aug 10.00–19.00), Sat 10.00–19.00, Sun 14.00–17.00.*

The Magazine The Newarke (50988–9). Museum of the Royal Leicestershire Regiment. *Open weekdays 10.00–17.00 (Apr & Sep 10.00–18.00, May to Aug 10.00–19.00), Sun 14.00–17.00.*

Museum of Technology Abbey Pumping Station, Corporation Road. Currently under development; following parts now open: Road Transport Gallery with horse-drawn vehicles, cycles, motor cycles and motor cars. *Open weekdays 10.00–17.00, Sun 14.00–17.00. Closed Tue.*

Newarke Houses Museum The Newarke (50988–9). Social history of the locality from 1500 to present day. Locally made clocks and a clock-maker's workshop. Also shows the history of the hosiery, costume and lace industries. *Open weekdays 10.00–17.00 (Apr & Sep 10.00–18.00, May to Aug 10.00–19.00), Sun 14.00–17.00. Closed G. Fri & Xmas.*

Railway Museum London Road, Stoneygate. A collection of items showing local railway history. *Open Thur & Fri 14.00–17.00, Sat & Sun 11.00–17.00.*

Road Transport Museum Oxford Street. Motor cars, motor cycles, bicycles and horse-drawn vehicles. Arranged to show the development of road transport. *Open weekdays 10.00–17.00, Sun 14.00–17.00. Closed Tue, G. Fri & Xmas.*

Market Harborough

Market Harborough Archaeological & Historical Society Museum The County Library (2649). *Open weekdays 10.00–12.30, 13.30–17.00.*

NORTHAMPTONSHIRE

Northampton

Central Museum & Art Gallery Guildhall Road (34881 weekdays, 39131 evenings and weekends). Archaeology, antiquities, paintings, furniture and the finest collection of historical footwear in Europe, including Queen Victoria's wedding shoes and ballet shoes of Nijinsky. *Open weekdays 10.00–18.00, Thur & Sat 10.00–20.00.*

Abington Park

Abington Museum (31454). 15thC manor house, partly rebuilt 1745. Period rooms, including Victorian 'street'. Folk material, Chinese ceramics. Ethnographical and natural history material. *Open weekdays Apr to Sep 10.00–12.30, 14.00–18.00, Sun 14.30–17.00. Weekdays only Oct to Mar.*

The Northampton Regiment Museum *Open weekdays Apr to Sep 10.00–12.30, 14.00–18.00, Sun 14.30–17.30*

Stoke Bruerne

*Waterways Museum (off A508, 3½ miles S of M1 Junction) (Northampton 862229). Canalside, on Grand Union Canal. Housed in a fine old stone granary, this unique collection brings to life the rich history of over 200 years of canals. Exhibits include a traditional narrowboat and boat-weighing machine displayed outdoors, a reconstructed butty boat cabin, steam and diesel engines, and extensive displays of clothing, cabinware, brasses, signs, models, paintings, photographs, plans and documents. Museum shop selling canal literature, maps, postcards, souvenirs and other ephemera. *Open daily 10.00–12.30, 14.00–17.00 & in summer, 18.00–19.30. Closed winter Mons, Xmas and Box.* (For further information on Stoke Bruerne, see the section on 'Where to see canals'.)

Wootton

Royal Pioneer Corps Museum Simpson Barracks (2 miles S of Northampton, on A508) (62742). *Open weekdays 09.00–17.00.*

NOTTINGHAMSHIRE

Nottingham

Nottingham City Museum & Art Gallery The Castle (43615). The 17thC Castle contains a museum with ceramics, glass, silver, woodwork, ironwork, costume, textiles, lace. 17th and 18thC vehicles and Nottingham mediaeval alabaster carvings. Art Gallery: paintings and drawings (mainly English) from 14thC to present day. The Castle also houses **The Sherwood Foresters Regimental Museum.** (43615). *Open weekdays 10.00–18.45, Sun 10.00–16.45.*

Wollaton

Natural History Museum Wollaton Hall (2 miles W of Nottingham, on A609) (281 333). An Elizabethan mansion partly by Robert Smythson, dating from 1580–88, in a large park. Natural history collections, departments of zoology, botany and geology, and extensive British and foreign herbaria. *Open weekdays Apr to Sep 10.00–19.00, Oct to Mar 10.00–16.30; Sun Mar to Oct 14.00–17.00, Nov to Feb 13.30–16.30.*

Industrial Museum Wollaton Hall Stables. A new museum featuring Nottingham industry with special reference to lacemaking. *Open Thur & Sat Apr to Sep 10.00–19.00, Oct to Mar 10.00–17.30; Sun 14.00–16.30.*

University Art Gallery (Dept of Fine Art), Portland Building, University Park (56101). Exhibitions change three times a term. *Open weekdays 11.00–21.30, Sat 11.00–17.00.*

SALOP

Telford

*Ironbridge Gorge Museum Southside, Church Hill (3522). Lies between the river Severn and the B4380. An open-air industrial museum covering 6 square miles. The emphasis placed on original, working exhibits makes it a particularly exciting place to visit. It is set in the area which is regarded as being the cradle of the Industrial Revolution. It was here, in the Coalbrookdale furnace, that Abraham Darby first smelted iron with coke, making feasible the manufacture of iron rails, boats, aqueducts and building frames. Visitors can see the world's first iron bridge (constructed in 1779), Tar Tunnel, driven by miners in the 18thC, a pottery, giant steam blowing engines and the Hay Inclined Plane, which connected the upper and lower levels of the Shropshire Canal (restoration work is currently in progress). There is an information centre in the tollhouse, near the Iron Bridge. *Open daily throughout year: 10.00–18.00 Apr to Oct, closes earlier during winter.*

STAFFORDSHIRE

Blithfield

Museum of Childhood & Costume Blithfield Hall, near Rugeley (near Blithfield Reservoir, 4 miles N of Rugeley, off B5013) (Dapple Heath 249). Fine Great Hall, carved oak staircase and Stuart relics. Attractive grounds, orangery and rose garden. Museum contains children's toys, books, furniture, Georgian costumes and uniforms. Exhibitions of needlework figures, toy and miniature theatres. *Open G. Fri to first Sun in Oct, Wed, Thur & weekends 14.30–18.00. Also Easter, spring & late summer B. Hol Mon 12.00–19.00, Tue following 14.30–18.00.*

Burton-on-Trent

Museum & Art Gallery Guild Street (0283 3042). Museum largely devoted to local history. *Open weekdays 11.00–17.00. Closed Sun & B. Hol.*

Great Haywood

*Museum of Staffordshire Life Shugborough Hall, Great Haywood (near the Staffs & Worcs Canal). An excellent museum housed in the 'outbuildings' of Shugborough Hall. Skilful layout and design show off to its best a collection of sporting guns, old vehicles, farm implements and rural bygones. The old estate brewhouse and laundry, restored to their original condition, give a valuable glimpse of manorial life in the 18thC. *Open weekdays 11.00–17.30, Sun & B. Hols 14.00–17.30. Closed Mon.*

Leek

Art Gallery Nicholson Institute (2615). Small permanent collection supplemented by travelling exhibitions. *Open daily 10.00–21.00, Sat 10.00–17.00.*

*Cheddleton Flint Mill (8 miles NNW of Cheadle on A520, on Caldon Canal). Twin water mills on river Churnet, preserved with undershot wheels and machinery, operate flint grinding pans. Museum collection of machinery used in pottery milling includes 100 hp steam engine. *Open weekend pm Apr to Oct & often in other months).*

Lichfield

Art Gallery & Museum Bird Street (2177). Small museum specialising in local history. Art Gallery shows loan and local exhibitions throughout the year. Exhibitions are held in the Norman Castle. *Open weekdays 10.00–18.00.*

Dr Johnson's Birthplace Bread Market Street. Relics and pictures of Dr Johnson and his contemporaries. *Open weekdays Apr to Oct & summer B. Hol 10.00–13.00, 14.00–17.00. Closed Mon. Weekdays Nov to Mar 10.00–13.00, 14.00–16.00. Closed Mon, Xmas, Box & G. Fri. Sun Jun to Sep 14.30–17.00.*

The Staffordshire Regiment (The Prince of Wales's) Regimental Museum Whittington Barracks (3 miles SE of Lichfield, off Tamworth Road, A51) (2971 ex 220). *Open weekdays 09.00–16.30, weekends & B. Hols by arrangement.*

Newcastle-under-Lyme

Newcastle-under-Lyme Borough Museum & Art Gallery Brampton Park (69705). Collections of local history including Royal charters, natural science, textiles, geology and general science, 18th and 19thC English watercolours, fine art, firearms, and a specialist ceramic collection. *Open weekdays 09.30–13.00, 14.00–18.00, Sun May to Sep 14.00–17.30.*

Shugborough

Staffordshire County Museum & Mansion House near Stafford (5 miles SE of Stafford, off A513) (Little Haywood 388). The central block of the house dates from 1693, with wings of 1748 and additions by Samuel Wyatt. Fine plasterwork, pictures and furnishings and a notable garden. *Open weekdays 11.00–17.30, Sun & B. Hols 14.00–17.30. Closed Mon.* The museum is in the stable block; its exhibits focus on Staffordshire country life. See Great Haywood entry (above).

Stafford

Izaak Walton's Cottage Shallowford (5 miles NW of Stafford, between Norton Bridge and Great

Bridgford, off A520) (Yarnfield 278). The restored country cottage of the author of 'The Compleat Angler'. *Open daily 10.00–13.00, 14.30–16.30. Closed Tue.*

Stafford Museum & Art Gallery The Green (2151). Small museum relating to the history, social life, art and industry of the locality. Art Gallery shows loan and local exhibitions. *Open weekdays 10.00–19.00, Sat 10.00–17.00.*

Stoke-on-Trent

Arnold Bennett Museum 205 Waterloo Road, Cobridge (between Hanley and Burslem, on A50) (25426). The writer's early home with two rooms showing drawings and personal relics. *Open Mon, Wed, Thur & Sat 14.00–17.00.*

City Museum & Art Gallery Broad Street, Hanley (22714–5). Important collections of Staffordshire pottery and porcelain, also Continental, South American, Near Eastern and oriental pottery, collections of 18thC English watercolours and painting since 1900, sculpture, costume, samplers, dolls and Staffordshire archaeological collections. Natural history section contains a collection of Staffordshire birds and mammals. *Open weekdays 10.00–18.00, Sun 14.30–17.00.*

Spode-Copeland Museum & Art Gallery Church Street (48557). The Works Museum contains examples of 18th to 20thC Spode pottery; the Family Museum displays a comprehensive collection of international pottery from early Chinese onwards. Very fine collection of early Spode blueprinted ware, bone china and stone china. *Open weekdays only 10.00–16.00 (by appointment only). Tours of factory arranged by appointment at 10.15 and 14.15.*

The Wedgwood Museum Josiah Wedgwood & Sons Ltd, Barlaston (4 miles S of Stoke-on-Trent, between A34 and A520) (Barlaston 2141). An extensive collection of early Wedgwood ware. *Admission by appointment with the curator.* The Trent & Mersey Canal is only a few yards from the Museum.

Tamworth

Tamworth Castle Museum The Holloway. (3561). The Norman Castle, with Tudor Banqueting Hall and Jacobean State Apartments, houses a recently re-organised local history museum. *Open weekdays Mar to Oct 10.00–20.00, Sun 14.00–20.00; weekdays Nov to Feb 10.00–16.00, Sun 14.00–16.00. Closed Fri.*

Wall

Letocetum Museum (2 miles SW of Lichfield, off A5). Remains of baths and finds from the excavated Roman garrison 'Letocetum' at the junction of the Roman roads Watling Street and Ryknild Street. *Open daily Mar, Apr & Oct 09.30–17.30 (Sun 14.00–17.30), May to Sep 09.30–19.00 (Sun 14.00–19.00), Nov to Feb 09.30–16.00 (Sun 14.00–16.00).*

Walsall

E. M. Flint Art Gallery Lichfield Street. Paintings include the Sister Dora, Jerome K. Jerome and Loriners collections. Also a collection of works by Lock (at Willenhall). Regular exhibitions of pictures from national sources.

The Museum of Leathercraft Central Library & Art Gallery, Lichfield Street (23920). 'Leather in Life' permanent exhibition. *Open daily 10.00–19.00, Sat 10.00–17.30.*

West Bromwich

Oak House Museum Oak Road (021-553 0759). A beautiful 16thC half-timbered house, furnished in period style. *Open weekdays 10.00–16.00, Sun summer only 14.30–17.00. Closed Thur pm.*

Wolverhampton

Bantock House Bantock Park (24548). Fine collections of English painted enamels and japanned ware. Worcester porcelain and Staffordshire and Wedgwood pottery. Dolls, old costumes, ivory and local collections. *Open weekdays 10.00–18.00, Sun 14.00–17.00.*

Bilston Museum & Art Gallery Mount Pleasant (42097). English painted enamels and Staffordshire pottery. *Open Mon, Tue, Thur & Fri 10.00–19.00, Wed & Sat 10.00–17.00.*

Central Art Gallery Lichfield Street (24549). 18th and 19thC English watercolours and oil paintings including works by Bonington, Fuseli, Gainsborough and Wilson. Modern prints, paintings and drawings. Sculpture by local artist. Oriental collections. *Open weekdays 10.00–18.00.*

WARWICKSHIRE

Birmingham

The Assay Office Newhall Street (021-236 6951-2-3). Collection of old Birmingham and other silverware, coins, tokens and medals. Library dealing with all aspects of gold and silver work. Collection of correspondence of Matthew Boulton comprising some thousands of letters, c 1760–1810. *By appointment only.*

Aston Hall Trinity Road, Aston (2 miles N of city, off A34). A Jacobean house surrounded by a park and built by Sir Thomas Holte in 1618–35. There are impressive friezes and ceilings. Of particular interest is the Coke collection of Tudor oak furniture, which includes four magnificent court chests. *Open summer weekdays 10.00–17.00, Sun 14.00–17.00, winter weekdays 10.00–dusk.*

Avery Historical Museum Soho Foundry (021-558 1112). A collection of machines, instruments, weights, records, etc., relating to the history of weighing. *Open during factory hours by appointment.*

Barber Institute of Fine Arts The University, Edgbaston (021-472 0962). Galleries of the Institute contain the first-class art collection belonging to the Trustees. *Open weekdays 10.00–17.00, Sat 10.00–13.00. Closed Suns, B. Hols & University general hols.*

Birmingham City Museum & Art Gallery Congreve Street. One of the most important museums outside London with departments of archaeology, art, ethnography, local history, natural history, science and industry. Fine Old Master paintings and an exceptional collection of Pre-Raphaelites. Famous Pinto collections of wooden bygones and an unusual number of industrial relics. *For opening times ring information bureau (021-2364051).*

Cannon Hill Museum Pershore Road (2½ miles SSW of city, on A441). Designed primarily for children. Illustrated leisure-time pursuits including bird-watching, bee-keeping, fishing and pets. Safari hut around which the sounds, sights and smells of the African bush are recreated. *Open weekdays 10.00–20.00 (winter 10.00–17.00), Sun 14.00–17.00.*

Geological Departmental Museum The University, Edgbaston (021-472 1301 ex134). Collections in palaeontology, stratigraphy, petrology, mineralogy and physical geology, including the Holcroft collection of fossils and the Lapworth collection of graptolites. *Open daily 09.00–17.00 by arrangement.*

Weoley Castle Alwold Road (021-427 4270). Remains of a fortified manor house surrounded by a moat and constructed, with alterations, between 1100 and 1320. Rich and varied archaeological finds housed in a small museum on the site. *Open Wed 14.00–20.00 (or dusk), Sat 10.00–17.00, Thur, Fri & Sun 14.00–17.00. Closed Mon and Tue, G. Fri, Xmas and Box.*

Coventry

Herbert Art Gallery & Museum Jordan Well (25555). Local collections include natural history and industry (including Coventry-built cars). The Art Gallery displays contemporary British painting, sculpture, water-colours, oil paintings, topography, and portraiture of local interest. Also works by local artists, and the Iliffe collection of Sutherland tapestry sketches. *Open Mon, Thur, Fri & Sat 10.00–18.00, Tue & Wed 10.00–20.00, Sun 14.00–17.00.*

Whitefriars Museum of Local History A branch of the Herbert Museum, housed in the cloister of the mediaeval White Friary. Contains archaeological exhibits, particularly of the mediaeval period. *Open Fri & Sat 10.00–18.00, Sun 14.00–17.00.*

Leamington Spa

Leamington Spa Art Gallery & Museum Avenue Road (25873). Paintings by Dutch and Flemish Masters, also 20thC oils and watercolours, mainly English. 16th to 19thC pottery and porcelain, 18thC and modern English glass. *Open weekdays 10.45–12.45, 14.30–17.00, Sun 14.30–17.00. Closed Wed pm.*

Nuneaton

Nuneaton Museum & Art Gallery Riversley Park (2683). Pre-history archaeology (including items from Roman and mediaeval Nuneaton), geology, mining, ethnography and anthropology, paintings and engravings, coins and medals, George Eliot personalia. *Open weekdays 12.00–19.00, weekends 10.00–19.00. Closes at 17.00 Nov to Mar.*

Rugby

Rugby Library, Exhibition Gallery & Museum St Matthew Street (2687). Regular loan exhibitions by local societies (Warwickshire agricultural and domestic collection in store). *Open daily 10.00–20.00.*

Stratford-upon-Avon

Shakespeare Birthplace Trust Properties *For details of opening times telephone Stratford 4016.*

Ann Hathaway's Cottage Shottery (1 mile W of Stratford-upon-Avon, off A422). The thatched and timbered Elizabethan cottage, birthplace of Shakespeare's wife, contains furniture and heirlooms from Tudor period onwards. Pretty garden and orchard.

Hall's Croft Old Town. The former home of Shakespeare's daughter Susannah, a Tudor town house containing rare Elizabethan and Jacobean furniture. Exhibition room showing the story of the Stratford Shakespeare Festival.

Harvard House High Street. A half-timbered house dating from 1596, former home of the mother of John Harvard, founder of the American University. *Open weekdays Apr to Sep 09.00–13.00, 14.00–18.00, Sun 14.00–18.00. Weekdays only Oct to Mar 10.00–13.00, 14.00–16.00.*

Mary Arden's House Wilmcote (5 miles NW of Stratford-upon-Avon, off A34). A 16thC half-timbered farmhouse, birthplace of Shakespeare's mother, furnished in period style. The barns contain old Warwickshire agricultural implements and bygones.

New Place & Nash's House Foundations of the house (destroyed in 1759) where Shakespeare died in 1616. Picturesque knot garden; ancient mulberry tree in the Great Garden of New Place. Nash's House contains material illustrative of the background of Shakespeare's England, together with local historical exhibits including Roman and Anglo-Saxon antiquities and David Garrick exhibits. *Open weekdays Apr to Oct 09.00–18.00, Sun 14.00–18.00. Weekdays only Nov to Mar 09.00–12.45, 14.00–16.00.*

The Royal Shakespeare Theatre Picture Gallery Original costumes and designs, portraits of famous actors and actresses. Exhibition of Shakespeare portraits. *Open daily 10.00–13.00, 14.00–18.00, Sun 14.00–18.00.*

Shakespeare's Birthplace Henley Street. The half-timbered house where Shakespeare was born in 1564, containing books, manuscripts, pictures and exhibits. Several rooms furnished in period style.

The Museum of the Queen's Own Warwickshire & Worcestershire Yeomanry T & AVR Centre, New Broad Street. *Open weekdays 09.00–17.00, weekends by arrangement.*

Sutton Coldfield

Old Smithy Driffold Corner, Birmingham Road. A 15thC timbered house with 17thC stone and brick extension, now used as a museum featuring local items, including old pictures and photographs of the town. *Open summer only Wed and Sat 14.30–17.30.*

Warwick

Doll Museum Oken's House, Castle Street. A half-timbered Elizabethan house, the 16thC birthplace of Thomas Oken, a benefactor of the town. Now a doll museum containing the Joy Robinson collection of antique and period dolls and toys. *Open weekdays 10.00–18.00, Sun 14.30–17.00.*

The Museum of the Queen's Own Hussars Lord Leycester Hospital, High Street. *Open weekdays: summer 10.00–18.00, winter 10.00–16.00.*

St John's House Coten End (43431 ex 132). A fine 17thC house, with gardens and notable wrought-iron gates, now a branch of the County Museum with local bygones, crafts, period costume and furniture. Also contains the **Regimental Museum of the Royal Warwickshire Regiment** (41653). *Open weekdays 10.00–12.30, 13.30–17.30, Sun (May to Sep) 14.30–17.00. Closed Tue.*

Warwick County Museum Market Place (43431 ex 329). Collections illustrate wild life, geology, archaeology and history of Warwickshire. A 17thC Sheldon tapestry is on show. *Open weekdays 10.00–17.30, Sun (May to Sep) 14.30–17.00.*

Yardley

Blakesley Hall Blakesley Road (6 miles SE of Birmingham, off A45) (021-783 2193). A half-timbered 16thC house, now a museum containing archaeological and local history exhibits. *Open daily 09.30–18.00, Sun 14.00–17.00. Closed G. Fri, Xmas and Box.*

WORCESTERSHIRE

Broadheath

Elgar Museum (2 miles NW of Worcester, off

B4204). The cottage where Sir Edward Elgar was born in 1857, now a small museum containing proof scores, books and relics. *Open daily 13.30–18.30. Closed Wed.*

Bromsgrove

Playthings Past Museum Beaconwood, Beacon Hill. Antique and period dolls, dolls' houses, toys and automata. *Opening times: by written application for appointment only (children under 12 years not admitted).*

Dudley

***Black Country Museum** at the junction of Tipton Road and the Birmingham–Wolverhampton road (56321). An exciting project being developed on a site near Dudley town centre with access from the A461; it is adjacent to the present museum and art gallery, and overlooks the entrance to Dudley Canal tunnel, from which the museum will be accessible. Exhibits illustrating the industrial, economic and social development of the Black Country will be shown, ranging from machine tools and colliery equipment to canal boats and trams. It is hoped that the museum will be opened during the first half of 1974; visits will be by appointment only during the initial period.

Brierley Hill Glass Museum & Art Gallery Moor Street (56321). A fine collection of local ('Stourbridge') and foreign glass and reference literature. Occasional temporary exhibitions. *Open weekdays 14.00–17.00, Sat 10.00–13.00. Closed Wed.*

Dudley Museum & Art Gallery St James's Road (56321). Permanent collection and temporary exhibitions throughout the year. Fine geological gallery, especially of local limestone and coal measure fossils. Reconstructed Black Country Nail Forge. Adjacent **Brooke-Robinson Museum** shows benefactor's personal collection of fine art and temporary exhibitions (*open occasionally as advertised*). *Open weekdays 10.00–18.00. Closed B. Hols.*

Hartlebury

Worcestershire County Museum Hartlebury Castle (5 miles S of Kidderminster on A449) (416). Situtated in the north wing of the Bishop's Castle, the museum includes the county archaeology and geology, crafts and industries, a restored cider mill, furniture, glass and costume, period furnishings, toys, dolls, horse-drawn vehicles and gipsy caravans. There is also a forge and wheelwright's shop. *Open Feb to Nov, Mon to Thur 10.00–18.00, weekends 14.00–18.00.*

Kidderminster

Art Gallery Market Street (62832/33). Loan exhibitions (from national collections and by individual artists), Brangwyn etchings, small permanent collection. *Open weekdays 10.00–18.00.*

Museum Local studies and archaeology. Official repository for the local archaeological and historical society. *Open as Art Gallery.*

Stoke Prior

The Avoncroft Museum of Buildings (1 mile S of Bromsgrove, at junction of B4091 and A4024) (Bromsgrove 31363). A new project which displays old buildings re-erected and saved from demolition. A 15thC timber-framed merchant's house, an old post mill, a windmill and a nailmaker's workshop are being restored. *Open weekends mid-Mar to mid-Oct 11.00–18.00, Wed & Thur 14.00–17.00.*

Worcester

City Museum & Art Gallery Foregate Street (22154). Expanding collections of folk-life material, antiques, archaeology, geology and natural history. The Art Gallery has travelling exhibitions and a permanent collection including particularly interesting local items. *Open weekdays 09.30–18.00 (Thur & Sat close at 17.00).* A large gallery is devoted to the **Museum of the Worcestershire Regiment** (24301). *Open weekdays 10.00–13.00, 14.00–18.00.*

The Dyson Perrins Museum of Worcester Porcelain The Royal Porcelain Works, Severn Street (23221). The finest and most comprehensive collection of old Worcester in the world. *Open weekdays 10.00–13.00, 14.00–17.00, Sat May to Sep. Tours of the works can be arranged. Week days 10.00–11.45, 14.00–15.45.*

***Tudor House Folk Museum** Friar Street. Displays illustrating the city's domestic life, also various themes such as 'The place of the river Severn in the history of Worcester'. *Open weekdays 10.30–17.00. Closed Thur.*

Tame Aqueduct, Fazeley

Restaurants

The following restaurants are all recommended by the Good Food Guide. L = Lunch, D = Dinner.

Albany Hotel, Four Seasons Restaurant St James's Street, Nottingham (40131). The standard of cooking is high and the menu, although expensive, offers such delicacies as champignons alsacienne (deep fried, with béarnaise sauce), suprême de faisan au suc d'orange, cooked at the table with fresh oranges and curaçao, and — occasionally — red mullet in a pastry case with champagne sauce.

Andalucia Restaurant 10 Henry Street, Rugby, Warwickshire (Rugby 6404). Genuine Spanish restaurant with a singing guitarist in the evenings. Recommended dishes include tortilla mimosa (with fresh asparagus), paella and medallones de langosta sanfaina (a combination of lobster, chicken and rice). There is a good selection of Spanish wines. Under a mile from the Oxford Canal.

Aylesford Restaurant 1 High Street, Warwick (42799). Lunch is served in the bistro-style Continental Room downstairs, and dinner is in the formal Regency Room above. The extensive menu offers seafood salad, stuffed aubergines, moules marinière, escalope Cordon Bleu, breast of pheasant, Dover sole Romano (with lobster and prawn sauce), oranges in Grand Marnier and profiteroles. *Closed Sun.*

Le Bistro 20 St James's Street, Nottingham (42993). Curtained booths for privacy and, on some evenings, a guitarist make this bistro unusual. Dishes include veal in cream, poulet basquaise and entrecôte. *D only. Closed Sun.*

La Capanna Hurst Street, Birmingham (021-622 2287). Small Italian restaurant with an imaginative menu. *Closed Sun.*

La Copper Kettle 151 Milcote Road, Bearwood, Birmingham (021-429 7920). A welcome addition to Birmingham's restaurants. Very simple lunches are served and, on three nights a week, slightly more elaborate dinners. On Wednesdays there is a cookery demonstration followed by a set dinner. On Mondays and Tuesdays, only prebooked private parties are served. Recommended dishes include soupe aux poissons, rillettes, scampi provençale and tarte aux pommes. Currently unlicensed; 25p corkage. *Closed Aug 1 to Sep 1; Sun; Mon & Tue D (exc parties).* Due west of city centre.

Cossington Mill Cossington, Leicestershire (Sileby 2205). An oak-beamed converted mill that has stood near the junction of the Soar and the Wreake for 700 years. *Closed 1 week over Xmas; Sun.* 5 miles N of Leicester near Rothley crossroads, off A6. Beside Cossington Lock on the river Soar.

Danish Food Centre 10 Stephenson Place, Birmingham (021-643 2837). Meals are served all day, from breakfast (09.30–11.30) in the Danwich Bar, to eat-as-you-please lunches and dinners and after-theatre supper in the Copenhagen Rooms. Schnapps and draught Tuborg are recommended. *Meals 10.00–17.00, 18.00–23.00. Closed Sun; Mon D.*

Dog and Partridge High Street, Tutbury, Staffordshire (Tutbury 2162 & 2182). A busy Truman pub with good food, including duck pâté, chicken Pavenham and bœuf en croûte. 4 miles NW of Burton-on-Trent, on A50.

Giorgio's 77 Narborough Road, Leicester (29267). Formerly 'La Gioconda'. Recommended dishes include smokies, scallops, ratatouille and zabaglione. *Closed Sun; Sat L.* Easily accessible from most of the bridges along the Grand Union Canal in Leicester.

Golden Pheasant Shelton Lock, Derbyshire (Derby 700112). A lavishly decorated, typical North Midland restaurant offering an à la carte menu and set meals, which include good pâté, escalope Marsala and an inviting selection of sweets. A quartet plays on Tue, Thur and Sat, for which there is a charge. *Closed Sun D.* 3 miles S of Derby on A514 (near the now-closed Derby Canal).

La Gondola 220 Osmaston Road, Derby (42383 & 32895). Converted Victorian house. The Italian-biased menu offers pasta, chicken and veal dishes. Dancing. *Closed Sun.*

Good Earth 19 Belvoir Street, Leicester (58584). Self-service vegetarian restaurant in the city centre, suitable for a quick lunch (12.00–15.00). Unlicensed. *Closed Sun; D.* Easily accessible from the Grand Union Canal.

Grange Farm Restaurant Toton, Nottinghamshire (Long Eaton 3413). A restaurant converted from cowsheds and stables. The farmhouse fare includes steak and kidney pie and hot cherries with ice cream. *Closed Sun.* 6 miles SW of Nottingham on B6003 (near the Erewash Canal).

Hundred House Great Witley, Worcestershire (Great Witley 215). Modernised Georgian house whose owners both cook. The short menu is 'French provincial' and frequently changes. The choice includes grilled scallops, smoked salmon, or the help-yourself hors d'œuvre table, lamb's kidneys in port and cream sauce, and a good selection of unusual puddings. The cold buffet lunch is also recommended. *Meals 12.00–14.00 (buffet), 20.00–20.45. Closed Sun & Mon D.* 11 miles NW of Worcester on A443 (4 miles W of the river Severn).

Koh-I-Noor 188–190 Alfreton Road, Nottingham (76864). A long-established Pakistani restaurant. The menu includes ample well-spiced dishes such as chicken vindaloo and biriani. *Orders taken until after midnight.*

Loon Wah 11 Bromsgrove Street, Birmingham (021-622 2697). Above average Chinese restaurant. Recommended dishes include beancurd in oyster sauce, steamed chicken with black beans and sliced beef with Chinese vegetables. Unlicensed. *Meals noon to midnight.*

Marianne 3 Greenhill Street, Stratford-upon-Avon, Warwickshire (Stratford 3563). Very French, with simple décor, and an adventurous menu. Pipérade, gratinée lyonnaise, guinea fowl, filet en croûte and the tartes maison are all recommended. *Closed for 'Stratford Mop' (on Oct 12); Sun.*

Newton Park Hotel, de Soligni Restaurant

Newton Solney, Derbyshire (Repton 3568). The French/English menu offers a wide variety of dishes, and there is a large selection of wines. 2 miles NE of Burton-on-Trent, off B5008 (3 miles SW of the Trent & Mersey Canal at Willington).

Old Farmhouse Restaurant Armitage, Staffordshire (Armitage 490353). Very popular English restaurant with many specialities, including Old Farmhouse smokies, lobster with cheese sauce, syllabub and strawberry gâteau. Essential to book. *Closed last week Jul, first week Aug; weekends; Mon L.* On A513 2 miles SE of Rugeley, just across the road from the Trent & Mersey Canal, which skirts Armitage.

Palm Court Duffield Road, Allestree. Derby (58107 & 50500). On the A6. Formerly called Court Barbecue, then Court Restaurant. Specialities are game and sea food. *Closed Mon; Sun D.*

Pattishall Grange Pattishall, Northamptonshire (Pattishall 217). A private Victorian house with a popular, small dining room for which it is essential to book well in advance. The short menu includes bortsch, ratatouille, bœuf Stroganoff and chicken Marengo. *Closed Sun,* 4 miles N of Towcester, off A5 (1 mile SW of the Grand Union Canal, near Gayton Junction).

Peacock Inn The Square, Market Harborough, Leicestershire (Market Harborough 2269). A stone-built pub decorated in William Morris style, owned by Poste Hotels. Recommended dishes include baked egg with shrimps dressed with cucumber, turkey breasts with garlic butter, and Melton ham. A ½-mile walk down from the canal basin at the end of the Market Harborough Arm.

Restaurant Beaudesert Birmingham Road, Henley-in-Arden, Warwickshire (Henley-in-Arden 2675). This small, comfortable restaurant runs dinner-dances on Fridays and Saturdays. The menu includes halibut poached in white wine, guinea fowl marinated in red wine, and various home-made ice creams. *Closed Aug 19 to Sep 9; Mon; Sun D; L (exc Sun).* 1 mile N of Henley-in-Arden on A34 (from the Stratford-upon-Avon Canal, 1½ miles, west of Preston Bagot along B4095).

Salamis Kebab House 178 Broad Street, Edgbaston, Birmingham (021-643 2997). Friendly Greek restaurant by Five Ways. Afelia and kebabs of lamb and pork are recommended, and appropriate Greek wines are suggested for different dishes. *D only (18.00–24.00). Closed B. Hols & preceding Suns.*

Sanremo 5 Sadler Gate, Derby (41752). Simple trattoria in a pleasant Georgian side street near the cathedral. Recommended dishes include risotto alla marinara (with prawns, sole, turbot and mullet), lasagne, kidney Sicilian special and cassata. *Closed 2 weeks Jul to Aug; Sun.*

Sun Inn Marston Trussell, Leicestershire (Market Harborough 5531). An old pub restored and modernised with ambitious cooking. Specialities include quail with red wine and brandy sauce, seafood rosé à la crème and tournedos Soleil (with pâté, chicken liver and red wine sauce). The wines are chosen with care. 3 miles W of Market Harborough, off A427 (equidistant from Harborough and Foxton).

Swan House Hotel Wilmcote, Warwickshire (Stratford-upon-Avon 2030). A charming, small and comfortable Georgian hotel. Whiting Orly, trout stuffed with spinach and mushrooms, salmon mousse, duckling and Armenian lamb are recommended, and traditional roasts are served for Sunday lunch. *Closed Sun & Mon D; every 3rd Fri L.* 4 miles N of Stratford, off A34 (¼ mile from the Stratford-upon-Avon Canal in Wilmcote).

Swan's Nest Hotel, Bewick Restaurant Stratford-upon-Avon, Warwickshire (Stratford 66761). Attractive hotel by the Avon at Clopton Bridge. The menu includes coq au vin, scampi provençale, ratatouille and bilberry cheesecake.

Valentia Arms Hotel Upper Arley, Worcestershire (Arley 218). A pleasant old pub with a short, regularly changed menu which has included pear and walnut salad with fresh prawns, saddle of lamb in Madeira sauce and poached fresh peaches in brandy sauce. *Closed Sun & Mon D.* 4 miles NW of Kidderminster off A442. (On the unnavigable section of the river Severn upstream of Stourport.)

Woodhouse Hotel Princethorpe, Warwickshire (Marton 303). This comfortable hotel has an unusual menu which includes fresh trout from a tank, excellent bouillabaisse, a good selection of fresh vegetables, and a wide variety of sweets. 1½ miles W of Princethorpe on B4453, 6 miles NE of Leamington Spa.

La Zouch 29 Kilwardby Street, Ashby-de-la-Zouch, Leicestershire (Ashby-de-la-Zouch 2536). A small but remarkably international restaurant with a repertoire of 200 dishes. Onion soup, pork , chops in cream and wine sauce and hazelnut meringue gâteau are all recommended. *Closed Dec 23–30; Mon; Sun D.*

Circular weir near Stourton Junction

Stoke Bruerne, Grand Union Canal

Index

Abandoned canals 43
Abington Museum, Abington Park 147
Albany Hotel, Four Seasons Restaurant, Nottingham 153
Alrewas 63
Althorp, Northamptonshire 140
Alton Towers, Staffordshire 140
Alvecote Pools 111
Andulucia Restaurant, Warwickshire 153
Angling 131
Ann Hathaway's Cottage, Stratford-upon-Avon 150
Aqueducts 15
Arbury Hall, Warwickshire 141
Arnold Bennett Museum, Stoke-on-Trent 149
Ashby Canal 43, 131
Ashby Canal Association 32
Ashby-de-la-Zouch Castle, Leicestershire 137
Assay Office, The, Birmingham 149
Association of Pleasure Craft Operators 33
Aston Hall, Birmingham 149
Aston Locks 11
Atherstone Locks 12
Avery Historical Museum, Birmingham 149
Avon Aqueduct 13
Avoncraft Museum of Buildings, The, Stoke Prior 151
Aylesford Restaurant, Warwick 153
Aylestone 66

Bantock House, Wolverhampton 149
Barber Institute of Fine Arts, Birmingham 149
Basins 60
Bearley Aqueduct 14
Belgrave Hall, Leicester 147
Bilston Museum & Art Gallery, Wolverhampton 149
Bird life of the Trent & Mersey Canal 119
Birmingham Canal Navigations 47, 58, 134
Birmingham Canal Navigations Society 32
Birmingham City Museum & Art Gallery 149
Birmingham & Fazeley Canal 108, 127, 134
Birmingham Zoo, Warwickshire 144
Le Bistro Restaurant, Nottingham 153
Black Country Museum, Dudley 151
Blakesley Hall, Yardley 150
Blisworth Tunnel 15
Boat clubs 29
Boat trips 26

Boatyards 21
Botanical Gardens, Warwickshire 141
Bradgate Park, Leicestershire 143
Braunston 8
Braunston Tunnel 15
Bridges 58
Brierley Hill Glass Museum & Art Gallery, Dudley 151
Brindley, James 53, 54
Brinklow Aqueduct 14
Brooke-Robinson Museum, Dudley 151
Brooksbury Agricultural College, Leicestershire 137
Burton Dassett Hills Country Park, Warwickshire 143
Burton-on-Trent 63
Burton-on-Trent Museum & Art Gallery 148

Caldon Canal 51
Cambrian Wharf, Birmingham 10
Canal carrying companies 30
Canal feeder reservoirs & their bird life 117
Canal societies 32
Canal walks 125
Cannock Chase, Staffordshire 143
Cannon Hill Museum, Birmingham 149
Canons Ashby, Northamptonshire 140
La Capanna Restaurant, Birmingham 153
Central Art Gallery, Wolverhampton 149
Central Museum & Art Gallery, Northampton 147
Charlecote Park, Warwickshire 141
Charnwood Forest Canal 48
Cheddleton Flint Mill, Leek 148
Childhood & Costume Museum, Blithfield 148
Chillington Hall, Staffordshire 140
City Museum & Art Gallery, Stoke-on-Trent 149
City Museum & Art Gallery, Worcester 151
Clopton House, Warwickshire 141
Commandery, The, Worcestershire 142
La Copper Kettle Restaurant, Birmingham 153
Cossington Mill Restaurant, Leicestershire 153
Coton Manor Wildlife Garden, Northamptonshire 140
Cottages 60
Cottesbrooke Hall, Northamptonshire 140
Coughton Court, Warwickshire 141
Country parks 141
Coventry Canal 110, 131
Coventry Canal Society 32
Coventry Zoo Park, Warwickshire 144
Crick 67

Danish Food Centre, Birmingham 153
Davenham, Worcestershire 142
Dayboats for hire 28
Debdale Wharf 66
Delapré Abbey, Northamptonshire 140
Derby Canal 49
Derby Museum & Art Gallery 147
Dog and Partridge Restaurant,
 Staffordshire 153
Doll Museum, Warwick 150
Dosthill Quarry 109
Drainage 40
Draycote Water Country Park,
 Warwickshire 143
Drayton Manor Park & Zoo, Staffordshire
 144
Dr Johnson's Birthplace, Lichfield 148
Droitwich & Droitwich Junction Canals
 48
Dudley Canal 55, 134
Dudley Canal Trust 33
Dudley Castle, Staffordshire 142
Dudley Museum & Art Gallery 151
Dudley Tunnel 15
Dudley Zoo, Worcestershire 145
Duffield Castle, Derbyshire 137
Dyson Perrins Museum, Worcester 151

East Midlands canals 63
Ednaston Manor, Derbyshire 137
Elds Wood, Staffordshire 140
Elgar Museum, Broadheath 150
Elvaston Castle Country Park, Derbyshire
 143
E. M. Flint Art Gallery, Walsall 149
Erewash Canal 64
Erewash Canal Preservation &
 Development Association 33

Farmer's Bridge 11
Farnborough Hall, Warwickshire 141
Ford's Hospital, Warwickshire 141
Foremarke Hall, Derbyshire 137
'Forest Line' 65
Foxton 5, 67
Fradley Junction 9, 63

Galleries & museums 145
Gardens 137
Gas Street, Birmingham 10
Gayton (Northampton Arm) 68
Geological Departmental Museum,
 Birmingham 149
Giorgio's Restaurant, Leicester 153
Golden Pheasant Restaurant, Derbyshire
 153
La Gondola Restaurant, Derby 153
Good Earth Restaurant, Leicester 153
Grand Union Canal 58, 66, 131, 134
Grand Union Canal Society 33
Grange Farm Restaurant,
 Nottinghamshire 151
Grantham Canal 43
Grantham Canal Society 33
Great Haywood 11
Guildhall, Leicester 147

Hall's Croft, Stratford-upon-Avon 150
Hanbury Hall, Worcestershire 142
Hartlebury Castle, Worcestershire 142

Harvard House, Stratford-upon-Avon 150
Harvington Hall, Worcestershire 142
Hatton Locks 12
Hawkesbury 10
Henley-in-Arden Guildhall, Warwickshire
 141
Herbert Art Gallery & Museum, Coventry
 150
Highgate Common Country Park,
 Staffordshire 143
Himley Hall, Staffordshire 140
Hoar Cross Hall, Staffordshire 140
Holme Pierrepont Country Park,
 Nottinghamshire 143
Hopwas Wood 109
Houses and gardens 137
Hundred House Restaurant,
 Worcestershire 153
Husbands Bosworth 67

Industrial archaeology of the East
 Midland canals 63
Industrial archaeology of the West
 Midland canals 53
Industrial Museum, Wollaton 148
Inland Waterways Association 33
Invertebrate 114
Ironbridge Gorge Museum, Telford 148
Izaak Walton's Cottage, Stafford 148

Jewry Wall & Museum of Archaeology,
 Leicester 147

Kedleston Hall, Derbyshire 137
Kegworth 64
Kenilworth Castle, Warwickshire 141
Kidderminster Art Gallery & Museum 151
Kilby Bridge 66
Kingsford Country Park, Worcestershire
 143
Kinver Edge, Staffordshire 144
Kirby Muxloe Castle, Leicestershire 137
Koh-I-Noor Restaurant, Nottingham 153

Lapworth 8
Leamington Spa Art Gallery & Museum
 150
Leathercraft Museum, Walsall 149
Leek Art Gallery 148
Leicester Museum & Art Gallery 145
Leicester Navigation 64
Leicestershire: canal walks 127
Leicestershire & Northamptonshire Union
 Canal 66
Letocetum Museum, Wall 149
Lichfield Art Gallery & Museum 148
Locks 59
Loon Wah Restaurant, Birmingham 153
Lord Leycester Hospital, Warwickshire
 141
Loughborough 64
Loughborough Navigation 64
Lower Avon Navigation Trust 34

Magazine, The, Leicester 147
Marianne Restaurant, Stratford-upon-
 Avon 153
Market Harborough Archaeological &
 Historical Society Museum 147

Mary Arden's House, Stratford-upon-Avon 150
Melbourne Hall, Derbyshire 137
Melton Mowbray Navigation 51
Mines 60
Moseley Old Hall, Staffordshire 140
Mountsorrel 65
Museums & galleries 147

Napton Locks 12
Narrow Boat Trust 34
Nash's House, Stratford-upon-Avon 148
Natural history 105
Natural History Museum, Wollaton 148
Navigable canals 70
Navigation, touring circuits & distances 17
Netherton Tunnel 15, 58
New Cut, Leicester 66
New Place, Stratford-upon-Avon 150
Newarke Houses Museum, Leicester 147
Newbold Tunnel 16
Newcastle-under-Lyme Borough Museum & Art Gallery 148
Newcastle-under-Lyme canals 46
Newton Park Hotel, de Soligni Restaurant, Derbyshire 153
Norbury Manor, Derbyshire 137
Northampton Locks 12
Northamptonshire Regiment Museum, Abington Park 147
Nottingham Canal 46
Nottingham City Museum & Art Gallery 148
Nuneaton Museum & Art Gallery 150
Nuneaton Zoological Garden, Warwickshire 144
Nutbrook Canal 49

Oakham Canal 52
Oak House Museum, West Bromwich 149
Old Farmhouse Restaurant, Staffordshire 154
Old Smithy, Sutton Coldfield 150
Old Union Canals Society 34
Oxford Canal 56, 131

Packwood House, Warwickshire 141
Palm Court Restaurant, Derby 152
Patterns of water life 113
Pattishall Grange Restaurant, Northamptonshire 154
Peacock Inn, Market Harborough 154
Places to visit in the countryside 143
Planning a cruise 17
Plant life 113
Playthings Past Museum, Bromsgrove 151
Pleck Gardens, The, Warwickshire 141

Quarries 60
Queen's Own Hussars Museum, Warwick 150
Queen's Own Warwickshire & Worcestershire Yeomanry Museum, Stratford-upon-Avon 150

Ragley Hall, Warwickshire 141
Railway & Canal Historical Society 34

Railway Museum, Leicester 147
Restaurant Beaudesert, Warwickshire 154
Restaurants 153
River Derwent 63
River Severn 107
River Soar Navigation 65
River Trent 63
Road Transport Museum, Leicester 147
Royal Pioneer Corps Museum, Wootton 147
Royal Shakespeare Theatre Picture Gallery, Stratford-upon-Avon 150
Royal Warwickshire Regimental Museum, Warwick 150
Rugby Library, Exhibition Gallery & Museum 150
Rugeley Aqueduct 16
Ryland Aqueduct 14

Salamis Kebab House, Birmingham 154
Sandon Park, Staffordshire 140
Sanremo Restaurant, Derby 154
Selly Manor House & Minworth Greaves, Warwickshire 142
Shakespeare Birthplace Trust Properties, Stratford-upon-Avon 150
Shardlow 10, 63
Sherwood Foresters Regimental Museum, Nottingham 148
Sherwood Zoo, Nottinghamshire 144
Shrewley Tunnel 16
Shropshire Union Canal 51, 126
Shropshire Union Canal Society 34
Shugborough, Staffordshire 140
Sir John Moore Junior School, Leicestershire 137
Soar Navigation 134
Southam Zoo Farm, Warwickshire 144
Spetchley Park, Worcestershire 142
Spode Copeland Museum & Art Gallery, Stoke-on-Trent 149
Stafford Museum & Art Gallery 149
Staffordshire County Museum & Mansion House, Shugborough 148
Staffordshire Life Museum, Great Haywood 148
Staffordshire Regimental Museum, Lichfield 148
Staffordshire & Worcestershire Canal 53, 107, 126, 134
Staffordshire & Worcestershire Canal Society 34
Stanford Hall, Leicestershire 137
Stapleford Lion Reserve, Leicestershire 144
Steam Boat Association of Great Britain 34
St John's House, Warwick 150
St Mary's Guild Hall, Warwickshire 142
Stoke Bruerne 5
Stoke Park Pavilions, Northamptonshire 140
Stourbridge Canal 134
Stourport 9
Stratford-upon-Avon Canal 55, 125, 134
Stratford-upon-Avon Canal Society 34
Stretton Aqueduct 14
Sudbury Hall, Derbyshire 137
Sun Inn, Leicestershire 154
Swan House Hotel, Warwickshire 154

Swan's Nest Hotel, Bewick Restaurant, Stratford-upon-Avon 154
Swarkestone Junction 63

Tame Aqueduct 13
Tamworth Castle Museum 149
Tardebigge 9
Technology Museum, Leicester 147
Telford, Thomas 56
Toll Houses 60
Transport Trust 35
Trent Junction 9
Trent Lock 63, 64
Trent & Mersey Canal 63, 119, 127, 134
Trentham Gardens, Staffordshire 140
Tudor House Folk Museum, Worcester 151
Tunnels 16
Tutbury Castle, Staffordshire 140
Twycross Zoo Park, Warwickshire 144

University Art Gallery, Wollaton 148
Upper Avon Navigation Trust 35
Upton House Warwickshire 142

Valentia Arms Hotel, Worcestershire 154
Vertebrates 115

Warwick canals 55
Warwick Castle 142
Warwick County Museum 150
Water supply 37
Waterways Museum Stoke Bruerne 147
Waterway Recovery Group 35

Watford (Northants) 67
Wedgwood Museum, The, Stoke-on-Trent 149
Welford 67
Weoley Castle, Birmingham 150
West Bridge, Leicester 66
West Midlands canals 53
Weston Park, Staffordshire 140
Wharves 60
Whatton House, Leicestershire 137
Where to see canals 5
Whitefriars Museum of Local History, Coventry 150
Wightwick Manor, Staffordshire 141
William Salt Library, Staffordshire 141
Wolverhampton Locks 11
Woodhouse Hotel, Warwickshire 154
Worcester 107
Worcester Bar Basin, Birmingham 10
Worcester & Birmingham Canal 54, 107, 125, 134
Worcester & Birmingham Canal Society 35
Worcester Guildhall 142
Worcestershire County Museum, Hartlebury 151
Worcestershire: natural history 105
Worcestershire Regiment Museum, Worcester 151
Working narrowboats 34

Zoos 142
La Zouch restaurant, Leicestershire 154